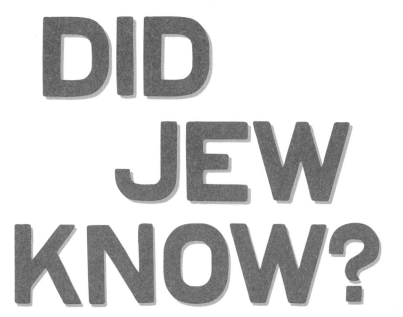

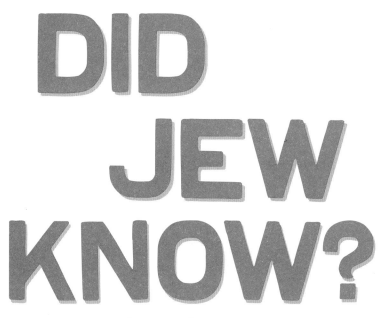

DID JEW KNOW?

A Handy Primer on the
CUSTOMS, CULTURE & PRACTICE
of the Chosen People

Emily Stone

CHRONICLE BOOKS

Library of Congress Cataloging-in-Publication Data:
Stone, Emily, 1969–
Did Jew know? : a handy primer on the customs, culture, and
    practice of the chosen people / Emily Stone.
256page cm
ISBN 978-1-4521-1896-3 (hardback)
1. Jews—Humor. I. Title.

PN6231.J5S755 2013
818.5402—dc23

2013013656

Manufactured in China

PH P&S

Packaged by powerHouse Packaging & Supply, Inc
37 Main Street
Brooklyn, NY 11201

Designed by Lana Le

10 9 8 7 6

Chronicle Books, LLC
680 Second Street
San Francisco, California 94107
www.chroniclebooks.com

For Ben, Isaac and Naomi

ACKNOWLEDGEMENTS:

The first and most essential source for this book is my cousin/on-call late-night rebbe Mikey Stone whose sagacity and depth of knowledge in all things Jewish earns him the well-deserved moniker "The Gaon of 77th Street." This book would not have been possible without him. Additionally, the following learned beings provided crucial information, explanation and analysis: Rabbi Ken Spiro of Aish.com, Rabbi Joseph Telushkin and Rabbi Joe Potasnik. Additionally, I am deeply grateful to the many other sources whose scholarship informed my research. Although I do not have the space to give them full mention here, a more thorough list can be found at www.chroniclebooks.com/didjewknow.

Other important humorists, scholars and supporters of this project and its author include Shawn Nacol, Marcel Brea, Amy Clemens, Francesca Bove, Jake Laub, Jillian Turecki-Baer, Chachi Luna Cruz, Damon Suede, Lauren Portada, Jordan Beckerman, Shawn Milnes, KG, David Bar Katz, Tina Benko, Jillian Gould, Mary Dana Abbott, Jessica Castro, Liz O'Connor, Jasmine Tarkeshi, Marc "The Gentle Gentile" Ryning, Niki Russ Federman, Angela Norton, Aliza Stone Howard, Rebecca Stone, the always fabulous Michelle Tovah Barge, Park Bench and EDNA.

Additional props to my uncle Richard Stone for his input, my cousin Ilana Stone for the chance, my beloved brother and sister-in-law Daniel Stone and Ellie Carmody for shelter during the storm, amazing Shabbat dinners and elucidating d'var Torah and finally, my amazing, wise and loving Jewish parents Harvey and Danna Stone for everything.

Contents

CHAPTER 1

FROM CANAAN TO NEW CANAAN: A Short History of the Jews

S'iz shver tsu zayn a Yid.
(It's tough to be a Jew.)

—YIDDISH FOLK SAYING

Welcome to Jew Hist 101, a (condensed) history of how the People of the Book became the People of the Book—before there was even a book! Speaking of book, this one is not meant to be a comprehensive history of the world and the Jewish people in it (I leave that to the great historian Mel Brooks); instead, it offers some essential highlights (and low points) of Jewish history, from Canaan to the Catskills, from capitalism to communism, and from God to now. So, whether you understand the Bible as metaphorical, historical, or hysterical, whether you think the history of Israel and its people is literal or biblical, whether you believe Jesus was the Messiah or just a complex if misguided cult leader from 2,000 years ago, this book is your captain through a journey that is bigger than your local miniseries and twice as racy and dramatic. In other words, Mel Gibson wishes he had it so good!

Indeed, as we will see, no literate people have suffered and survived so much and written, theorized, or sung half as much about it. But before we get into the Chosen Tribe's massive contribution to world literature, entertainment, science, fashion, food, or intellectual history, let's go back to about 1900ish BCE, when the world was a still a patch of inhospitable sand and the Jews became the Jews.

THE WANDERING JEW: How Stamina (and Schlepping) Built the Nation of Israel

---

Back in the Bronze Age (and possibly before), the Jews were just a Semitic tribe of desert nomads worshipping a mountain and looking for a land to call their own. It was the dog days of Sumer, and Abraham—then Abram—and his stalwart crew of swarthy sophisticates had just schlepped all the way to Haran (Turkey) from the city of Ur (Iraq). They were sitting around kibitzing and pondering how to improve their prospects when a disembodied, heavenly voice (allegedly) spoke to Abraham.

> "Get thee out of thy country, and from thy kindred, and from thy father's house, unto a land that I will shew thee."
>
> (GENESIS 12:1)

Right away Abram knew it was the voice of God. After all, who else would say "shew"? So he, his wife Sarah—then Sarai—and other assorted kinfolk left the creature comforts of the known world to follow the Voice to the land of Canaan, there to dwell.

As un-luck would have it, a grievous famine fell upon the land of Canaan. Famished and schvitzy as heck, not to mention seventy-plus years old, Abraham and Sarah didst sojourn to Egypt. There, in the land of the Sphinx, they didst pull a fast one on Pharaoh and told him Sarah was Abraham's sister, lest Pharaoh kill

Abraham and steal his wife. Only, by the time Pharaoh discovered this little ruse, he had already tried to play hide the nonkosher salami in she who is a Jewish princess, and the Lord had sent plagues upon him—a rift between Egyptian and Hebrew that would not be healed until the Camp David Accords in 1978, not to mention possibly the moment when the age-old notion that Jewish girls are easy was born, but let's not get ahead of ourselves.

Back to Canaan didst our J.Crew go, where the Lord eventually proclaimed unto Abe, "All the land which thou seest, to thee I will give it, and to thy seed forever." (Genesis 13:15) And so it came to pass that in this desert wilderness Abraham and Sarah (Israel's founding patriarch and matriarch) birthed the people in a book (the Hebrew Bible) that would much later be the People of the Book (the Jews) in a land that would later still become none other than the Holy Land itself (the modern-day State of Israel). Thanks, God! Next time, though, consider Boca: nicer neighbors, better bagels.

Unable to produce spawn, Sarah offered Hagar, her Egyptian handmaiden, to her holy hubby so that the Father of Many Nations might fill somebody's womb with his mighty, monotheistic seed. As more un-luck for the Jews would have it, this emission proved successful, and Hagar conceived none other than Ishmael, prophet and patriarch of Islam. "And he will be a wild man; his hand will be against every man, and every man's hand will be against him." (Genesis 16:12)

DID JEW KNOW? The name Abraham means "father of the multitude," and Sarah's name means "she who is princess." Originally Abraham's and Sarah's names were Abram and Sarai, but when they left behind the life and the people they knew for the brave Jew world of Canaan and monotheism, the aspirated *h* syllable was added to their names. This addition signifies their connection to God by incorporating part of the unspoken name of God (YHWH).

Hebrew Bible Quiz

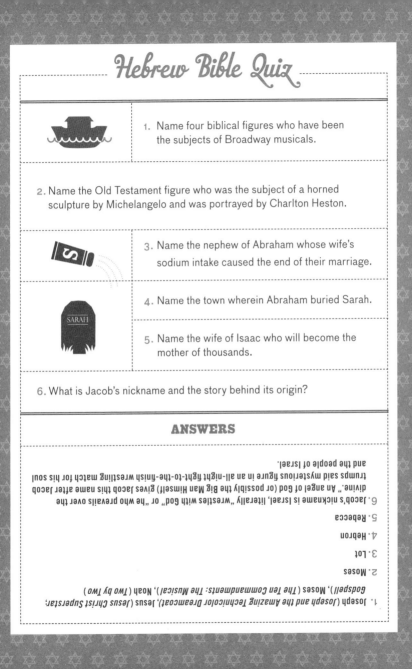

1. Name four biblical figures who have been the subjects of Broadway musicals.

2. Name the Old Testament figure who was the subject of a horned sculpture by Michelangelo and was portrayed by Charlton Heston.

3. Name the nephew of Abraham whose wife's sodium intake caused the end of their marriage.

4. Name the town wherein Abraham buried Sarah.

5. Name the wife of Isaac who will become the mother of thousands.

6. What is Jacob's nickname and the story behind its origin?

ANSWERS

1. Joseph (*Joseph and the Amazing Technicolor Dreamcoat*), Jesus (*Jesus Christ Superstar, Godspell*), Moses (*The Ten Commandments: The Musical*), Noah (*Two by Two*)

2. Moses

3. Lot

4. Hebron

5. Rebecca

6. Jacob's nickname is Israel, literally "wrestles with God," or "he who prevails over the divine." An angel of God (or possibly the Big Man Himself) gives Jacob this name after Jacob trumps said mysterious figure in an all-night fight-to-the-finish wrestling match for his soul and the people of Israel.

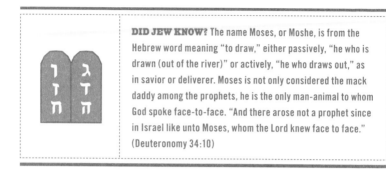

DID JEW KNOW? The name Moses, or Moshe, is from the Hebrew word meaning "to draw," either passively, "he who is drawn (out of the river)" or actively, "he who draws out," as in savior or deliverer. Moses is not only considered the mack daddy among the prophets, he is the only man-animal to whom God spoke face-to-face. "And there arose not a prophet since in Israel like unto Moses, whom the Lord knew face to face." (Deuteronomy 34:10)

Reason number 1,007 why you should never, ever, ever hire a hot housekeeper, secretary, or nanny.

Meanwhile, to make up for the whole race of mortal enemies shebang, the Lord granted Abraham not only the joy of experiencing adult circumcision, but also a son. Mazel tov! Upon hearing this news, Abraham fell upon his face! And not just to protect his poor *schmeckle,* but because Sarah was a hundred and even God has His limits!

Blown away by God's power—who wouldn't be?—Abraham and Sarah begat Isaac, who begat Jacob, who begat Joseph, and everyone had a very nice bris. Due to intense sibling rivalry issues, Joseph ended up in Egypt, where a semidecent pharaoh capitalized on his planning skills and made him a vizier, a high-ranking adviser in the Egyptian government, a post that Joseph carried out with great foresight and panache.

About seventy years later, another pharaoh, Ramses II, showed up on the scene—a mean and jealous pharaoh who knew not Joseph or musicals about dreamcoats and who, let's face it, wasn't such a big fan of Jews. Cut to: a burning bush that talks to a prophet named Moses, the ten plagues, the invention of matzo, the parting of the Red Sea, more schlepping in the Sinai, and the giving of the Ten Commandments and the Torah—events that Jews the world over now commemorate by getting drunk on Manischewitz and eating gefilte fish.

Time After Time: Jewish Dating Systems

A brief word from the fantastic Rabbi Ken Spiro on Jewish dating systems (as opposed to calendrical): Though ye olde Jewish and Christian dating systems can vary by as many as 164 years during the Babylonian period, by the Christian year 1 this discrepancy all but disappears. The reasons for this are many. One: As time went on, both historical records and methods of tracking elaborate patterns in the sky—i.e., time before the invention of the clock—improved and universalized across the board. Two: Until the birth of You Know Who, every empire measured the passage of time using culturally specific and often chaotic and divergent astrological criteria.

Meantime, the Hebrew dating system comes from a book called *Seder Olam Rabbah*, literally *The Great Order of the World*, a second-century Hebrew tome that chronologizes biblical events from creation through Alexander the Great. The *Seder Olam*, as it is often called in the Talmud, also bases said chronology on highly "accurate astronomical phenomena" and "rabbinic traditions recorded in the Talmud" and is therefore possibly more exact.

As scholars of the late nineteenth and early twentieth centuries began to cull scant info from historical records and archaeological finds, they worked backward to arrive at actual dates on which major ancient and/or biblical events may have occurred. Clearly these modern systems also leave margin for discrepancy and debate, which is why one Gentile scholar might say Abraham began his migration from Ur in 1900 BCE while another puts it at 1750 BCE. Since this book is about Jews, and because Jews consider Jewish chronology more Jewish (and therefore more accurate), *Did Jew Know?* uses the traditional—and preferable!—Jdates. It's what your mother would have wanted!

JEW HIST 101:
From the Torah to the Talmud

1272 BCE After the death of Moses, Joshua leads the Twelve Tribes of Israel and conquers and settles the Promised Land, a large chunk o' Canaan that also includes Jericho. At this point the Canaanites are just a bunch of immoral idolators, and the time is nigh for serious neighborhood gentrification. The first and most famous

DID JEW KNOW? Whence the Jews-have-horns myth: As any person who has been lucky enough to feast their peepers on Michelangelo's famous statue of Moses will tell you, something lumpy is growing out of our progenitor's temples! Rabbi Rifat Sonsino suggests that the reason for this depiction may stem from a biblical word describing Moses' appearance post–Mount Sinai: the Hebrew word *karan* (meaning "shine") could have been confused with the word *keren* (meaning "horn"). When the Bible became the Vulgate (Latin version), karan/keren became "horn," though it wasn't until the time of the Crusades that Moses' horns picked up the unmistakably pejorative association with the devil.

battle is none other than Jericho, portal city to the core of Canaan. Historians posit that the reason the walls of Jericho came a tumblin' down so easily may have been a well-timed earthquake. Thanks, God!

1106–879 BCE Period of Judges. After Joshua dies, the Jews are independent in their homeland yet lack a central authority. The judges become interim champions of YWYH who handle all traditional legal matters as well as issues pertaining to warfare and religious mores. Famous judges include Deborah and Samson.

879 BCE Reign of Saul, the first king of Israel. Lacking a charismatic leader since the time of Moses (about 400 years at this point), the Jews ask for a king "like all nations." Even though God is none too thrilled about this prospect, He tells the equally unthrilled prophet Samuel to anoint Saul. Next time Saul bumps into Samuel and asks if he knows where he might find some lost donkeys, Samuel replies, "Yes. And while we're on the subject of ass, you're the king of Israel." Saul attempts to defend his people against the Philistines but is unsuccessful and commits suicide by falling on his sword.

877 BCE Reign of David, second king of Israel. Among other righteous acts, including killing the giant Goliath, vanquishing the Philistines, writing the book of Psalms, and uniting the kingdom, David collects materials with which to build the Temple in Jerusalem and brings the Ark of the Covenant to Jerusalem. More important, he is also one hot Jew: "Now he was ruddy, and withal of a beautiful countenance, and goodly to look upon." (1 Samuel 16:12)

DID JEW KNOW? One theory as to why some of the Ten Tribes were lost is that God stymied them with the raging, unnavigable rapids of the Sambatyon River. During the week, the river seethed and churned, resting only on Shabbat (or *Shabbos*, as it's referred to in Yiddish). Since the Ten Tribes were too Jewish to whitewater raft, not to mention too pious to schlep on Shabbat, they stayed put and thus got lost in the shuffle.

Peoples who have claimed to be descended from the Lost Tribes of Israel include the Kurds, the Mormons, the Kaifeng Jews of China, the Afghans, the Falashas, the Northern and Southern Native Americans, the Indians, the Yoruba, the Irish, and the Japanese.

836 BCE Reign of King Solomon begins. The son of David, and the third king of Israel, Solomon is a great king. His reign is the most peaceful forty years in Israel's history and saw the completion and dedication of the First Temple in 825 BCE.

796 BCE The Northern Kingdom of Israel splits from the Southern Kingdom of Judah (containing Jerusalem). Idolatry occurs, especially among the Ten Tribes up north.

555 BCE Assyrians overtake the Northern Kingdom of Israel, and ten of the Twelve Tribes of Israel (descendants of the twelve sons of Jacob) are lost, i.e., dispersed and assimilated by other nearby and far-flung peoples. The southern tribes of Judah, Benjamin, and Levi miraculously survive the Assyrians but eventually fall to the Babylonians. Eventually, they are allowed to return to Israel, in 370 BCE.

The Lost Tribe: Jews in Africa

You may call them Falashas (the lost ones) but these African Jews call themselves Beta Israel (the House of Israel). Several theories exist as to their origin: Some say they can trace their lineage back to the powerful tribe of Dan, others that they are descendants of Solomon and Sheba or Jews who fled for Egypt after the destruction of the First Temple. Regardless of origin, these intrepid souls ended up living in Ethiopia, surrounded by Christian and Muslim tribesmen and eating *injera*.

In the early 1980s, the Ethiopian government forbade the practice of Judaism or the learning of Hebrew, and many members of Beta Israel were imprisoned on false charges. To add insult to injury, extreme famine, the threat of war, and forced conscription for boys at the ripe old age of twelve made the position of Ethiopian Jewry more and more precarious. On November 21, 1984, Operation Moses, a six-week covert operation to evacuate members of Beta Israel from Sudanese refugee camps, rescued 8,000 Jews and brought them to the land of milk and hummus. Unfortunately, news leaks truncated the mission as Arab nations pressed the Sudanese government to cease the operation, and around 15,000 Jews, mostly women, children, and the infirm, were left behind in Ethiopia.

In 1985, Vice President George Bush arranged Operation Joshua, a CIA-sponsored covert op that brought 500 more Ethiopian Jews from the Sudan to Israel. Between 1985 and 1991, however, Ethiopian Jews became human pawns in a battle between rebel forces and Colonel Mengistu Haile Mariam, whose Marxist-Leninist dictatorship threatened the fate of Beta Israel. His aim was to use Ethiopian Jewry as a bargaining chip for both money and arms from the United States.

On Friday, May 24, 1991, Americans assisted the Israeli government in Operation Solomon, a massive rescue operation that brought 14,000 Jews to Israel. In order to facilitate this massive operation, Israeli Prime Minister Yitzhak Shamir issued a special permit for El Al, the Israeli airline, to fly on Shabbat. For the next thirty-six hours, thirty-four El Al jumbo jets and Hercules C-130s, all with the seats removed to accommodate the maximum number of passengers, airlifted almost the entire Jewish community of Ethiopia from Addis Ababa and returned them to their motherland—a dream 2,000 years in the making. More than 120,000 Ethiopian Jews now live in Israel.

Harry Krishna: Jews in India

These diasporites, some of whom arrived in India as early as 2,500 years ago, during the time of the Kingdom of Judah, and others slightly later as some of the Ten Lost Tribes (or so they claim), wisely ended up hangin' with the Hindus, one of the few world religions to leave the Jews in peace and papadum. In the 1950s, the Jewish population of India hovered at around 35,000. Since then, about 20,000 have immigrated to Israel, leaving 7,000 to 8,000 still living in India. In addition to Jewish ex-pats and recent immigrants, India boasts five native Jewish communities:

- Cochin Jews: Oldest group of Jews in India, who trace their roots back to the reign of King Solomon. They now live in Kerala.
- Bene Israel: A handful o' Jews who fled persecutions in Palestine only to be ship-wrecked on the shores of India sometime before the destruction of the Second Temple. From the loins of these brave few sprang as many as 20,000 Jews—the largest Jewish population in India—living in and around Mumbai. Other theories as to the origins of the Bene Israel include the descendants of Babylonian Jews or Yemenite Jews who fled persecution by the Muslims.

- The Baghadadi Jews: Jews from Iraq and other Arab countries who, fleeing persecution, immigrated to India about 250 years ago.
- The B'nei Menashe: A group of headhunters and animists in Manipur who practiced a form of biblical Judaism and claimed to be descended from the Lost Tribes of Israel. Many were converted to Christianity at the beginning of the twentieth century but then converted to Orthodox Judaism under the guidance of Rabbi Eliyahu Avichail in the 1970s. (Avichail was the founder of Amishav, an Israeli organization dedicated to locating the lost tribes and schlepping them to Israel.)
- B'nei Ephraim a.k.a. the "Telugu Jews": Established in 1981 in Andhra Pradesh by a group of Christianized Madiga who claimed to be descendants of the Lost Tribes of Israel, the Ephraim now study Torah and learn Hebrew. Aside from the fact that they have enjoyed visits from several groups of rabbis, the Ephraim have not been afforded the same recognition as the B'nei Menashe.

Kosher Mu Shu (NO MSG!): Jews in China

A thriving Jewish community has existed in Kaifeng, a city in central China, since as early as the first century. Historians hypothesize that itinerant Jewish merchant communities from India and Persia ended up in Kaifeng as they were wending their way east along the Silk Route. According to historian Mark Avrum Ehrlich, during the Ming Dynasty, a Ming emperor gave seven Chinese sinifications (Ai, Shi, Gao, Jin, Li, Zhang, and Zhao) to Jewish surnames, including Ezra, Shimon, Cohen, Gilbert, and Levy.

Whoever Hoid of a Jewish Priest: The Kohanim and How They Got That Way

The Kohanim are a priestly group of Jews descended from the Tribe of Levi, the sons of Jacob. A little backstory: Originally, firstborn sons were the priests of the Jewish Nation. That is, until after the Torah was given on Mount Sinai and

---

SOUNDS LIKE: MAH-JONGG AND ERICA JONG

The ancient Chinese parlor game mah-jongg became a craze in the United States when Ezra Fitch tapped into the United States' newfound interest in the "mysticism" of the East, an interest that simultaneously made Chinese food a dinner go-to for the Chosen Tribe. Mah-jongg stayed popular among American Jewish women and was even the subject of a song by Eddie Cantor, "Since Ma Is Playing Mah Jong." Erica Jong, on the other hand, is a Jewish novelist who canonized the zipless *schtup* as a form of sexual freedom in her 1973 novel *Fear of Flying*. Among her four husbands was a Chinese American, Allan Jong.

---

the Jewish people made the brilliant mistake of worshipping a golden calf. The one tribe that abstained from this *shanda* was the Tribe of Levi. Thus, priestly status was conferred upon the Levites.

Luckily Moses and his brother Aaron were both Levites. Since Moses was getting all the press, God made the descendants of Aaron—the first *kohen gadol* (high priest) of Israel—Kohanim. Becuse Kohanim are expected to perform sacred functions such as sacrificial offerings or reciting the priestly blessing, their behavior is restricted by a number of rules: They can marry neither a divorcée nor a convert; they cannot go to a cemetery or have sex with a prostitute.

JEW HIST 101, PART DEUX:
From the Torah to the Talmud, Continued

434 BCE In an attempt to undermine the Kingdom of Judah, Babylonian King Nebuchadnezzar marches on Jerusalem and deports the wealthy, smartypants Jews to Babylon while he allows the average, ordinary folk to remain in Judea and appoints Zedekiah, a puppet king, to oversee them. This little move of Nebuchadnezzar's ultimately backfires, as all the nerdniks have a chance to set up a serious Jewish infrastructure *before* the rest of the Jew Crew arrives on the shores of Babylon, thus keeping the Jews on point.

423 BCE Nebuchadnezzar overtakes Jerusalem, and the First Temple is destroyed by fire. The Diaspora begins as some Jews flee to Egypt and the rest are expelled to Babylon where, unlike the Lost Tribes, they manage to retain their religious leaders, practices, and philosophies. Additionally, unlike the prior period of exile in Egypt, the Babylonian captivity is relatively benign, if not intellectually and spiritually fecund; Lamentations, the books of Esther and Daniel, and some of the Psalms are written. Also, the Bible is sealed, as in it's a wrap, kids; the Bible has left the building.

DID JEW KNOW? Mr. Spock's Vulcan greeting is a space-age variant of the historic Kohanic gesture of blessing (in which the hands come together to form the Hebrew letter *shin*, which stands for the Hebrew word *Shaddai*, another name for God). In a celluloid homage to his observant roots, Leonard Nimoy adapted this traditional gesture into the single-hand Trekkie salute that says "Live long and prosper" to Heebs and dweebs of all nations.

370 BCE Jews are allowed to return to Jerusalem, though some remain in Egypt and others choose to remain in Babylon.

352–353 BCE Construction of Second Temple begins under King Darius.

312 BCE It's all Greek to me! The conquests of Alexander the Great at the beginning of the fourth century BCE cast the golden net of Greek philosophy over a significant chunk of the Middle East. As a result, many Jews are exposed to the beauty of Greek logic and the Platonic ideal.

37 BCE Romans appoint Herod as King of Judea. The Second Temple gets an extreme makeover.

The Moshiach of Schnoz: How a Charismatic Handyman Became the Son of God

Somewhere between 6 and 4 BCE, along came Jesus, the political rabble-rouser from Bethlehem who took a bath with John the Baptist, thought his mother was a virgin, and got nailed to a piece of wood for saying people should be nice to each other.

After Jesus left his body, his loyal backup band of gospel singers, a.k.a. the apostles, went around preaching that he was the son of God and therefore the Messiah. In fact, where Jesus had preached mostly to Jews, Paul took it to the next level by going on tour and preaching Christ's gospel to the Gentiles all over the Roman Empire. Regardless of efforts of the Romans to squelch this new cult religion, the Christian church continued to pick up steam, the banner moment occurring in 312–313 BCE when Emperor Constantine and his Western compadre Licinius issued the Edict of Milan—a proclamation that promulgated religious tolerance for Christianity within the Roman Empire.

From the Carpenter With a Heart of Gold to the Inquisition

66 CE Jewish rebel forces overtake the Roman garrison at Masada, the mountain plateau with a view of the Dead Sea on which Herod had built a massive fortress.

70 CE Titus attacks Jerusalem, eventually penetrating the Temple Mount. The Great Jewish Revolt against the Romans ends with the destruction of the Second Temple, an event that occurs on the ninth of Av, the same day the First Temple was destroyed. One thousand Jewish Zealots manage to escape and hole up at Masada.

> **DID JEW KNOW?**
> More than a ruined fortress with a killer view, Masada is now one of the Jewish people's greatest symbols. In fact, Israeli soldiers continue to swear an oath there that Masada will not fall again. It is also a popular spot for bar mitzvahs.

Meanwhile, a wise rabbi by the name of Yochanan ben Zakkai decides to go lo pro and assembles an essential legal infrastructure that allows the Jews to survive without the Temple and its service. As a result of Yochanan and his council, there is a marked shift in focus/method of worship wherein the priesthood is replaced by the rabbinate, animal sacrifice by prayer, and the synagogue becomes the center of Jewish life.

73 CE The Romans lay siege to Masada. According to Roman Jewish historian Titus Flavius Josephus, author of *The Jewish War*, the Jewish defenders decided to burn the fortress and kill themselves rather than be taken alive by the Romans. They then cast lots to select ten men to kill the remaining 960 defenders and one man to kill the survivors. The last Jew standing then killed himself.

JEW HIST 202:
From Bar Kochba to the State of Israel

132 CE The rebellion of Bar Kochba. Just when Jews thought it was safe to go back in the water, Emperor Hadrian decides to destroy Judaism by forbidding its ritual observance. This is the last straw for a great Jewish leader by the name of Simon Bar Kochba, who organizes a guerrilla army and somehow succeeds in booting the Romans out of Jerusalem, briefly establishing an independent Jewish state. His success causes many to believe that he is the Messiah.

DID JEW KNOW?

Jesus' real name was Jehoshua (or Yahshua) Ben Yosef Natzri (as opposed to Jesus H. Christ). In fact, *Jesus* means "Jehovah is salvation" and *Christ* is actually Greek for "anointed one."

134 CE In an attempt to obliterate what they considered the last shard of Judaism, the Romans murder teachers of Judaism, including Rabbi Akiva, one of the all-time great Jewish sages, along with many other important rabbis.

135 CE In what is one of the most brutal attacks in Jewish history, the Romans sack Jerusalem. The city falls on the ninth of Av, the same date that both the First and Second Temple were destroyed. Additionally, Hadrian decides that the time has come to separate the Jews once and for all from their land and levels Jerusalem, building a pagan city atop its sacred rubble.

190-200 CE The Mishnah, a definitive and esoteric written version of the oral law from the time of Mount Sinai, is completed.

DID JEW KNOW? The Sephardim (Hebrew for "Spaniard") are the descendants of Spanish or Portuguese Jews who hung out in the Iberian Peninsula in and around the time of the Inquisition. On the other hand, the Ashkenazi are descendants of the significantly less tanned though equally noteworthy medieval Jewish communities in Germany. A third group, the Mizrahi, are the Jews who stayed in Babylon after the destruction of the First Temple. The Mizrahi also include Moroccan, Egyptian, and Persian Jews.

200–500 CE Countdown to Babylon. After the Romans destroy the Second Temple, centuries of Jewish persecution follow and many rabbis hightail it back to Babylon. Concerned that the Mishnah alone will no longer suffice as an explanation of the oral law now that the Jews are so dispersed, the various Judge Jew-dys of Babylon decide that the time has come to compile their legal discourses in writing, and thus the Gemara, the written-down rabbinic discussions on the Mishnah, is born. Next thing Jew know, the legal combo platter of the Mishnah and the Gemara forms the Babylonian Talmud—the central text of rabbinic Judaism. (See chapter 8.) Meanwhile, slightly before the composition of the Babylonian Talmud, another posse of rabbis in Jerusalem is holding similar discussions that will become the Jerusalem Talmud.

As the saying goes, when life gives you lemons, make lemonade! When life gives you tallow, write the Talmud!

312 CE Jew can't go back to Constantinople. The Roman Empire goes Christian under Emperor Constantine and his world-changing Edict of Milan.

1095 The Crusades are launched to control the spread of Islam. Unluckily, the Gentile mob get impatient on their way to Jerusalem and decide to take their aggression out on the Jews as well. The Crusades mark the beginning of European mob violence against the Jews, establishing a pattern for the next 800-plus years. In fact, as Christian reconquest of Muslim territories picked up speed, Jews were, as usual, the targets of increasingly brutal persecutions. As my mother would say, "No new information."

THE MIDDLE AGES:
a.k.a. Everybody Hates the Jews

1328 As the Black Death was systematically wiping out about half the population of Europe, rumors began to circulate that the Jews were to blame for this gangrenous scourge on society. In a dastardly prequel to the next several centuries, there followed pernicious scapegoating of the Jews, not to mention amped persecution in the form of torture, mob violence, and mass extermination. For instance, the Strasbourg massacre, which occurred on February 14, 1349, witnessed the public immolation of as many as 900 Jews in a town where the plague had yet to hit. This public barbecue was one of the first pogroms of pre-modern history.

Jew Better (NOT) Believe It: The Spanish Inquisition and the Crypto-Jews

About a hundred years after the Crusades, King Ferdinand and Queen Isabella decided to go all-Catholic-all-the-time in order to unify the people of Spain. Implicit in this decision is none other than Tomás de Torquemada, the infamous Dominican friar and grand inquisitor of Spain who, in 1484, promulgated many articles outlining a range of "criminal personalities" including but not limited to Jews, sorcerers, heretics, sodomites, blasphemers, usurers (a.k.a. Jews), polygamists, Mariscos (Muslims who converted to Christianity), and worst of all, Jews! Oddly enough, Torquemada was actually descended from Jewish converts to Christianity, and Isabella also claimed some Jewish ancestry!

Smitten by Torquemada—he was, after all, Isabella's confessor—and longing for ritual purity, Isabella and Ferdinand announced to the pope that it was high time to start expelling Protestants, Jews, and other nonbelievers. The pope concurred and started exiling Jews left and right and/or proffering the catch-22 chance to convert or die. Cut to the Spanish Inquisition: a tribunal for maintaining the devotion and orthodoxy of those who converted to Catholicism from Judaism,

---

BOUGHETTO CHIC: THE GHETTOS OF EUROPE

The word *ghetto* comes from the Italian word *borghetto*, a diminutive of *borgo*, meaning "borough" or "fortified settlement." These fortifications could either be locked from the inside to protect the inhabitants against pogroms or from the outside to keep the Jews from spoiling Christmas and Easter by showing up in the town square and eating all the ham.

Islam, Protestantism, or (D) all of the above. One of the ways the cleansing of Jews and Jewish practices was carried out was via auto-da-fé, ritual public penance of Jews, Muslims, and other heretics. These mock trials often culminated in public burnings and other equally wonderful forms of execution.

The only glitch in this otherwise foolproof 300-year plan was controlling and maintaining the Catholic practices of the *conversos* (Sephardic Jews who were forcibly converted during the fourteenth and fifteenth centuries). Other synonyms for conversos include *marranos*, which is Arabic for "forbidden" and carries the connotation "pig," *anusim*, which is Hebrew for "coerced," and crypto-Jews (conversos who publicly appeared Catholic but secretly practiced rabbinic Judaism).

JEW HIST 202, PART DEUX:
The Best of Times and the Voist of Times

1543 German Reformation leader Martin Luther pens *On the Jews and Their Lies*, a document that details the various blasphemies of the Jews and outlines methods for containing and subverting them, which the Nazis will later incorporate into their anti-Semitic propaganda.

1563 Rabbi Yosef Caro of Safed writes the Shulchan Aruch, literally "Code of Law," a concise Halakhic code/compendium based on the rulings of the Talmud and its interpreters. Aside from ratifying the itty-bitty nitty-gritty of Jewish daily life, the Shulchan Aruch also represented a radical move toward establishing a more universal interpretation of Jewish law. Now Jew and Jew alike were at last able to consult the same guidebook to find the answers to questions on various ritual observances and legalities rather than merely consulting their local rabbi.

1648–1649 Chmielnicki Massacres. After a long period of unprecedented and unimagined rights and privileges, the Jews of Poland fall under the attack of the Ukrainian Cossack Bogdan Chmielnicki, one of the top ten anti-Semites in world history. Chmielnicki and his followers manage to wipe out 100,000 Jews, immortalizing the attack as the worst and most gruesomely sadistic pogroms of all time. And that's saying something.

1648 Sabbatai Zevi, a Turkish mystic, rebbe, and Kabbalist, claims to be the Messiah, and the Jews fall for it hook, line, and sinker, mostly because they were so demoralized by the Chmielnicki Massacres. When Zevi makes the mistake of telling the Sultan of the Ottoman Empire he is the Messiah, the Sultan throws his *tuchus* in jail and tells Zevi he will torture him to death unless he converts to Islam . . . so Zevi does. This only further demoralizes the Jews.

CIRCA 1736 The Ba'al Shem Tov founds Hasidism, an ecstatic movement that emphasizes prayer, connection to God, and mysticism. According to this movement, anyone with true intention can connect both deeply and spiritually with Hashem, not just scholars, intellectuals, or Tom Cruise. On some level, Hasidism is spiritual Prozac for lingering despair caused by Chmielnicki and Sabbatai Zevi.

LATE 1700s Jews are allowed to participate in secular European society and given rights as citizens. Oddly enough, as Napoleon marches though Europe, he liberates Jews from the ghettos in which they had been summarily stuffed and oppressed. This marks the beginning of the rise of the secular Jew, or the "Jewish Enlightenment," in Western Europe.

1791 Russian Jews are herded into the Pale of Settlement—a region of Imperial Russia in which Jews could have permanent residency and beyond which permanent residency for Jews is a big no-no. Needless to say, life for Jews in the Pale is difficult, poverty-stricken, and chock-full of pogroms.

1894 In France, artillery officer Captain Alfred Dreyfus (Jewish) is wrongly accused of treason and sentenced to life in prison. Two years later, it turns out that another soldier (a non-Jew) is the real culprit, but the French Army continues to point *le doigt* at Dreyfus. Upon discovering this cover-up, prominent intellectual Emile Zola (author and father of French naturalism) writes *J'accuse*—an open letter to the newspaper about the framing of Dreyfus. The scandal over the Dreyfus Affair divides France (and causes quite a ruckus abroad). Eventually, Dreyfus is exonerated.

JEW HIST 202, PART 3: BRAVE JEW WORLD
The Holocaust, Israel, and the Americas

As Adolf Hitler began his meteoric rise to power in 1933, the German economy was deep in the doldrums from the lasting effects of World War I and the Great Depression. Already anti-Semitic, Germans were disillusioned with their government, desperate for stability, and looking for someone to blame for their defeat in WWI. Guess whom they picked! You guessed it! Commies and Jews! True, Hitler's message was supported and disseminated by one of the fiercest propaganda machines of all time, but the German people were already in a spot to receive and run with it.

Adolf Hitler: The Uni-Balled Austrian Homunculus and The Final Solution

Long before he became chancellor of Germany in 1933, Adolf Hitler had already authored *Mein Kampf* (published in 1925), an anti-Semitic, anticommunist manifesto that became the bible of Nazism and sold an unprecedented 5 million copies by 1939. After Hitler was appointed chancellor, he summarily turned the Weimar Republic into the Third Reich—a dictatorship based on the totalitarian and autocratic Nazi ideal. Part of this ideal included the notion that the Aryans were the master race, superior to all other races, and that in order to achieve racial purity, the Nazis had to eliminate by any means necessary all Jews, Romani, homosexuals, and the mentally and physically disabled.

1938 A Jewish youth assassinates German diplomat Ernst vom Rath, an event that was the pretext for Kristallnacht, a series of government-sanctioned pogroms that took place in Germany and Austria from November 8 to November 9. On the command of Propaganda Minister Joseph Goebbels, German civilians and brown-shirted Stormtroopers burned synagogues, ransacked and/or looted, and destroyed Jewish homes, hospitals, businesses, and schools. At least 91 Jews were killed, and an estimated 30,000 Jews were arrested and deported to concentration camps.

TELL YOUR FRIENDS THEY'RE ACTUALLY JEWISH!

Some common surnames of conversos: Alva, Alonzo, Alvares, Baez, Castellanos, Cruz, Diaz, Duarte, Enriquez, Espinosa, Fernandez, Fonseca, Franco, Garcia, Gomez, Hernandez, Leon, Lopez, Machado, Mendez, Muñoz, Olivera, Ortiz, Perez, Pimentel, Ramirez, Rodriguez, Sanchez, Silvera, Torres, Vaez, Vega, Ximenez, Zerda.

Take My Nazi, Please!

In 1942, Hitler and his buddy Heinrich Himmler, head of the SS, devised and implemented the Final Solution to the Jewish Question—a euphemism for the systematic genocide of the Jewish people. Extermination camps were built, ghettos were liquidated, and mass slaughter was the name of the game. Thankfully, the Allied forces arrived on the scene in 1945, the camps were liberated, and World War II was won with a mighty hand and an outstretched arm.

With the next big problem (a.k.a. Stalin) just around the corner, a number of Jews who miraculously survived the Holocaust decided it was time to hightail it to countries like Israel, the United States, and Canada, where they might not only be free but also have full rights of citizenship.

And so, much like their ancestors' ancestors' ancestors in Canaan, the Hebrews and Shebrews packed their bags and headed for greener pastures, teeming tenements and the land of milk and money. But first, a flashback.

JEW HIST 303: The State of Israel, or How a Bunch of Lefty Intellectuals Reclaimed a Patch of Desert Sand and Built a Nation

1882–1903 The First Aliyah (immigration to Israel). Some 30,000 Jews immigrate to Palestine from Eastern Europe and Yemen. Cause: anti-Semitism.

1897 Theodor Herzl (1860–1904), the Austro-Hungarian journalist and father of Zionism, founds the Zionist Organization, a group that espouses Jewish nationalism and advocates a Jewish nation-state in Uganda. After closely following the Dreyfus Affair (see page 24), Herzl came to believe that the only future for the Jews was to create/restore their own state in the homeland of Israel.

1904–1914 The Second Aliyah. Approximately 40,000 Jews immigrate to Palestine from Yemen and the Russian Empire. Cause: anti-Semitism in the form of pogroms.

1909 A group of mostly Eastern European workers from Sejera, the first Jewish settlement in Galilee, found Degania, the first kibbutz. A kibbutz is a utopian cooperative community that blends both socialist and Zionist ideals. Originally, kibbutzim (what you say instead of kibbutzes) were all about collective farming and irrigating the desert, but now it seems like they mostly center on Jewish teens and college students making out and taking MDMA with other Jewish teens and college students.

1917 The Balfour Declaration announces British support for the creation of a Jewish homeland in Palestine.

1923–1948 The British Mandate. British rule replaces 400-some-odd years of Ottoman rule. The Brits remain on the scene until 1948.

1919–1923 The Third Aliyah. Another 40,000 Jews immigrate to Palestine from Russia, Poland, Romania, and Lithuania. Cause: anti-Semitism and the October Revolution.

1922 The League of Nations established the British Mandate for Palestine, a commission meant to administer the territory of Israel, the West Bank, the Gaza Strip, and Jordan. The mandate created two distinct protectorates: Palestine, a national home for the Jews that includes Jerusalem, from the West Bank to the Gaza Strip; and the Transjordan, an Emirate municipality of considerably greater square footage than the literal dot on the map that comprises Palestine.

1924–1928 The Fourth Aliyah. About 80,000 Jews immigrate to Palestine from Eastern Europe and Asia. Cause: anti-Semitism.

1929–1939 The Fifth Aliyah. Between 225,000 and 300,000 European Jews immigrate to Palestine. Cause: Hitler.

1945 Allies defeat the Axis Powers. Auschwitz is liberated. From the end of World War II until the establishment of Israel in 1948, Jewish immigrants from Europe enter Israel illegally due to the Brits' quota of 18,000 per year. In 1947, the Mandatory government sends the 4,500 immigrants aboard the SS *Exodus* back to Europe.

1947 The United Nations recommends the adoption of the partition plan of Mandatory Palestine (a plan that established two independent Jewish and Arab states). The plan stipulates that both states grant full civil rights to all people dwelling within their borders. Let's just say that the Jews went for this plan and the Arabs did not.

1948 David Ben-Gurion (first prime minister and founding father of Israel) declares the establishment of the State of Israel. A day later, Arab armies invade.

1948–1949 Ben-Gurion leads Israel in the Arab-Israeli War. After a yearlong initiative, Israel now controls the Negev and the Galilee—a larger territory than that which had been allotted by the U.N. Partition agreement. Jerusalem is divided, and the Old City, including the Western Wall, is under Jordanian rule. Egypt and Jordan now occupy the Gaza Strip and the West Bank.

Whose Strip Is It Anyway?
Israel and the Eternal Battle of What's Yours Is Mine

As we have seen, all of Jewish history, and indeed all of human history, comes down to real estate. What's more, since its inception, the State of Israel and its Arab neighbors have been a-fightin', a-feudin', and a-fussin' over who gets the West Bank, the Golan Heights, and the Gaza Strip. This turf war traces its roots back to Genesis, when Hashem tells Abraham that he will give to him and to his offspring "the whole of the land of Canaan as an everlasting possession." (Genesis 17:8) Shortly thereafter, He tells Abraham that Ishmael, Abe's first child by Hagar, will beget twelve princes and become a great nation, but that He will maintain His Covenant through Isaac. (Genesis 17:20–21) And therein lies the rub to end all rubs.

1949 After the U.S. and the U.K. withdraw their pledge to fund the Aswan Dam as a result of Egypt's increased alliance with the Soviet Union, the Egyptians close the Suez Canal to Israeli shipping.

1956 As a result of this blockade, Egyptian President Gamal Abdel Nasser's import of arms from the Soviet Union, and increased attacks of the Fedayeen (Arab terrorists) against Israel, Israel is compelled to attack Egypt. Though the United States does not back Israel in this move, England and France ally with

STAR TRACKS

Rabbi Shraga Simmons posits a few reasons why the Star of David became a Jewish icon: While it has no mention in the Torah or the Talmud, its shape nonetheless connotes the quintessence of Judaism. For one, just as God took six days to create the world and rested on the seventh day, the Star of David has six points surrounding the "core" of Judaism, a.k.a. Shabbat. Meanwhile, over in Kabbalah territory, the two triangles represent the binaries of good and evil or spirit and matter or even the reciprocal relationship between God and the People of Israel. Also, the star's twelve sides may represent the Twelve Tribes of Israel. The hexagram is also regarded as a Messianic symbol.

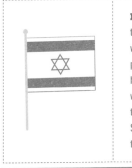

DID JEW KNOW? The First Zionist Congress designed the Israeli flag in 1897. According to Rabbi Ken Spiro, the white background represents the notion of newness and purity, and the blue stripes symbolize both the color of heaven and the stripes of a *tallit* (Jewish prayer shawl), which is meant to convey the "transmission of the Jewish tradition." At the flag's center is the Magen David, the Star (or Shield) of David, a symbol of Jewish identity since the eleventh century.

Israel. One hundred hours later, though Israel holds the Gaza Strip, pressure from the U.S. results in Israeli withdrawal from all areas it conquered without any kind of concession from the Egyptians. This little oversight forms the impetus for what will later be the 1967 War.

1967 The Six-Day War ends with victory for Israel. Gaza, Golan Heights, the West Bank, and East Jerusalem revert to Israeli control. Subsequently, Jews begin building settlements on this recaptured land. Problems ensue.

1969 Golda "Best Man in the Government" Meir is elected fourth prime minister of Israel. A committed socialist, Meir left the United States to live on a kibbutz in Palestine in 1921. When she married her husband in 1917, settling in Palestine was part of the prenup.

1973 Yom Kippur War. Syria and Egypt launch a surprise attack against Israel. Following two years of back-and-forth negotiation, Israel withdraws from parts of the territories.

1979 Camp David Accords. The peace treaty, brokered by U.S. President Jimmy Carter, is signed by Menachem Begin (Israeli prime minister) and Anwar El Sadat (Egyptian president).

1987 The First Intifada (Arab uprising) against Israeli occupation of the West Bank and Gaza.

1990–1991 The Gulf War. Iraq fires missiles at Israel.

1995 Yigal Amir assassinates Israeli Prime Minister Yitzhak Rabin as Rabin is attending a rally for the Oslo Accords, an agreement between Israel and the PLO that created and ultimately called for the withdrawal of Israeli Defense forces from the West Bank and parts of the Gaza Strip. Amir, a right-wing Orthodox Jew, deeply opposed Rabin's signing of these accords.

2000 The Second Intifada. Israeli Prime Minister Ehud Barak, Palestine Liberation Organization Chairman Yasser Arafat, and U.S. President Bill Clinton chew the fat at the Camp David Summit. Arafat rejects the Israeli prime minister's plan to establish a Palestinian state.

2004 Palestinian President Yasser Arafat dies.

2005 Israeli Prime Minister Ariel Sharon enacts the Disengagement Plan (a plan to resettle all Israelis currently residing in the Gaza Strip). Israeli security forces evict all citizens who refused to comply with the government mandate.

2006 The Second Lebanon War. July 12: Hezbollah terrorists infiltrate Israel's border and attack Israeli soldiers, killing three and taking two hostage. Hezbollah also initiates a series of rocket attacks on Israel. Subsequently, Israel carries out

DID JEW KNOW? According to the Israeli Bureau of Statistics, as of 2012, 5,978,600 Jews live in Israel. That's 75.4 percent of the population of Israel and about 44 percent of the world's Jews. Meanwhile, as of 2011, the Berman Institute counts about 5,275,000 living in the United States—about 40 percent of world Jewry—with approximately 1,635,020 residing in the New York metropolitan area. NOTE: NYC also holds the largest Jewish population on the planet outside of Israel. Next we have France, with a whopping 3.6 percent. The Canadian census lists 370,505 Jews, or 2.8 percent of world Jewry, living in Canada as of December 2012, with the most living in Toronto, followed by Montreal. The U.K. boasts a whopping 2.2 percent of the world's Jews, while Australia has slightly over .8 percent. Finally, southeast Florida (particularly the so-called Jewish Riviera: Miami, Boca, and Jew-piter) boasts more than 535,000 Jews. Only five of them are under seventy.

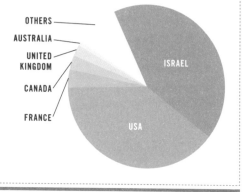

a massive bombing of Lebanon. On August 11, the U.N. calls for a ceasefire, the return of the hostage Israeli soldiers, and Israel's withdrawal from Lebanon. In June 2008, Hezbollah returns the bodies of the two kidnapped Israeli soldiers in exchange for Lebanese terrorist Samir Kuntar and assorted Hezbollah guerrillas captured during the war.

2008 Egypt negotiates a ceasefire between Israel and Hamas. Hamas agrees to prevent militant groups from launching rockets at Israel. Israel agrees to allow increased imports into Gaza.

2010 Israeli air strike kills four Islamic Jihad operatives, most notably Awad Abu Nasir.

2011 On March 11, Palestinians Amjad Awad and Hakim Awad butcher five members of the Fogel family in the Israeli settlement of Itamar, a small farming community in the West Bank. The victims were Ehud Fogel, his wife Ruth Fogel, and three of their six children.

2012 Under pressure from America and Egypt, Israel and Hamas agree to a ceasefire after eight days of conflict in Gaza.

Freedom's Just Another Word for Nothing Left to Lose

While most Jews came to the Americas during the two great waves of Jewish immigration, a fair share o' Jews washed up onto her Shores of Freedom as early as the colonial era, and some intrepid travelers even managed to schlep along earlier.

1584 Joachim Gans is possibly the first Jew to set foot on American soil. Some historians place this distinction on a Spanish converso by the name of Luis de Carabajal y Cueva, who possibly arrived in what is now Texas in 1554, before there was even a single decent Chinese restaurant!

1654 The first group of Sephardic settlers arrives in New Amsterdam from Brazil.

1779 Thomas Jefferson writes The Virginia Statute for Religious Freedom, a statute that grants legal equality to all religious minorities in the state of Virginia. Seven years later, the statute is enacted into law by the legislature.

1790 None other than George Washington pens a responsum to Moses Seixas, synagogue president of Hebrew Congregation of Newport, Rhode Island, asserting that the Chosen Tribe can indeed expect to enjoy the same political and religious freedoms implicit in the Declaration of Independence: "May the Children of the Stock of Abraham, who dwell in this land, continue to merit and enjoy the good will of the other inhabitants; while every one shall sit in safety under his own vine and fig-tree, and there shall be none to make him afraid."

1791 The First Amendment ratifies the New World's commitment to religious freedom, including the freedom of its 2,500 or so Jews. "Congress shall make no law respecting an establishment of religion, or prohibiting the free exercise thereof." The one catch to all of this fabulous freedom is whether or not a Jew can hold public office. In fact, eight of the original thirteen states deny this privilege to their Jewish citizens, Maryland being especially crabby on this topic.

1797 The Jews of the Old Line State begins petitioning for the right to hold public office. This bill, called, fittingly, "the Jew Bill," isn't introduced until 1818 and is ultimately defeated. In 1826, a redux of said bill finally becomes law. From there on out, Jews eventually gain legal equality in every state.

To the 'Burbs Gladly: The American Diaspora

Fleeing virulent anti-Semitism, the Jews began arriving on the shores of North America in droves in the 1800s through 1924 and again after World War II. Since America offered not only religious freedom but also economic and social opportunity, it was the ideal destination for a people escaping horrendous living conditions and looking to start a new life. Nevertheless, until as late as the 1960s, Jews were restricted from certain white-shoe companies, neighborhoods, and country clubs. Additionally, certain universities had quotas on how many Jews could be admitted. That said, the United States was the first country to present Jews with any real possibility of assimilation—for some this was the dream of a lifetime, while for others, especially the Orthodox Jews of Eastern Europe, this represented the death knell of religious life and therefore Judaism in general.

DID JEW KNOW?

German Jewish immigrants founded such enduring American Jewish institutions as B'nai B'rith, the American Jewish Committee, and the National Council of Jewish Women.

1840s German Jews begin arriving in America. By World War I, some 250,000 German Jews, many from affluent families, have made it to the land of opportunity.

1880s–1924 Eastern European Jews arrive in the United States. Between 1880 and the start of immigration quotas in 1924, two million Jews from Russia and Eastern Europe show up on the scene, making Ashkenazi Jews the majority. For the most part, these old-world laborers settle in the poorer areas of major cities such as New York, Chicago, Baltimore, and Philadelphia.

Let's just say that living conditions in these urban jungles were anything but ideal; crowded, squalid neighborhoods were the norm, and it was challenging to make a buck even in the best of times. Either because of this challenge or because of their ties to socialist causes in the Old Country, Jewish workers became active in the labor movement, supporting socialist and communist causes and advocating or striking on behalf of the worker. As a result, the Ashkenazim established the American Jew's stronghold in liberal politics.

The New York Diaspora: How the Jews Invented the Suburbs

While a fair number of Jews ended up in Canada and Argentina, two and a half million came to the United States. Of these, 85 percent came to New York City, of whom 75 percent settled Manhattan's Lower East Side, the South Bronx, and parts of Brooklyn. Subsequently, many of these New World pioneers skipped town for the lighter, brighter suburbs. In fact, historian Arthur Hertzberg estimated that between 1945 and 1965, one out of three Jews left the big cities for the 'burbs, "a rate higher than that of other Americans." These days, most of New York City's original Jewish stores and restaurants have closed and been replaced by restaurants whose menus boast artisanal ingredients and bars that feature mixologists. Some LES points of interest: the only Greek synagogue in the Western hemisphere and the Angel Orensanz Center, the fourth-oldest synagogue building in the United States.

> "Being Jewish in the South is like being Gentile in New York."
> —ELI EVANS

Jews Invent the Baby Boom!

The white-picket-fence, green-lawn suburb was invented (and prefabricated) by Jewish real-estate developer William Levitt. In 1946, Levitt and Sons acquired 4,000 acres (1,618 hectares) of potato fields in Hempstead, Long Island, where they built not only the largest development by a single developer to date, but

DID JEW KNOW? Approximately 3,000 of America's bravest Yids fought for the Confederacy. Additionally, General Robert E. Lee was menschy enough to allow Jewish soldiers to observe their holy days. Meantime, in 1862, Ulysses S. Grant issued General Order Number 11—an order that expelled all Jews from Mississippi, Kentucky, and Tennessee and is considered the United States' most blatant and officially sanctioned order of anti-Semitism. Grant's intention was to eliminate the black market in cotton, which he felt was run mostly by Jews.

also the largest housing development the United States had ever seen: 17,400 homes for 82,000 people. These homes were available for rent with an option to buy for $6,990 after a year. They required little or no down payment, were mass-produced via assembly line, and even came with their own modern kitchen appliances. Picture, if Jew will, a Tupperware party in the kitchen while Dad naps in a hammock out back. Due to the fast rate at which the good citizens of Levittown were pumping out babies, the town came to be known both as "Fertility Valley" and "the Rabbit Hutch."

While the citizens of Levittown reflected the melting pot well enough—Jews, Italians, and Irish people revving up the power lawnmower in relative harmony— African Americans were excluded from renting or purchasing homes in the community. In fact, every rental lease and contract expressly barred those who weren't members of the Caucasian race. This move didn't come from Levitt and Sons per se as much as the Federal Housing Administration, who were the development's financial backers, though Levitt would continue to defend the restriction on the grounds that he was following the social mores of the era and appealing to his customers. Though the 1948 U.S. Supreme Court Decision in Shelley v. Kraemer determined racial covenants are unconstitutional, Levitt did not agree to desegregate until 1960.

Jews of the American South

Lest you think that Jewish life in the United States only happens in the Northeast and Los Angeles, shalom, y'all! While less than 1 percent of the South's population is Jewish, the cities of New Orleans, Atlanta, Austin, and Jacksonville and (of course) the Florida coastline boast some seriously southern-fried communities.

That said, Southern Jews are not your typical bagels-and-lox Jews of the East Coast. Indeed, Jews of the South have their own distinctly Southern persona and foodways, a quality that journalist Wilbur J. Cash calls "a nation within a nation." Embracing both aspects of their identity, Southern Jews like their matzo balls fried, their brisket barbecued, and their lox with grits on a bagel. By the same token, they moved toward assimilation and acculturation somewhat more quickly than their Yankee counterparts and considered themselves an essential part of the Southern landscape, from *les bons temps rouler* to the Civil Rights movement.

While Jews settled in many cities across the American South, in 1800, the city of Charleston, South Carolina, boasted more Jews than any other North American city. This may well be because the Carolina Charter granted "liberty of conscience" to all settlers, including "Jews, Heathens, and dissenters." According to journalist Nell Porter Brown, Carolina also claimed the "first professing Jew elected to public office" and the second-oldest synagogue in America.

In an unfortunate episode of the American Jew, the Black Code of the French Colonial Period (mid-1700s) decreed that all Jews be expelled before they arrived! That said, no one really enforced the code. In New Orleans, the Jewish community was small but prominent, and anti-Semitism was rare. While Jews were sometimes excluded from social organizations and elite Mardi Gras Krewes, the Krewe of Rex's first King of Carnival in 1872 was Jewish. The Crescent City is currently home to some 13,000 Jews, including the author of *Did Jew Know*'s grandmother, who was born Bogalusa, Louisiana, in 1915 and knows from crawfish étouffée!

KOSHER COWBOYS

As the first wave of Jewish immigrants was making its way to the Americas between 1880 and World War I, some 50,000 Jews fleeing the increase of pogroms in the Pale of Settlement came to Argentina. Check this: A German Jewish millionaire and philanthropist, Baron Maurice de Hirsch, bought enormous swaths of land in Canada, the United States, and Argentina with the idea of the Jews going back to their roots and living off the land. And so each family took over a hundred-some-odd-acre plot of land in Argentina and began farming and raising cattle. As time went on, sixteen Jewish colonies formed in Argentina, each with Yiddish as the primary language!

The only glitch in this otherwise perfect offer was that the Jews of Eastern Europe were often scholars, rabbis, and merchants and found it difficult to adapt to this new outdoorsy lifestyle. Thus they began opening stores and eventually migrated toward Buenos Aires. These days, the communities have dwindled considerably, but the legend of the *gauchos judios*, Jewish cowboys, endures.

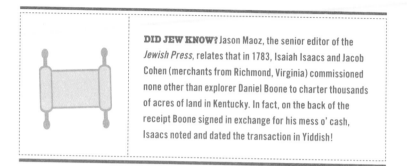

DID JEW KNOW? Jason Maoz, the senior editor of the *Jewish Press*, relates that in 1783, Isaiah Isaacs and Jacob Cohen (merchants from Richmond, Virginia) commissioned none other than explorer Daniel Boone to charter thousands of acres of land in Kentucky. In fact, on the back of the receipt Boone signed in exchange for his mess o' cash, Isaacs noted and dated the transaction in Yiddish!

Baby, It's Cold Outside: The Jews of Alaska

As the largest state in the union, Alaska unsurprisingly boasts thriving Jewish communities in Anchorage, Fairbanks, and Juneau. They may be small communities (only 6,000 Jews in a state bigger than Texas), but they still know how to get their Jew on. Dr. Gerhard Falk asserts that 70 percent of Alaskan Jews light Shabbat candles, while only 30 percent manage to light up in New York City. Time to put on your snowshoes and step it up, Big Apple!

Jews in Space!

While the above phrase may instantly remind one of Mel Brooks, there are actually some bona fide, bona Jewish astronauts who have both put their math skills to good use and evolved the ancient ways of the desert nomad into a penchant for space travel. Meet some Jewish boys (and a girl) who took the word *astronaut* beyond the old goldfish-bowl-on-the-head trick. Up next: Mezuzote on Mars?

- Boris Valentinovich Volynov (born 1934) was a Siberian-born Soviet cosmonaut who was also the world's first officially Jewish cosmonaut, flying two successful space missions under the Soyuz Program, in 1969 and 1975 respectively.
- Judy Resnik was the first Jewish astronaut and the first woman to go into space. She died in 1986 when the *Challenger* broke apart almost seventy-three seconds after liftoff for its tenth mission.
- Jeffrey Hoffman was the first American Jew in space, not to mention the first person to bring a Torah into space.
- Garrett Reisman was the first nice Jewish boy from New Jersey to live on the International Space Station.
- Ilan Ramon was the first Israeli astronaut. He died in 2003 when the space shuttle *Columbia* disintegrated on reentry.

Kiss My Diaspora

And there Jew have it: a history of the Chosen Tribe from the moment they were chosen well into the twenty-first century. Indeed, their story is so much more than a globetrotting travelogue for people with bad stomachs and brown curly hair. Like all great pioneering suburbanites, the proto-Jews left the urban hustle-bustle for various versions of a one-donkey town with neither decent restaurants nor schools. And so, from town to town, Canaan to Canaan, didst our weary travelers wander in search of a brave Jew world, beset from all sides by those who would as soon destroy them as hire them to do their taxes.

For uprooted souls who might never have left their hometowns, the various diasporas provided an opportunity for the Nation of Israel to connect and affect cultures on several continents. With no specific real estate to call their own, the Chosen Tribe became citizens of the world, their millennial mission to boldly Jew where no Jew had Jewed before.

CHAPTER 2

JEWIER THAN THOU:
Hasidic to Reform and Everything in Between

A Jewish sailor is shipwrecked on a desert island on which he builds a house and two synagogues. After many long and lonely years, a rescue crew from his original fleet manages to find him. Taking a tour of the island, they notice his house and the synagogues and ask him why he built two. "Oh, that other one?" he replied. "I would never go there."

—CLASSIC JEWISH JOKE

When the People of the Book became the People of the Book, there was just one people and one book. In other words, for approximately 3,000 years, Jewish life, though fraught with imminent destruction, was pretty straightforward: Everyone went to the same Temple, kept kosher, witnessed the same miracles, worshipped the same way, and, give or take reasonable adjustments for climate and income level, wore the same bedsheets. Even after the advent of pants, Judaism was still Judaism and Jews were still Jews; they wore specific ritual garments, ate kosher foods, and kept Shabbat as the Lord instructed. Everything was, if not hunky-dory, at least like the wedding scene from *Fiddler on the Roof* only without the dream sequence and the killer Klezmer band.

Cut to the late eighteenth and early nineteenth centuries and the birth of two distinct movements in Judaism: Hasidism and the German Reform Movement. Suddenly the Chosen Tribe became the Chosen Tribes: new movements of Judaism whose main differences derived from the stringency in which Halakhah, Jewish law, was observed. While fundamentally each Jew was still as Jewish as the next Jew, different levels and methods of observance began to define an evolving Jewish identity based not only on what Hashem originally instructed Moses and Aaron in the desert, but also on which rabbi ran the roost, not to mention what the roost in question thought about all the other roosts.

These days, the Jewish community, especially in the United States and Canada, has splintered into so many factions that the differences between the groups sometimes outweigh the similarities. To someone who is Reform or Conservative, a Hasidic person might seem Amish rather than Hamische, a throwback to a time when cousins married cousins and you died in the bed you were born in. Meantime, to an Orthodox Jew, a Reform Jew is little more than a foreskin away from being a goy, regardless of his primordial love for pastrami on rye or the size of his proboscis. And yet, technically, both are Jews. It's a quandary perhaps best summed up by the following joke:

> At an Orthodox wedding, the mother of the bride may be pregnant. At a Conservative wedding, the bride may be pregnant. At a Reform wedding, the rabbi may be pregnant. At a Reconstructionist wedding, the groom may be pregnant.

DID JEW(S) KNOW? Aside from Hasidic and Reform, the various delineations, including modern Orthodox, ultra-Orthodox, Conservadox, Conservative, Reform, Reconstructionist, Renewal, Jews for Jesus, and everything in between, wouldn't be invented until Jews immigrated to the United States and Canada. Also, most European Jews and Israelis consider themselves either Orthodox or secular, and there isn't as much of a brouhaha over who sits where in which pants and for how long in what temple.

So, before we make another value judgment about our black-hat-wearing or tattooed hipster Jewish neighbors, let's first examine their history, rituals, and customs. Who knows, you may have more in common with them than you think. Besides, who doesn't look good in black?

SINGIN' IN THE 'KRAINE:
Hasidim and How They Got That Way

As the Hare Krishnas are to Hinduism, so the Hasidim are to Judaism: an ecstatic offshoot of a parent religion where devotion is foremost and the outfit is questionable. A similar analogy may be drawn between the Hasidic movement and its goyishe (and older and blander) correlative the Protestant Church. Just as Protestantism offered its adherents universal access to God, the Hasidic movement espoused the radical idea that the common folk could enjoy their own personal love connection with God merely by singing, dancing, and praying. In fact, the word *Hasidic* actually means "pious ones" or "loving kindness."

Q: How many Hasidim does it take to change a lightbulb?

A: However many it took their grandparents to change it.

Yet, while Hasidism was more ecstatic/devotional and Protestantism more ascetic, both were a solution to the serious issue that the religious system at the time was not suiting the emotional and spiritual needs of its common folk. What's more, both movements shifted away from study (or excess) toward a universal method of worship whose message was "love me and serve me" rather than "devote your life to studying me and/or making paintings or mosaics of me." Suddenly, Gimpel the Fool could be a devout Jew without studying the Torah or understanding the Talmud. He just had to pray.

In terms of Hasidism, this distillation was in direct response to events that were horrible and demoralizing. Here's what went down: In the 1600s, the horrors of the

---

DOES THIS COME IN ANY OTHER COLOR BESIDES BLACK?

Way back in the 1700s, rabbis decreed that black garments be worn out of the home lest non-Jews become resentful and a pogrom break out. Additionally, when tsarist decrees started referring to the "Jewish kaftan," many wise Jews went for the Prince Albert cutaway instead. No, not *that* Prince Albert!

Chmielnicki Massacre and the debacle of Sabbatai Zevi had left Jewish morale at an all-time low; the time was ripe for revival. Enter Israel Ben Eliezer, a.k.a. the Ba'al Shem Tov or "Master of the Good Name," the charismatic Jew-ru who founded Hasidic Judaism on the principles of piety, devotion, and deep refinement of the inner-self. The Ba'al Shem Tov, or Besht, believed that God placed tremendous value on devotion and sincerity of spirit rather than on intellect alone. In general,

the essential teachings of Hasidism are twofold: Everything has elements of godliness, and God and man have an unlimited family plan. As a result, the Hasidim were originally viewed as heretics, and not just because they wore black wool suits and fur hats in August!

The Ba'al Shem Tov Versus the Vilna Gaon

One guy who thought the Hasidim were especially heretical and nutty was the Vilna Gaon (1720–1797), literally "the genius of Vilna," the Orthodox rebbe and leader of the Misnagdim—opponents of Hasidim. Where the Vilna Gaon placed tremendous importance on Jewish learning and asceticism, the Besht felt that because God was the world, it was high time to put the joy back in oy. In fact, to the outside observer, the Hasidic prayer service, with all its singing and *shuckling* (shaking), could almost look like a gay wedding that turned into a rave—minus the ABBA tunes and the glow sticks.

What most riled the Gaon was the fear that Hasidism would spark another messianic movement, something he felt would be the final, devastating blow to Eastern European Jewry. So, he issued a ban of excommunication upon the Hasidim and forbade Jews to conduct business with them or to marry them. Ultimately, this rift between the Misnagdim and the Hasidim proved to be small change in terms of outside factions threatening to decimate the Jewish population. Today, the Orthodox and Hasidic Orthodox venerate both the Besht and the Gaon as two of the three most influential Jews in terms of articulating the three initial streams of Judaism: Hasidic, Orthodox, and Reform. The other Jew was Moses Mendelssohn. But more on him in a few.

Jew-cy Haute Couture for the Kosher Set

HE Black pants (or knickers tucked into white socks), three-quarter-length black coat, white shirt, *tzitzit* (ritual fringes) either tucked in or out, no tie, *rekel* (long black coat worn on weekdays) versus the *bekishe* (holy-day coat similar to a *rekel*

Rebbe to Wear

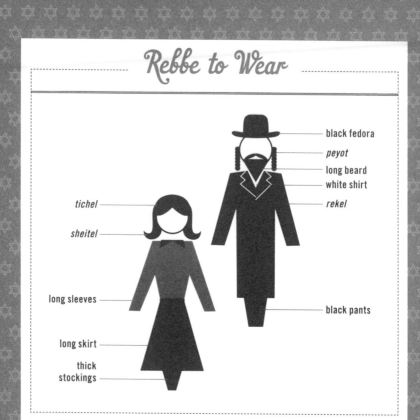

tichel

sheitel

long sleeves

long skirt

thick
stockings

black fedora

peyot

long beard

white shirt

rekel

black pants

DID JEW KNOW? The reason Satmar Hasidic women and those of a few other Hasidic groups shave their heads entirely is not so much because of *tzniut*, but because of a controversial stringency relating to the *mikveh*, ritual bath (see chapter 3) and the need to have no separation between hair and state for the mikveh's purification to be legit. All other groups, including other Hasidim, yeshivish, and especially modern Orthodox, can actually grow their hair as long as they want even after marriage, although they may cover it with a *sheitel* or a *tichel* depending on how *frum* they are. Get it?

but made out of satin), *gartel* (belt worn during prayer), black hat (under which is *kippah*—skullcap), *peyot* (earlocks), long beard. On special days, most Hasidim wear a *shtreimel*: a donut-shaped fur hat (also likened to a UFO). Polish Hasidim wear a *spodik* (similar to a *shtreimel* but long instead of wide). At the behest of their rebbe, Chabad Lubavitch forgo the *shtreimel*, in favor of traditional black fedora, whence the general moniker "black hats" for Hasidim. **NOTE:** *Many ultra-Orthodox Jews sport similar ensembles to those worn by their Hasidic brethren, save for the knickers, furry hats, and long coats, which, let's face it, are tough to pull off, even in Crown Heights, Brooklyn!*

And in case you thought all black hats look alike, take another look, my friend! Not all black hats are created equal!

Black fedora: Following that great millinery trendsetter otherwise known as the Lubavitcher Rebbe, Chabad Hasidim pinch their hats to form a triangle on the top.

Open-crown hats: The placement of the pinch and the size of the brim can delineate affiliation, not dissimilar to the way a gangbanger might wear colors.

Samet hat: Hungarian gents sometimes opt for a *samet* (black velvet hat) during the week, while others wear it only on Shabbat. There are two types of *samet* hat: the high and the flat. The Satmar tend to rock the flat variety.

SHE Thick stockings (opaque if Satmar); longish skirt, either ankle-length or considerably past the knees; flat shoes (no toes or toe cleavage); shirtsleeves beyond the elbow (in general nothing flashy or "showing," because of laws pertaining to *tzniut*, modesty); and no visible collarbone. Married women wear a *sheitel* (wig) or a *tichel* (scarf) over shortish/modest hair. Sometimes the übermodest wear a *tichel* over a *sheitel*. No pants! Why? Because wearing what pertains to a man is verboten, and vice versa if you're a guy; i.e., no slacks for Sarah and no *sheitel* for Schlomo! Cross-dressing is out!

By the 1830s, the majority of Jews in Poland, Galicia/Ukraine, significant chunks o' Belarus and Hungary had up and gone Hasidic. Next thing Jew know, a fair share of Hasidim schlepped to America during the great waves of Jewish emigration in the 1880s and then again in greater numbers after the Holocaust.

FRUM, FRUM, FRUM WENT MY HEARTSTRINGS

The Yiddish adjective *frum* means "devout" or "pious" and is synonymous with Orthodox Judaism. People who are *frum* observe all of the 613 commandments. *Frei*, on the other hand, is Yiddish for "free" and pertains to someone who is lax when it comes to certain of these commandments. *Orthodox* means "correct belief" in Greek.

While all Hasidim share certain similarities, such as living in insular communities, wearing traditional garb, and keeping Yiddish alive, there are more than thirty major sects, each hailing from different towns, following different rabbis, and practicing slightly different rituals. Let's break a few of them down:

Bobover Hasidim: A sect that originated in Bobowa, Galicia, the Bobov were almost entirely wiped out during the Holocaust, when the Germans murdered the Second Rebbe along with thousands of his followers. The Rebbe's son Shlomo Halberstam then became the Third Rebbe and made it his mission to rebuild the community, eventually setting up shop in Borough Park, Brooklyn, where the Bobovers are currently headquartered. When Rebbe Halberstam died, the tally of his mourners exceeded those of his father in prewar Poland! Other Bobov branches can be found in Montreal, Toronto, London, Antwerp, and Jerusalem.

The Breslov: Possibly the most ecstatic and spiritual sect, founded by Rebbe Nachman of Breslov, the Ba'al Shem Tov's great-grandson. The Breslovers espouse the importance of going to the forest to "talk" to God. This practice is called *hisbodedus*, literally "self-seclusion." If God doesn't answer, they keep calling until He picks up.

Chabad Lubavitch: One of the world's best-known Hasidic sects, not to mention the largest Jewish organization in the world. The Lubavitch, or Chabadniks, as they are sometimes known, derive their name from Lyubavichi, the Russian/Ukrainian town where the sect was based.

While some Chabadniks immigrated to America in the great Jewish migrations of the 1800s, it wasn't until 1940, when Lubavitcher Rebbe Yosef Yitzchak Schneersohn sailed into New York harbor, that the Lubavitch spiritual command center moved to Crown Heights, Brooklyn. Shortly thereafter, Rabbi Menachem

Mendel Schneerson, the Hasidic Jew-ru to end all Jew-rus, followed his father-in-law Yosef Yitzchak Schneersohn to Brooklyn, where he became the rabbinic superstar of the global Lubavitch community. The rest, as they say, is chistory!

Funnily enough, while the Lubavitchers set themselves apart from other Jews in terms of how they live, dress, and pray, they believe in love for all Jews no matter their level of observance or fashion sense, or lack thereof. When one Jew sins, it affects all Jews everywhere, even Madonna (just kidding; she's not a real Jew). But when a Jew fulfills even one mitzvah, everything is wine and roses for the Jewish people. Thus, the Lubavitch practice nonstop outreach and send *schlichim*, emissaries, all over the world not only to bring the light of the Torah to all Jews everywhere, but also to keep God's chosen partying like it's 1740.

In the Chabadnik spirit of "you've got to give it away to keep it," the Lubavitchers will also be happy to bring the party to Jew. Following their rebbe's orders to become active in *kiruv*, bringing secular Jews back to their Orthodox roots, the Lubavitchers routinely uproot themselves and move to whatever city the rebbe chooses. This practice of outreach is the Chabad method, ushering in the Messianic age by spreading Jewish ritual observance. To quote Rabbi Yosef Shlomo Kahaneman, "I have found two things in every city I have visited, Coca-Cola and Lubavitcher Hasidim."

Satmar Hasidim: A sect comprising mostly descendants of Hungarian and Romanian Holocaust survivors, the Satmar form the largest group in America. Founded by Rabbi Moshe Teitelbaum, the Satmar take their name from the town Szatmárnémeti (now Satu Mare in Romania). Though a goodly number actually live in Israel and all revere the Holy Land, the Satmars vehemently denounce Zionism. Here's why: The Talmud explains that the Jews have been foresworn by "three strong oaths neither to ascend the Holy Land by force, nor rebel against countries in which Jews live, nor by sin lest we prolong the coming of the Messiah."

THE 613 COMMANDMENTS

The 613 commandments are the principles of law that derive from the first Five Books of Moses, or the Torah. These commandments are either positive (as in, "thou must do") or negative (as in, "thou must NOT do.") The 365 negative commandments correspond to the number of days in the solar calendar year, and the 248 positive commandments correspond to the number of bones and major organs of the human body. While some of the commandments are more "I shouldn't do it, but if I do, I can make up for it on Yom Kippur," three negative commandments fall under the one-should-opt-for-death-rather-than-violate-it category: murder, idolatry, and forbidden sexual relations, such as incest or adultery.

Miss-Conception!

A TRUE/FALSE QUIZ ON HASIDISM

T | F   1. Hasidim and/or ultra-Orthodox couples have sex through a hole in a sheet.

T | F   2. *Peyot*, a.k.a. earlocks, are curlicues of hair worn Nellie Oleson–style in front of each ear by Hasidic and ultra-Orthodox males in accordance with the biblical prohibition against clipping hair at the temples.

T | F   3. Hasidic sartorial style is based on the way Polish nobles dressed in the 1700s.

T | F   4. Hasidic men wear a *gartel* (belt) during prayer so as to keep a barrier between their genitals and their heads.

T | F   5. All Hasidic and/or ultra-Orthodox women are bald under those wigs.

T | F   6. Hasidic men of certain sects sometimes wear black knickers tucked into white socks (rather than long pants) to keep their trouser buttons from touching the ground to obey a biblical mandate against being wasteful.

ANSWERS

1. **False.** Jewish law actually prohibits having sex while wearing clothes; in fact, anything that forms any kind of barrier between you and your partner, including condoms, is not allowed.

2. **True.**

3. **False.** Hasidic dress has little to do with the way Polish nobles once dressed. Some scholars believe that this myth was promulgated in the 1800s in an attempt to lure younger Jews toward a more secular-seeming style of dress. Additionally, the ensemble may have a Babylonian origin, which was then adopted by Jews, then the Persians, then the Turks, and THEN Polish nobility. So technically they copied us.

4. **True.** Jewish law requires that there be a barrier between the *schvantz* and the heart during prayer. This separation is intended to help keep a lid on the base instincts of the lower region so that the mind and lips (intellect and its expression) stay pure and true during prayer in accordance with the biblical command, "Prepare to meet your God, O Israel." And do it with your pants on.

5. **False.** Only Satmar women shave their heads completely; most ultra-Orthodox women cut their hair and wear it short under their *sheitels*.

6. **Truish.** May also be to avoid getting mud on their cuffs.

In America, the Satmar command center is in Williamsburg, Brooklyn, though there are other Satmar communities in Antwerp, Buenos Aires, and Jerusalem.

WHO WEARS THE PANTS:
Ultra vs. Modern Orthodox

Separation of Shul and State:
Ultra-Orthodox and Segregation of the Sexes

In general, while a main tenet of Judaism is family togetherness, this is maintained among the ultra-Orthodox through stringent separation of males from females outside the family structure, much like the tenet that keeps Jews separate from Gentiles, Shabbat from regular days, milk from meat, and so on. In Ortho world, boys and girls go to different schools and are kept apart as much as possible until they are married. Men and women also sit in separate sections of the synagogue and ride different parts of the bus. Some extreme ultra-Orthodox may even walk down separate sides of the street in places like Mea Shearim, which is one of the oldest Jewish neighborhoods in Jerusalem.

Other restrictions of the ultra-Orthodox can include:

- Study of secular subjects—though this can happen at certain schools after study of Jewish subjects and in a somewhat limited fashion
- Watching television or films (even if it's *Fiddler on the Roof* or *Yentl*)
- Listening to the radio or secular music
- Internet usage—may be allowed with a filter so as to ensure no one meanders into any naughty sites or chat rooms
- Reading secular newspapers

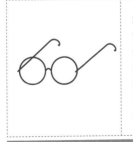

DID JEW KNOW? The Yiddish word *rebbe* means teacher, master, or mentor and derives from the Hebrew word *rebbi* or *rav*, meaning "great man" or "teacher." The Hasidim often use this honorific when referring to their rabbi/leader. The Lubavitch Hasidim believe that the Hebrew letters that comprise the word *rabbi* are also an acronym for Rosh B'nei Yisroel or "Head of Israel."

In general, the *Haredi*—a Hebrew term used to describe the ultra-Orthodox—regard any non-Orthodox streams as a deviation from "authentic Judiasm," as do the modern Orthodox, though they are considerably gentler about it. As you might guess, most Haredim live in Israel, North America, and Western Europe. Due to a high birthrate—the Haredim eschew the use of birth control—the ultra-Orthodox population doubles every twelve to twenty years!

Q: How many Orthodox Jews does it take to change a lightbulb?

A: Change?

While non-Orthodox peeps, North Americans especially, get all hung up on who wears a wig and whether or not the womenfolk are allowed to wear pants, the main difference between the ultra- and the modern Orthodox is that the modern view themselves as adhering just as strictly to the law as the ultra-Orthodox but are more open to the modern world, regardless of the fact that men and women still don't sit together in shul.

What's more, while few modern Orthodox rabbis would permit women to wear pants—and certainly never tight pants—they may make certain allowances for a modern/secular lifestyle, for example attending either religious or secular high schools and attending university and/or pursuing advanced degrees, both of which are mostly a no-go for ultra- and Hasidic Orthodox. Another difference: Unlike many ultra- and Hasidic Orthodox, the modern Orthodox see the religious significance of the State of Israel as a Jewish state rather than just a safe haven or a holy land.

This doesn't mean that the modern Orthodox are technically less stringent or observant, though that can sometimes be the case. The supreme value of modern

Orthodoxy is still to follow the Torah as it was writ from Sinai on. In other words, they might throw on some pants now and then, but they still *shomer* (observe) with the best of 'em.

REFORM JUDAISM: Good Idea, or Last Stop Before the Unitarian Church?

While the Orthodox Jews of Eastern Europe were busy leading their insular lives, a humpbacked German Jewish philosopher named Moses Mendelssohn (1729–1786) was busy translating the Torah into German and birthing the Haskala—the Jewish Enlightenment. Even though he was a religious Jew, Mendelssohn would later come to be known as the Father of the Reform Movement.

> Q: How many Reform Jews does it take to change a lightbulb?
> A: None. Anyone can change it whenever they want!

Nu, how did this *shanda* happen? I'll tell Jew: Unlike his fellow yeshiva *buchers*, Mendelssohn educated himself on secular topics and went on to become a highly regarded philosopher who once beat out none other than Immanuel Kant in an essay contest! Mendelssohn's study of German thought and philosophy made him realize the need for modern education, a combination of both Jewish and secular topics. It was his dream for Jews to acquire a rigorous education such that Germans might one day view Jews as equals—a mighty tall order considering the depth of German anti-Semitism at that time, but a man can dream.

Another radical belief of Mendelssohn's was that Jewish laws did not necessarily contain universal truths. His followers espoused this concept and urged Jews to ditch what they labeled a "medieval mindset." Their idea was to meld the best of Jewish thought with the best of the secular world to make for a well-educated and less provincial Jew. To Orthodox Jews, the idea of assimilation of this nature was nothing less than the death of Judaism.

DID JEW KNOW? Moses Mendelssohn may have been the father of the Reform Movement, but four of his six children converted to Christianity. Talk about *shanda*! However, the famous early-Romantic composer Felix Mendelssohn was his grandson. So, he got one thing right.

A few years down the road, Mendelssohn's Enlightenment would evolve—or devolve, depending on your perspective—into the Reform Tradition. Let's break it down: Reform Judaism introduced the vernacular, in this case, German, into the synagogue service rather than having the service conducted solely in Hebrew. To add insult to injury, they added an organist even though Jewish law forbids playing an instrument on Shabbat. Next thing you know, Reform Judaism dropped the notion that Jews are "a people." Instead, Judaism was seen simply as a religion, and Jews as, well, Jewish.

Another significant departure from Orthodox belief was the Reform concept that the Torah and many other Jewish texts, though meaningful, are not authoritative, i.e., written by humans, not God, and thus open to interpretation. What's more, the Reform movement viewed Orthodox belief as an overly literal interpretation of the Torah that conflicted with modern thought and science. For a Reform Jew, the one true obligation is to be ethical and believe in God, rather than to conform unquestioningly to the 613 commandments. Thus the focus shifted from rituals to

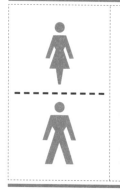

DID JEW KNOW? A *mechitza* is the physical divider that separates the men's section from the women's section in Orthodox synagogues and also at other religious celebrations such as weddings. Why? Because mingling of the sexes is distracting and therefore less conducive to prayer. The *mechitza* is often opaque to prevent the distracting practice of gazing. In recent times, the *mechitza* may divide the synagogue into left and right sides as opposed to the traditional front (male) and back (female). This division seems more "separate but equal," since the women aren't farther away from the service than the men.

"ethical monotheism," the notion that God's primary concern is that human beings behave ethically and make choices thusly, rather than for the sake of ritual alone.

These days, Reform temples in the Americas often conduct most of the service in English with a smattering of Hebrew, usually just for the biggie prayers such as the *Sh'ma*. Men and women sit together in the sanctuary. Also, Reform liturgy tends toward the gender-neutral, often swapping out the word *forefather* with *ancestor* and using *humankind* for *mankind*. Some Reform prayer books even try not to refer to God as a He. Finally, Reform Jews are about as likely to keep Kosher as a Chabadnik might one day tear into a plate of fried calamari.

Another big change catalyzed by the American Reform Movement is permitting ladyfolk to become rabbis and cantors. This is remarkable because Jewish law states that a cantor must be a Jewish male over the age of thirteen, the end. In 1968, Sally J. Preisand was the first female student accepted to rabbinical school, at Hebrew Union College. When she was ordained in 1972, she became the first female rabbi in America. In '75, Barbara Ostfeld-Horowitz became the first woman to be ordained as a cantor. Who wears the pants? We do! We do!

CONSERVATIVES ARE LIBERAL:
Conservative Judaism and the Remembrance of Things Past

The post-Haskala concept of Conservative Judaism, though still more lax than its *frum* brethren might like, arose in response to the liberal ideas of the Reform Movement in Germany and then flourished in North America. The descriptive Conservative—or *Masorti* ("traditional" in Hebrew) in all other countries outside the United States and Canada—implies the movement's aim, which was to conserve Jewish traditions of old rather than change them or kick them to the curb entirely. While Orthodox Judaism upholds the belief that God revealed the Torah to Moses on Mount Sinai, Conservative Judaism is more likely to offer multiple stances on this topic:

a) God and Moses did not pull an all-nighter, but God may have inspired Moses and the later prophets to write the Tanakh.

b) If God inspired the prophets to write the Tanakh, He did it nonverbally, as in by rolling His eyes and moaning until they felt guilty enough to write it down.

c) Since the Torah was a compilation album of material from varied sources, it's totally acceptable to employ modern methods of lit crit and historical analysis to both contextualize and understand it, but only if you do so at an Ivy League university. Because that's why your father worked so hard to send you to private school.

Q: How many Conservative Jews does it take to change a lightbulb?

A: I don't know. Call a committee meeting!

In terms of daily life, depending on how Conservative (as in neither Orthodox or Reform) a community of Jews may be, the boundary between Conservative and modern Orthodox can be somewhat blurry. A Conservative service might be conducted mostly in Hebrew, but men and women will generally sit together in synagogue, though, depending on the congregation, neither of these statements is necessarily always true. Also, a Conservative person may or may not keep kosher, while a modern Orthodox person pretty much always will. Some Conservative Jews may keep kosher at home but be decidedly more lax about eating out, while their modern Orthodox brethren generally eat only in kosher restaurants. Some modern Orthodox will eat in regular restaurants but won't eat *treif* or will only eat cold food in a nonkosher restaurant. As my father would say, "This is America! Everyone can have everything that they want."

Meanwhile, Conservative Judaism views Jewish law as binding, but allows that it must evolve to continue to meet the *mise-en-scene* of modern times, for example, driving to synagogue on Shabbat or wearing a tight dress to synagogue in order to attract a rich husband. In fact, the whole idea of Conservative Jewish thinking is to align with modern values, even if at first glance it seems that the lay person's level of commitment to the 613 commandments hovers at ten to twenty commandments. Also, since Conservative Jews are more open to modern ideas, it's no big deal if women wear pants, keep their hair long after marriage, or study secular topics.

If It Ain't Broke, Keep Fixing It:
Reconstructionist Judaism and the Solution of Evolution

Reconstructionist Judaism is a splinter group of Conservative Judaism cofounded by Rabbi Mordecai Kaplan (1881–1983) and his son-in-law, Rabbi Ira Eisenstein (1906–2001). The main tenet of Reconstructionism is that Judaism is an evolving expression of the traditional Jewish practice, as in Abraham's faith and era were one thing, Solomon's Temple another. By the same token, Jewish life in pre–World War II Europe is not Jewish life in the postwar era or the time of the Internet. Enter

DID JEW KNOW? *Shul* is the Yiddish word for "school" but is generally used to refer to "synagogue" in popular parlance among Ashkenazi Jews. Generally speaking, Orthodox and Hasidim use the word *shul* to refer to the *beit knesset*—Hebrew for "house of study." By the same token, Conservative Jews mostly say "synagogue," while Reform Jews are inclined to say "temple."

The Velveteen Rabbi

ORTHODOX:
Rabbi with a long beard
in a *bekishe*
and a *shtreimel*

CONSERVATIVE:
Rabbi in a suit with
a *kippah* and a *tallit*

REFORM:
Woman wearing jeans
and Teva sandals
with a guitar and an
OM necklace

WHY ORTHODOX JEWS CAN'T GET TATTOOS BUT CAN PIERCE THEIR EARS

The Torah is fine with ear piercing, for boys and girls. For example, when Abraham's servant Eliezer met Rebekah at the well, she gave him water for his camels, and he rewarded her with a nose ring and took her home to marry Isaac. When Aaron wanted the Jews to help make the golden calf, he asked the men for their wives' earrings. According to the Torah, God was not so big on Jewish people willingly marring their bodies. "Ye shall not make any cuttings in your flesh for the dead, nor print any marks upon you." (Leviticus 19:28) Another reason tattoos were verboten may be that many of the pagan cultures at the time of Moses used tattoos as part of their ritual practice. But even if you get drunk one night and wake up with a tramp stamp, don't vorry. You won't have to take an electric sander to your *tuchus* when the time comes to meet your maker. There is a general accord among rabbis that the notion that tattooed Jews can't be buried in a Jewish cemetery is ridiculous. Why? Jews are always supposed to honor their dead. And get this: Some Orthodox cemeteries have a separate section for tattooed Jews!

Reconstructionism! The ever-morphing mouthpiece of the People of the Scroll, the People of the Book, and the People of the Tablet!

Here's the 411 on Reconstructionist theory: In keeping with their Reform cousins, Reconstructionists believe that secular ethics and morality take precedence over the law. But Kaplan believed that it would be downright silly for modern Jews to continue to adhere to the mothership's static definition of God and His law in light of advances in science and technology. In other words, it's not so much about whether you keep kosher or wear pants as much as how your definition of kosher and pants stays au courant.

> Q: How many Reconstructionist Jews does it take to change a lightbulb?
>
> A: None. Who needs a lightbulb when you have a solar panel?

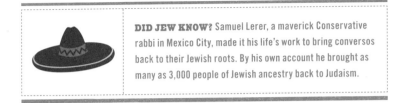

For example, rather than an old white man with a beard, the Reconstructionist God is more of an impersonal being who comprises all the natural (and unnatural) processes that humans need to become self-actualized Jews in His image. In other words, Reform Jews pray to God, and Reconstructionists pray to Whom It May Concern.

Fifty Shades of Oy Vey

And so the People of the Book didst become the Peoples of the Books, a journey that has ultimately been as arduous and divisive as it has been fruitful and fashion-forward. Where once the Temple was the Temple, the Torah the Torah, and a Jew was a Jew was a Jew, the expression of Judaism, especially in North America, has become a panoply of options and outfits as diverse as the cereal aisle at your local supermarket. Only here's the rub: Not only are there many options within the supermarket itself, but there are also myriad supermarkets and many types of shoppers with many different needs. In other words, these days even your choices have choices. The question is, which one will Jew choose, where will Jew sit, and who will be wearing the pants?

BEYOND THE NOSE: PIERCING YOUR SECRET NO-NO PLACE

Here's where the-Bible-says-I-can-pierce-myself-wherever-I-want gets tricky: genital and nipple piercing. Some rabbis might argue that genital piecing is not in sync with the notion of "human creation in the divine image." Regardless of your interpretation of divine image versus your grandparents' version of same, the Jewish law of *tzniut*, or modesty, is definitely called into question. This begs the question, who exactly is piercing your hoo-ha, and for what purposes? And if it would better your chances on JDate, might the Talmud actually greenlight it?

CHAPTER 3

THE CHOSEN VIBE: Jewish Rituals and Customs

For I am the Lord your God; sanctify yourself and be holy, for I am holy.

LEVITICUS II:44

For any Reform or Conservative Jew who has actually read the entire Torah, Leviticus at first seems like the biblical precursor to the Weight Watchers points system; only in the Good Book, points accrued don't help you fit into your skinny jeans as much as keep you in God's good graces until you finally lay off the dessert. That said, the entire Torah spells out the laws and precepts that essentially form the warp and weft of what it means to live, eat, and die as a kosher Jew, while still being able to have a little kosher fun the way God intended.

While some of these biblical precepts seem to state the obvious, as in don't eat bugs, make out with lepers, or canoodle your sister, others have an irrational quality, as though God were pulling a fast one on the Israelites when He came up with them, for instance using the ashes of a red heifer to purify someone who has come into contact with a corpse. (Numbers 19:18–19) Regardless of whether these laws seem rational, irrational, or downright weird, God's word on them is final and meant to be followed to the letter; otherwise, why would He have spent so much time in the desert dictating them to Moses?

KASHRUT: What's Kosher; What Isn't; and Why, God? Why?

Sometimes God has an eating disorder. Or so it seemed when He was laying down those crazy dietary laws to Moses *und* Aaron in Leviticus. At first glance, His injunctions regarding what not to eat and why make perfect sense for some desert nomad and his friendly neighborhood camel. On the other tablet, some rules seem almost passive-aggressive, for instance, the amount of time a Jew is expected to wait between meat and dairy consumption and what to do if said Jew should accidentally drop a pat of butter into the turkey chili. Especially when you consider the fact that the ancient Israelites were lucky to have even two pots and a pan and were basically wandering the desert with said pots and pan getting skin cancer for forty years. I mean, come on, God! Give a Jew a break!

EVERYBODY'S DOING IT ... NOT

These days, only the Orthodox make these ancient laws their raison d'être. Reform Jews ... not so much. This do-or-die versus I'll-die-if-I-do-it stance forms the great divide between the various sects, most notably Orthodox versus Conservative/Reform, many of whom wouldn't know the ashes of a red heifer from a ham sandwich if it hit them over the head with a Talmud tractate.

Tender Vittles: What It Means to Keep Kosher

Kosher is the Yiddish word for "fit" and applies to food that is ritually fit, correct, or pure. This Yiddish variant stems from the Hebrew word *kasher*, meaning "fit, proper, or lawful." While it specifically applies to the laws governing what foods observant Jews can and cannot eat and how they must be prepared and served, the word *kosher* has also come to have a more generalized meaning of spiritually correct, copacetic, or legit. *Treif*, on the other hand, is a Yiddish derivative of the Hebrew word *teref*, meaning "torn." It originally referred to nonkosher meat that was "from an animal torn in the field." (Exodus 22:30) As time went on, *treif* expanded to become an umbrella term for anything nonkosher, including situations and behaviors, such as stealing towels from your gym or having a tawdry one-night stand with a Gentile even if he's really hot.

While most Jews, even the most secular, know that it is decidedly *treif* to eat the product of the pig, they generally attribute the reason for this divine directive to ye olde methods of hygienic safety. But here's the thing: Since Judaism is basically an all-or-nothing deal, the laws of kashrut pertain not just to a healthy body but also to a healthy mind and soul. As Rabbi Hayim Halevy Donin points out, the food-related designations *tahor*, "clean," and *tamei*, "unclean," actually refer to the overarching concepts of holiness and defilement rather than simply sanitary and unsanitary, as many people think. The animals designated as *tamei* were fit neither for human consumption nor animal sacrifice, and not just to keep God from getting trichinosis. "For I am the Lord your God; sanctify yourself and be holy, for I am holy." (Leviticus 11:44)

Meantime, while Jews are busy keepin' it clean, they are also keeping it apart, not just clean from unclean, but milk from meat, and, of course, the old favorite of Jew from Gentile. "I am the Lord your God who has set you apart from all nations. You shall therefore separate the clean beast and the unclean." (Leviticus 20:24) To put it another way, for Jews to live as God intended, they must not only keep separate the clean from the unclean, but also keep themselves apart from non-Jews so that the nation of Israel can be fruitful and multiply while it enjoys a nice roast chicken.

DID JEW KNOW? God's commandments fall under two categories: *mishpatim,* meaning logical laws or judgments, such as prohibitions against murder or adultery; and *chukkim,* meaning because-I'm-God-and-I-say-so, such as the laws of family purity or dietary restrictions. Regardless of the incomprehensibility of the laws, Orthodox Jews accept *chukkim* as divine ordinance even when on the go or on vacation.

Hooves and Hechshers
SO WHAT THE HECK CAN I EAT?

ALLOWED (i.e., *kosher*)

HERBIVOROUS ANIMALS that have both cloven hooves and chew their own cud—sheep, cattle, goats, deer, and giraffe. **NOTE:** Not all herbivorous animals are kosher (for instance, camels)

FISH THAT HAVE BOTH FINS AND SCALES that can be easily removed without tearing the skin of the fish: salmon, tuna, sea bass, trout, cod, haddock, halibut, sole, whitefish, herring

CHICKEN, GEESE, DUCKS, DOVES

LOCUST, certain species

FORBIDDEN (i.e., *treif*)

ANIMALS that chew their own cud but don't have cloven hooves or animals that have cloven hooves but don't chew their own cud, i.e., pig, hare, rock badger, and camel

FISH THAT DON'T HAVE FINS OR SCALES: catfish, lobster, shrimp, crab, oysters, clams, eels, squid

BIRDS OF PREY: hawks, vultures, ravels, owls, herons, storks

ANYTHING THAT CRAWLS "UPON THE BELLY" like a snake, a snail, a rodent, or a lizard, or is a "winged swarming thing" such as an insect or a bat

PRODUCTS THAT COME FROM NONKOSHER CREATURES: The only exception to this rule is honey from bees

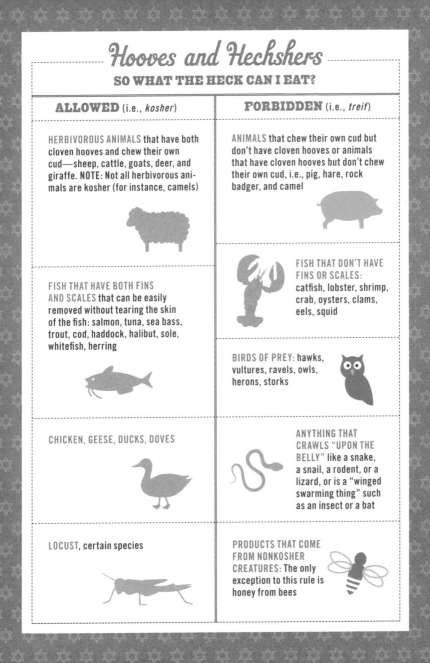

Finally, the laws of kashrut sanctify even the simple act of chewing and swallowing. An observant Jew who observes the mitzvot of kashrut cannot eat even a single peanut M&M without remembering that s/he is a Jew and that the Great Equalizer didst sanctify and command his people Israel to eat junk food. Let's examine God's divine Points Plus system.

Milkhik, Fleyshik, and the Triumph of Nothingness

So, while there are foods that are kosher and foods that are *treif*, never the twain shall meet and mate. In fact, the verse "You shall not boil a kid in its mother's milk" (Deuteronomy 14:21) is repeated three times in the Torah. From this injunction, the Talmud gleans the prohibition against eating milk and meat together. In other woids, here's where we get to the seemingly irrational (and challenging) anti-cheeseburger injunction.

Just as a Jew must keep separate the clean from the unclean, a Jew must never, under any circumstances mix *milkhik* (Yiddish for milk) with *fleyshik* (Yiddish for meat and/or fowl). There also exists a third, wishy-washy category called *pareve*, meaning that which contains neither milk nor meat and can therefore be eaten with milk and meat.

But wait, there's more: All *milkhik* must be kept separate from *fleyshik* AT ALL TIMES. As in, hope you have a big kitchen, because you're gonna need four sets of dishes: *milkhik, fleyshik,* and *milkhik* and *fleyshik* for Passover (more on this later). You also ideally need two dishwashers and two sinks, or you're going to spend a lot of time boiling everything.

Finally, if you eat a meat meal, you must wait anywhere from one to six hours before consuming dairy. Jews from Holland wait only an hour, while German Jews wait three. Everywhere else, the rabbis insist on six. If you want to pop a kosher chicken McNuggetberg after a dairy meal, the wait is about half an hour—but only after a thorough mouth rinsing.

AT-A-GLANCE GUIDE TO HECHSHERS

A *hechsher* is a symbol that means "kosher approved" and is found on the packaging of foods to let kosher consumers know that the food has been packaged in a kosher factory as well as under rabbinic supervision.

The most common *hechsher* is the U inside the letter O, the trademark for the Orthodox Union.

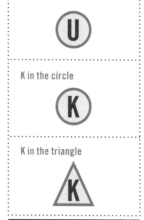

K in the circle

K in the triangle

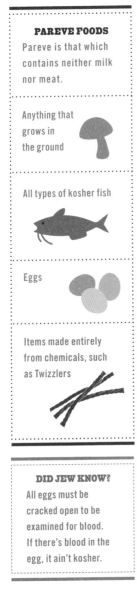

SHECHITAH (RITUAL SLAUGHTER) and Bloodletting Among the Kosher Set

In order to be considered kosher, all meat must not only hail from a kosher bird or beast, but it must also be slaughtered in a kosher manner by a *schochet* (ritual slaughterer). The *schochet* must be a righteous Jew who keeps Shabbat; otherwise that supposedly kosher filet mignon might as well be a bacon double cheeseburger. In other words, you cannot come upon a dead cow in the field, hack off its *tuchus,* and go home to prepare a nice rump roast, even if you went to fancy-schmancy charcuterie school. Here's why: You cannot eat *tuchus* AND the Torah forbids the eating of animals that died of natural causes (Deuteronomy 14:21).

The Torah also forbids the eating of blood from kosher animals, as well as any fat surrounding their vital organs. The reason for this rule stems from the time of the Tabernacle till the destruction of the Second Temple, when animal sacrifice was still de rigueur and blood symbolized the souls of the Israelites themselves. "For the soul of the flesh is in the blood and I have assigned it for you upon the altar to provide atonement for your souls." (Leviticus 17:11) **NOTE:** *These rules do not apply to fish or anyone in the cast and crew of* Twilight.

Killing Me Softly: How to Slaughter Kindly and Kosher-ly

According to the Oral Torah, the *schochet* must cut the beast's throat quickly, horizontally, and cleanly with a very sharp and smooth blade. Then all the blood must be drained from the meat before it has a chance to congeal, which would render the meat *treif.* In other words, I'll take my carpaccio well done, please.

After the blood is entirely drained, the meat must then be broiled or soaked and salted in order to remove any remaining blood. If soaking and salting, the meat is washed and then allowed to soak in cool water for half an hour. Next, it is covered with coarse salt and left to sit for an hour, during which time the remaining blood is drawn from the meat. Finally, the salt is rinsed off, and you're ready for Ruchel Ray.

Oops, I Did It Again: How to Re-Kosherize Plates and Flatware

If you or your cleaning person should unintentionally shake Parmesan cheese on a meat plate or stick a *fleyshik* spoon into a dairy pot, it's OK if both are cold. But if this happens when one or both are hot, you have to *kasher*, or re-kosherize, the item in question by boiling it in water or passing it over a flame until glowing. Some people bury unkoshered utensils in the ground for three days before kashering, though this tradition has no precedent in the official rulebooks. Some scholars posit that back in the day, earth was used as an abrasive agent when cleaning knives, and this led to the practice of burying utensils when circumstance demanded that they be kashered. Meantime, according to most sources, glass is considered neutral.

If you happen to serve cheese on *bubbe's* fine *fleyshik* china from the Old Country and it's too precious and delicate an item for boiling or blow torching, don't have a conniption. Just set the blessed dish aside for the period of one year, after which it may be rinsed and used without further concern.

THE FAMILY THAT PRAYS TOGETHER PRAYS TOGETHER: How a Jew Worships the Great Equalizer

Praying is how Jews converse with God. For this holy convo to be kosher, it must be pure, sincere, and from the heart. This was something that Abraham totally understood and excelled at back in the day. He just up and prayed unto God every morning in his own brilliant words. Now, this was all well and good for Abraham and his high-scoring descendants but mighty daunting for the rest of us nincompoops. Also, after the First Temple was destroyed, a uniform liturgy became essential. Suddenly, there was no Temple in which to offer up animal sacrifice or witness miracles. Somebody had to come up with something to say, and fast! That somebody was none other than Ezra the Scribe.

As the Second Temple was under construction, Ezra established the Great Assembly, a gang of 120 prophets, scribes, and sages who officially institutionalized the traditional synagogue service, including the Amidah, or the "Eighteen Benedictions," and the reading of the Torah. Without Ezra, we would still be sitting around Babylon complaining to God that our apartment's too small and the rent's too high and calling it prayer.

A Funny Thing Happened on the Way to the Quorum: What's a Minyan and Why Do You Need One?

According to the Mishnah, you need a klatch of ten males thirteen years of age or older to recite the essential prayers such as the Amidah or the Kaddish. Ditto for the Torah reading. This klatch is called a minyan, literally "to count," and is basically God's hearing aid for the prayers of the Chosen Tribe. In certain smaller congregations, it is often the custom to wait for more guys to show up or to get proactive and start pulling them in off the street. It's like a Jewish singles mixer: not enough men and most of them are bald.

Funnily enough, or sadly enough, sinners and idiots count as part of an Orthodox minyan, but not women. In fact, the Shulchan Aruch, Code of Jewish Law, states that even a man-animal who has committed a capital offense can still be counted among the ten, unless part of his punishment be some kind of religious ban.

SIX FEET UNDER: Jews and Death

Just as there is a kosher way to eat and to pray, there is also a kosher way to bury and mourn the dead, as well as a kosher way to handle the corpse in its brief sojourn from death to burial. Even though a Jew is buried ASAP, usually no more than three days after death, the body isn't just stuffed in a box and dumped in the ground. Rather, a series of elaborate rituals and customs are in place both to ensure the body is buried according to Jewish law and to respect the body as the earthly apartment complex of the soul.

Putting the *Fun* Back in Funeral: How to Bury and Mourn a Jew Like a Jew

In Judaism, life is the supreme value, with real estate coming in at a close second. In fact, the Talmud states that all people originate from a single person. Therefore taking a life is tantamount to destroying the world, and saving a life is the equivalent of saving the world, even if the life in question is that of Mel Gibson. And death, being part of life, is God's natural recycling process and the start of our imminent journey from this world to the next. As such, not only are specific mourning rituals part of God's sanctified requirements, but abundant carbs are too. God pretty much spells this out for Adam when He says, "By the sweat of your brow you shall eat bread until you will return to the ground from which you were taken. For you are dust, and to dust you shall return." (Genesis 3:19)

Shemirah: Guarding the Body of the Deceased

Immediately after a Jewish person dies, the body must be covered with a sheet. From the actual moment of death until the person is interred, usually no more than three days, a guard stands watch over the body to prevent any manner of disrespect or desecration. In the Talmud, one of the purposes of *shemirah* is to keep rodents at bay, though ostensibly it also works on annoying relatives.

Who Got the Props

JEWISH PRAYER ACCESSORIES AND THEIR ORIGINS

KIPPAH: (a.k.a. yarmulke or skullcap) For many Jews, wearing a *kippah* is a symbol of commitment to the Jewish people. Possible origin: In ancient Rome, a head covering was mandatory for all servants. Jews may have adopted this practice while at prayer to show that they were servants of the Lord. According to the Schulchan Aruch, a Jewish man should walk no more than four cubits (about seven feet or two meters) without his *kippah* on his head and even wear it while standing still. Where you don't have to wear it: in bed or in the shower.

TALLIT GADOL: Literally, "big sheet." The Torah commands men to wear tzitzit, a ritual fringe, at the four corners of their garments to serve as a reminder of the mitzvot. "You shall make for yourselves twisted threads on the four corners of your garment with which you cover yourself." (Deuteronomy 22:12) Since modern garments aren't four-cornered, the *tallit* was invented.

TALIT KATAN OR "SMALL TALLIT": Otherwise known as the tzitzit poncho, this is a four-cornered, fringed garment worn under the clothing by Orthodox males, like a lucky if somewhat unsexy undershirt.

MEZUZAH: A piece of parchment encased in a cute decorative case that is summarily affixed to the doorpost of a Jewish home. On this parchment is inscribed the Shema, the prayer in which the commandment to post these words "on the doorposts of thy house" is elucidated.

TEFILLIN/PHYLACTERIES: A set of two small black leather boxes containing parchment scrolls worn by observant Jewish males during the weekday morning prayer services. The hand tefillin is worn on the upper arm, while the head tefillin is placed above the forehead. The purpose of the tefillin, like the *tallit*, is to serve as a reminder that God led the Jews out of Egypt (and possibly that He had a bondage fetish).

Additionally, the mourners rend their garments, on the left if it's for a parent and on the right if it's for anyone else. This tearing is to symbolize the great void that the deceased has left in the life of the mourner. Rather than tearing their beloved Hugo Boss, Reform Jews often tear a piece of cloth and pin it to their lapel.

Another more palatable purpose of *shemirah* is to keep the soul of the person company so that they don't feel lonely while in such a liminal state. According to Kabbalah, when a person dies, their *neshama*, or soul, hovers in the vicinity of its earthly container, a.k.a. the body. During this time, the guard might read Psalms to the corpse to keep the *neshama*'s mind off the whole box-in-the-ground thing. Another important task of the guard is to make sure that it is Aunt Rose who actually ends up in Aunt Rose's coffin for all eternity and not some other dead Jew.

> "I don't believe in an afterlife, although I am bringing a change of underwear."
> —WOODY ALLEN

TAHARA: Just as a newborn is washed when it enters the world, so too is the body of the deceased. After all, the soul is about to wend its way to the spirit world, and when it gets there, it wants to smell nice in case it bumps into any of its ex-boyfriends. The *Chevra Kadisha*, literally "holy society," perform *tahara* or thorough ritual cleansing and dressing of the body while reciting prayers of forgiveness and peace. While the *tahara* requires that the body be clean and presentable, Jewish law forbids all forms of embalming. Much as the blood of an animal is considered soulful, the blood of the deceased is also essential and must be buried along with the body rather than callously discarded as biohazard. Additionally, since the Jews don't do the open-casket thing—mostly because it is seen as undignified and disrespectful of the dead—embalming (and making the body appear "lifelike") is ultimately considered tacky and unnecessary.

TACHRICHIM (BURIAL SHROUDS): Since the *neshama* is about to face its final judgment, clothes aren't as important as good deeds. Thus a clean white linen shroud, or *tachrich*, supplants designer threads. In addition to the shroud, men are also wrapped in a *tallit* whose fringes have been cut to symbolize the fact that

---

FLORES PARA LOS MUERTOS

Since Jewish law demands immediate burial, flowers are considered superfluous. In general, non-Jews keep their dead around for a considerably longer time before burial, which back in the day dictated the need for flowers to distract from the smell of the decaying corpse. Subsequently, the flower-free scenario became a way to distinguish a Jewish funeral from a non-Jewish one, so the trend stuck.

earthly requirements, even those sanctified by God, are now kinda beside the point.

ARON (THE CASKET): This is where the whole "For you are dust and to dust you shall return" (Genesis 3:19) thing comes in. Since a Jew must be returned as-is to the earth, the casket must be made of a natural material such as pine to allow decomposition to take place. Metal caskets are therefore out of the question, as is any other nonbiodegradable material. In essence, you could say that the Jews invented recycling long before Al Gore went to Harvard.

KVURA (BURIAL): Since a Jew's gotta return to dust, Jewish law is unequivocal that the dead must be buried. In fact, the *neshama*'s return to God's 7-Eleven is dependent upon the body's return to the earth whence it came. "Thus the dust returns to the ground, as it was, and the spirit returns to God who gave it." (Ecclesiastes 12:7) To ensure this divine trade-off, mausoleums are verboten, as are cremation, mummification, and cryogenics. A word on cremation: Though on some level it could be viewed as a manner of returning to earth, especially if the ashes are sprinkled somewhere scenic, it's still a no go. For one, it's seen as disrespectful to Aunt Ruth for her to end up as a bag of bone chunks, and second, because the Torah requires burial. Also, who wants Aunt Ruth to end up in their eye?

After the coffin is lowered into the ground, the immediate mourners shovel earth onto the coffin themselves until a significant mound of dirt has accumulated. This is both to indicate respect for the dead and to leave nothing undone. Then, and only then, is it possible for true healing (and true eating) to begin.

Grave Matters

Regarding the actual gravestone, it is customary for a marker to be set in place after the eleven-month Kaddish period has ended. The unveiling ceremony is basically the funeral redux, only shorter and at the graveside. Just before leaving the cemetery, the mourner places a small stone to commemorate his or her visit. This tradition may reflect the pagan custom of covering a corpse with stones when proper burial wasn't possible, or it may result from the custom of writing notes to the deceased and then weighing down said notes with stones. Eventually, the custom became the laying on of stones sans note.

Strictly Speaking:
The Emily Postewitz Guide to Making Shivah Calls

Shivah is the seven-day period of mourning following burial. For Reform and Conservative traditions, shivah is basically an opulent Jewish wake, with better food and no booze. If you are making a shivah call and it's a Reform or Conservative shindig, you can show up with a platter of cookies or little sandwiches. This will always give you something to do in the kitchen if the proceedings get too intense.

Though the Torah is all hopped up on *Olam Ha-Zeh*, life on Earth or the here and now, it doesn't explicitly refer to the afterlife. Instead, rabbinic discussions of the afterlife have evolved in response to that most human of questions: What happens to me when I die? Is there reincarnation, and if so, can I come back as a blonde? That said, there are a few places where a Jew might end up:

OLAM HA-BA: In Hebrew, "the world to come," or the afterlife, is a physical realm that will exist after the Messiah has come and the righteous dead are resurrected to enjoy life number two. Though this term does not appear in the Hebrew Bible, the Talmud states that "all of Israel has a share in the world to come." Resurrection of the dead is also one of Maimonides's Thirteen Principles of Faith. (See chapter 8 for more Maimonides).

GAN EDEN: According to Ye Olde Rabbis, *Gan Eden*, literally, "Garden of Eden," often synonymous with *Olam Ha-Ba*, is a paradise for the righteous, either sometime after death or after resurrection. It is important to note that Jewish eschatology, unlike the Christian concept of the Rapture, focuses on the coming

- Mourners do not sit on normal-sized chairs, but on low stools. Male mourners neither shave nor get haircuts. Women refrain from use of cosmetics. People may not bathe as often. Try not to say, "Tzeitel, you look so tired." Or, "Yankel, you smell."

- Do not pull the sheets off the mirrors trying to "brighten the place up." They have been deliberately placed there to make sure that no one is facing a mirror at the time of prayer, which would be too distracting. The covered mirrors also indicate that vanity has been put aside out of respect for the dead.

- People coming to pay their respects sit on regular-sized chairs surrounding the mourners, saying nothing, not even a "Hi, Abie," until the mourner addresses them, so as to respect the depth and gravitas of their grief. While sitting around, refrain from small talk. Instead, try to solve algebraic equations in your head so you look appropriately concerned and mournful.

- Though there is food, the atmosphere is subdued. Friends of the mourners may bring a "meal of comfort," which often consists of hard-boiled eggs, a food that is a symbol both of mourning and rebirth. If you are making a shivah call at the home of an Orthodox Jew, better not to bring victuals, especially if you're confused about the laws of kashrut.

of the Messiah and its regathering of the Diaspora, the restoration of Israel, and the smiting of her enemies. Though the Babylonian Talmud discusses the coming of the Messiah, more evocative descriptions of this event and all the drama it will entail are also found in Isaiah.

GEHENNA/GEHINOM: This hell equivalent is punishment central for people who have led an immoral life. Originally, *Gehenna* was a term derived from the Valley of the Son of Hinnom, a scary no-man's-land outside of Jerusalem, where children were ostensibly burnt as a sacrifice to the Ammonite god Moloch, whose worship God expressly forbade. "You shall not present any of your children to pass through for Moloch, and do not profane the name of your God—I am Hashem." (Leviticus 18:21) This ritual eventually evolved to mean hellfire. While no one wants to go to hell, one nice feature of Gehenna is that no matter what you did on Earth, you only visit for twelve measly months and not the rest of eternity. What's more, a bad Jew is given the opportunity to repent at the gates of Gehenna, where he or she may be pardoned and sent to *Gan Eden*.

HOLD THE PICKLE:
The Covenant of Circumcision

Circumcision is the oldest ritual in Judaism. Abraham was instructed to remove his foreskin at the ripe age of ninety-nine and then to circumcise his thirteen-year-old son Ishmael; his son Isaac was circumcised eight days after his birth, as are all Jewish boys since.

What happened was this: One night a voice informed Abraham that the time was nigh to scrape some skin from his *schmeckle*. "You shall circumcise the flesh of your foreskin, and that shall be the sign of the covenant between Me and you. . . . Thus, My covenant shall be in your flesh for an everlasting covenant." (Genesis 17:11) Contrary to any normal response from an adult male commanded to remove his own foreskin, Abraham fell on his face laughing. How can a peeled *schmeckle* signify a covenant with God? The answer: It just does. Guess Jew could say the joke's on him.

Another great circumcision story in the Torah is the story of Moses, his wife Zipporah, their son, and a strange encounter they had with God (or an angel of God) at an inn.

One night the family of Moses stopped at an inn. Suddenly, God appeared and tried to kill Moses for neglecting to circumcise his son. Thinking on her feet, Zipporah took a flint from her purse and cut off her son's foreskin and touched either God or Moses' feet with it and said, "You are a bridegroom by blood to me." And God let Moses alone. The interpretation of this cuddly story is basically that Zipporah averted what could have been the end of the Jews as a people by performing the rite herself. Behold the power of the purse!

What it comes down to is this: For whatever reason, God decided that "an uncircumcised male who will not circumcise the flesh of his foreskin—that soul will be cut off from his people; he has invalidated My covenant." (Genesis 17:12–14)

WHY MEN GET ALL THE COOL ACCESSORIES
AND ALL THE LADIES GET IS A WIG

Some rabbis assert that the soul of a woman is actually more closely aligned with God's, so she doesn't need all the extra schwag to remind her to fulfill her religious duties, while a man, simple creature that he is, needs all the help he can get. I still say the men should have to wear the wigs.

Some rabbis interpret the act as a removal of any barriers between men and God. Others view it as a symbol of moral commitment. Whatever the case, it's definitely one of those times where it's better to be a girl.

Brit Milah and Why It's Good to Employ a Mohel

The bris or Brit Milah, "covenant of circumcision," is a ritual event in which a professional foreskin remover dost remove the foreskin from a Jewish male eight days following his birth. **NOTE:** *Circumcision without the Brit Milah ceremony does not fulfill the requirements of the commandment and is considered an incomplete that might jeopardize the baby's Jewish GPA.*

This ceremony is celebrated as a *simcha*, a "joyous event" in which the bouncing baby boychik is both Jew-ified and officially given his Hebrew name. While the boy's father is supposed to perform the circumcision himself, most dads are not necessarily up to this task and so they hire a mohel, a person specially trained in enacting this commandment as well as the rituals and liturgy that surround this ancient and holy ceremony.

Either in the actual synagogue (Orthodox) or at the parents' home, the infant is handed to the *sandek*, usually the grandfather or another man "learned in the Torah," whom the mohel then instructs to hold down the trusting tyke so that the covenant can take place. If the grandfather be squeamish, the mohel can remind him that Abraham removed his own foreskin and instruct him to man up.

I'M AN ADULT CONVERTING TO JUDAISM; DO I STILL HAVE TO HAVE A BRIS?

Technically, yes. Though if you are already circumcised, you can just lose a drop of blood from the head of your penis. Let me say that again. You can just lose a drop of blood from the head of your penis. This tiny pinprick, if you will, fulfills the law that the mohel must draw blood from the circumcision wound. Most mohels do this with a special suction device, but it is the practice among some Orthodox rabbis to use their mouths. On the baby, not the convert.

The mohel then recites the blessing of circumcision, as does the father. The guests echo this prayer with the hope that the boy will enter into the Torah, live a life of good deeds, and get married to a nice Jewish girl. Preferably one from a good family whose parents are attractive, still married, and went to first-tier colleges.

Next, the mohel takes a cup of wine and recites over it a prayer in which he gives the baby his Hebrew name. A drop of wine is then placed in the baby's mouth, and the father takes a slug from the cup and then passes it to the mother, who is traditionally not present for the ceremony but might need to knock back some of the sauce regardless. **NOTE:** *In Reform and Conservative Brit Milah, the mother is generally present in the room where the ceremony is taking place.*

Oddly enough, in Ortho world, the event is concluded with a meat meal. Most Reform and Conservative Jews climax with an all-you-can-eat carb fest in the form of a bagel, smoked fish, and egg-salad buffet.

The Emily Postewitz Guide to Attending a Bris, and Where You Should Look During Those Three Horrible Seconds

A bris is a joyous event. If you're the baby or the mother, you might not think so, but it's technically supposed to be. The bris occurs on the eighth day following the bouncing baby boychik's birth, usually in the morning so your guests can witness this rite and still make it to work on time. P.S. You bring neither food nor gifts to a bris.

During the actual slice, it is advised to look at your shoes or at the ceiling rather than directly at the site of foreskin removal, especially if you're sensitive or a person who also has genitals on the outside of your body. If you feel faint, take a walk outside or drink some orange juice.

YOU SCORE MORE WHEN YOU'RE *TAHOR* (PURE): The *Mikveh* and Ritual Purity

The word *mikveh* translates from the Hebrew as "collection," as in, of water, optimally about 127 gallons or 480 liters of rain or flowing spring water; i.e., no bathtubs or Jacuzzis. Biblical regulations are also pretty keen on the idea that full immersion in the *mikveh* is an absolute must if you want to attain ritual purity after periods of impurity, especially those that have to do with blood, such as when Aunt Flow comes to visit and/or following childbirth. That said, there are other instances in the Torah where a person is required by God the Father to immerse in water:

- Jewish high priests on the Day of Atonement (Leviticus 16:24)
- After one has expelled semen (Leviticus 15:16)
- After sex (Leviticus 15:18)
- After one has come into contact with someone who has a skin condition such as leprosy either by touching or by sitting upon a vessel on which said person with said skin condition has plopped their *tuchus*. (Leviticus 15:5–10)
- After contact with a corpse or a grave—in addition to the red heifer ritual (Numbers 19:19)
- After eating meat from an animal that suffered a natural death (Leviticus 17:15)

Here's the Part About Sex

The Torah prohibits all forms of boot knockin' during the woman's menstrual period and at other times of uterine bleeding, such as post-childbirth or as a result of disease. (Leviticus 15:19–24) In fact, it's forbidden to have sex for a full seven days after the woman has ceased bleeding. **NOTE:** *The rabbis later broadened this no-sex rule to include bed-sharing or any kind of touching. This seven-day period in which all matters of funny stuff is off limits is called* niddah, *which means "separated."*

Our Tampons, Ourselves

Generally speaking, the whole concept of *tahor* and *niddah* seem to get many non-Orthodox people's dander up, mostly on the basis that both this custom and the *mikveh* are A) misogynist, B) archaic, C) weird, or D) all of the above. Admitting that the mitzvah is supra-rational or a *chok* (decree that surpasses understanding) doesn't necessarily help the old girl win more votes, nor does the whole "women have to take a bath, but men have to lose skin from their penis, which is way worse" argument. That said, men are also considered *tamei* after they discharge semen. Many people misunderstand the word *purity* to mean simply "clean" and therefore view the ritual bath as an indication that both the red river and women are "dirty."

In actuality, some rabbis believe that life is the essence of purity and death is the essence of impurity. Therefore, a woman's menses is actually the death of a potential life. Or the potential of a potential life, depending on your take.

Immersion Excursion: How to Go to a *Mikveh*

The *mikveh* is not a bath in the sense of Rubber Ducky. Nor is it a spa. Rather, it is a body of water used for ritual immersion purposes only. Therefore, before we hit the hot tub, we have to get clean. Really clean. As in, a *mikveh* attendant is going to scrutinize every nook and cranny to make sure they have been acceptably cleaned *prior* to pool time. In other words, after you scrub down like a maniac, you must also empty your bladder and bowels, blow your nose, wash your hair, clean the corners of your eyes, clean your fingernails and toenails, remove all loose hairs and foreign substances (such as leftover adhesive from a Band-Aid), and scrub your elbows, knees, and feet to slough off dead skin. Why? Because all barriers between skin and water must be removed prior to immersion. Possible barriers include clothing and underclothing, *sheitels*, toupees, makeup, contact lenses, false teeth, hearing aids, removable prostheses, and nail polish.

Once it has been determined you're suitably fresh and so clean, you can finally hit the *mikveh*, immerse completely and remain under the water for a few moments. Then stand and utter appropriate blessing number one. Rinse, repeat.

So, Who Goes to the *Mikveh?*

Generally speaking, only Orthodox women go to the *mikveh* with real regularity. Since the assumption is that unmarried women are not making the beast with two *tuchuses*, only married women are allowed to go, regardless of the fact that this rule would apply to anyone who did not wish to be in *niddah*. The two exceptions to this rule are that a bride may go before she is married, and all female converts go regardless of marital status. Some Hasidic men go before the High Holidays or

DID JEW KNOW? Although the *mikveh*, or ritual bath, is a biblical mitzvah mostly associated with women and their menstrual cycle, its purpose is for ritual purification rather than simply personal hygiene. The *mikveh* is also a compulsory part of the Jewish wedding ritual for brides and customary for grooms as well as for those converting to Judaism. What's more, the Christian ritual of baptism comes from the *mikveh*. Copycats!

Sabbath, but they go to a separate bath or at a special men-only time. What do you think this is, the Grotto?

BOYS TO MEN: The Bar Mitzvah, or How to Sock Some Serious Dough Away for College

As any parent of a thirteen-year-old boy will tell you, getting your son over the bar may take several trips to one, and/or your local bakery, depending on your poison. Indeed, a bar mitzvah, literally "son of the commandments," is a *simcha* celebrating the watershed moment in a boy's life when he becomes a man. According to the Talmud, when a boy turns thirteen, he becomes bar mitzvah, regardless of whether he has an actual bar mitzvah ceremony. As a bar mitzvah, young Schlomo can now be counted in a minyan (see page 63), lay tefillin (if not necessarily get laid), and lead prayer services. In fact, from age thirteen on, a Jewish boy bears personal responsibility for his actions in terms of Jewish law and ethics even though, technically, he is still getting an allowance.

While the earliest reference to any kind of actual ceremony commemorating this milestone is from the time of the Second Temple, it wasn't until the Middle Ages that the central act of this new rite of passage became an aliyah—being called to bless or read from the Torah. Subsequently, other ritual elements were added to beef up the act, such as delivering discourses on the passage being read, and *seudat mitzvah*, literally a commanded celebratory meal that may or may not include a giant cake in the shape of Yankee Stadium.

These days the term *bar mitzvah* has become synonymous both with the religious ceremony and the fête that follows. Let's break it down: On the first Sabbath after he turns thirteen, young Schlomo is called up to read the weekly Torah portion as well as something called a haftarah portion, an excerpt from the Prophets section of the Hebrew Bible. In order to prepare for this undertaking, our newly minted man-child may practice (or pretend to practice) his Torah portion for a least a

DID JEW KNOW? Bar mitzvah ceremonies do not appear in the Hebrew Bible. In fact, it wasn't until the first century CE that age thirteen became the universal moment symbolizing the inception of male adulthood, a view ratified in the Talmud Aboth 5:25. Funnily enough, elsewhere in the Talmud, there are opinions that one is only obligated when one has two pubic hairs. Length not specified.

year or more, during which time he also prepares his *d'var Torah*, a speech on his Torah reading or another relevant Jewish topic (for example, what it means to be a Jewish man or how great it is that my grandparents survived the Nazis and came to America so I could get a giant bar mitzvah cake in the shape of Yankee Stadium).

In most North American cities, what follows this whole Jewish performance-art experience is mitzvapalooza—a lavish, ostentatious party that may or may not feature an ice sculpture of the bar mitzvah boy or a live performance by Jon Bon Jovi. Gifts are common; indeed, the bar mitzvah boy stands to rake in a considerable amount of gelt for his herculean memorization efforts. For instance, Irvine Robbins, the cofounder of Baskin-Robbins, started his ice cream empire with money he saved from his bar mitzvah!

THE TOP FIVE EXOTIC LOCALES TO GET A DESTINATION BAR/ BAT MITZVAH

1 The Western Wall in Jerusalem

2 Anne Frank's house in Amsterdam

3 Masada, overlooking the Dead Sea

4 San Juan, Puerto Rico

5 Barbra Streisand's backyard

When a Jewish Girl Becomes a Man: The Bat Mitzvah

In the Reform and Conservative traditions, girls become bat mitzvah, or "daughter of the law," at twelve and celebrate this coming of age in much the same way their brothers do, with a Torah reading and an ostentatious party. That said, in Orthodox circles, the bat mitzvah ceremony will not include little Ilana or Aliza leading a religious service, because women are technically ineligible to lead communal religious services. A few Orthodox congregations may allow the bat mitzvah girl to read the Torah in women-only prayer groups, but this is considered unusual. In congregations where women are not allowed to read from the Torah, they can deliver a prepared lecture on a Jewish topic to a large room of other bored teenagers.

DID JEW KNOW? The first bat mitzvah in America occurred on March 18, 1922. The little lady in question was none other than twelve-year-old Judith Kaplan Eisenstein, the daughter of Mordecai Kaplan, the rebel rabbi who founded the Reconstructionist movement. By the end of the twentieth century, practically all non-Orthodox congregations were jumping on the newly invented bat mitzvah bandwagon.

SUNRISE, SUNSET:
Jewish Marriage Customs

In Ortho world, the sole purpose of dating is to find one's *bashert*, i.e., destiny or soul mate, and is overseen by the prospective couple's progenitors and/or a professional matchmaker. In order to ensure that the *shidduch*, arranged marriage, will be a worthwhile union, both the bride's and groom's parents make inquiries about each partner's character, level of learning/religious observance, 401(K), and physical appearance. The bride- and groom-to-be may get together anywhere from a few times to regularly for a few months to discover if they will be able to tolerate one another for the long haul—note that getting together in no way implies *getting together*, at least until the hall has been paid for—and then the

> "It doesn't matter what happens at the temple, it's the party that counts."
> —*KEEPING UP WITH THE STEINS*

engagement is announced. In ultra-Orthodox and Hasidic circles, these *shidduch* dates can start as early as age eighteen. In more stringent communities, rather than going on an actual date, the couple goes to a *bashow*, in which the young male and his parents go to the gal's house and the prospective couple has an at-home date with both sets of parents present. While this custom may seem archaic and invasive, and makes it nearly impossible to get your sext on, at least it eliminates the sad reality of Internet dating.

IT'S OVER WHEN IT'S OVER: HAS AUNT FLOW REALLY LEFT THE BUILDING? ASK THE YOETZET HALACHA!

Time was, an Orthodox woman who was uncertain as to whether her time of *niddah* was complete would take her undergarments to be examined by her friendly neighborhood rabbi, who would then make a pronouncement as to the type of uterine discharge and whether or not the woman could resume having marital relations. Awkward! Enter the *Yoetzet Halacha*, literally "the adviser," a female Halakhic adviser on topics having to do with the laws of family purity and other related women's health issues that a nice Jewish girl might feel uncomfortable discussing in front of her rabbi. The concept of a *Yoetzet Halacha* is a relatively new development in the more modern streams of Orthodoxy and is considered ancillary to rabbinical ruling. Service also includes panty inspection.

In Reform land, a *shidduch* is any form of blind date where a friend or co-worker takes pity on you and sets you up with their husband's college roommate or friend from Zumba. Fun fact: If you arrange three *shidduchim* that end in marriage, you go to Jewish heaven.

Is There a Canopy in Store for Me?
What to Expect at a Jewish Wedding

Since Orthodox Jews don't follow the same protocol as a secular wedding celebration—the rehearsal dinner, the wedding, and then a brunch following—the *aufruf*, Yiddish for "calling up," is the spiritual equivalent of the rehearsal dinner. For Orthodox Ashkenazic Jews, the *aufruf* takes place on the Shabbat before the wedding. In the *aufruf*, the groom is called up for an aliyah. After the Torah reading, women pelt the groom with candies, and the groom's family invites everyone over for a festive Kiddush (see page 88). In accordance with the custom that the bride and groom must refrain from seeing each other for a week before the wedding, Orthodox brides don't attend the *aufruf*. Instead, on the Shabbat before the wedding, the bride's lady friends and relatives gather to keep the bride company and joke away her wedding jitters and/or just tell her to close her eyes and think of Jerusalem.

The *Ketubah*

The *ketubah* is essentially a Jewish prenup that sets forth the rights and responsibilities of the groom for his beloved: clothing, food, sex, *and* hopefully a nice wad of cash in the event of a divorce. The *ketubah* is signed by two witnesses and read aloud under the chuppah.

The Chuppah

A chuppah is the canopy under which the bride and groom stand during their wedding ceremony. It symbolizes both the new home that the couple will build together and the House of Israel, under which all Jews convene with the Big Man. Some chuppah fun facts:

- As the tent of Abraham remained open, so the chuppah is open on all four sides.
- Just as the *kippah* serves as a reminder that God is the Big Kahuna, the chuppah is also a symbol that the marriage ceremony is part of God's mysterious and loving master plan.

So What the Heck Is Going on Under There?

In many Jewish weddings the bride circles the groom either three or seven times under the chuppah before the rabbi begins the wedding ceremony. Both journeys have biblical precedents. The first stems from Hosea 2:21–22, when God tells the Jewish people that He betroths Himself to them forever, with righteousness, justice, kindness, mercy, and, finally, fidelity. It may also imply the groom's three obligations to his little lady: food, clothing, sex. The seven circles commemorate Joshua's circling the walls of Jericho seven times before they fell. Thus the bride circles her man and the walls between them come a-tumblin' down and their souls are forever united. An additional Kabbalistic interpretation is that the seven circles also symbolize the seven days of creation.

Then What?

After the whole "bride as holy hula hoop" situation, there follows the *kiddushin*, betrothal; followed by the *nissuin*, nuptials; and finally the chanting of the Sheva Brachot, or seven blessings, and finally the infamously ubiquitous glass-stomping routine.

Mazel Tov! Breaking the Glass

At the end of the wedding ceremony, the groom stomps on a glass (or the more user-friendly lightbulb wrapped in a napkin) with his right foot. There are a few hypotheses as to the origin of this custom, the most widely held being that the broken glass serves as a reminder not only of the First and Second Temples, but also the Third and more glorious one that has not been built. So, while the wedding is a *simcha*, Jews mourn the lost Temple(s) regardless.

DID JEW KNOW? The Hora . . . The Hora! However unnerving or neurosis-inducing it may seem for the bride and the groom clutching the seat of their chairs for dear life as their friends and relations hoist them sky high and enthusiastically bounce them up and down, the hora is actually meant to be a joyful experience. In fact, the wedding guests are obligated by the Talmud to make sure the bride and groom enjoy their wedding. The song accompanying this whole chair dance number is, of course, "Hava Nagila," or "let us rejoice" in Hebrew.

When to Consummate a Jewish Marriage

Strictly speaking, one of the requirements of an Orthodox wedding is to consummate the marriage right at the wedding ceremony. While the bride and groom may not actually be getting busy at that exact juncture, they must spend some time secluded in a room together "sharing a meal" just after the wedding ceremony. This seclusion is called *yichud*. While *yichud* is taking place, the wedding guests loudly chew their appetizers so they don't have to hear Yankel and Rebecca's first foray into the golden palace of the Himalayas, and so Yankel and Rebecca can hear Aunt Sadie complaining that her tea isn't hot enough, forever cementing the aphrodisiac quality of lamentation that pervades every Jewish home. This practice is absent from Reform and Conservative wedding traditions.

Meanwhile, here's the kicker: The hora isn't even originally Jewish. It's a Romanian wedding ritual that went Jewish at some point during the last century! Another hora origin theory is that it may also hail from the tradition of carrying royalty aloft on chairs, in this instance signifying the bride and groom's proximity to the divine as a result of their divine union.

Along with the "Banana Boat Song," "*Hava Nagila*" was one of Harry Belafonte's signature numbers. In fact, Belafonte once uttered the following amazing statement: "Most Jews in America learned that song from me."

Gotta Getta Get: Jewish Divorce

Much as nobody likes to bring up the *D* word, sometimes even Jewish marriages don't work out. *What?* On such rare, rare occasions, a husband must present a get, a Jewish divorce document, to his soon-to-be-ex wife. **NOTE:** *The get is not a civil divorce; that's a whole other expensive shebang.*

Here's what the get actually says: "You are hereby permitted to all men." As in, now that you are no longer my ball-and-chain, the rules against adultery are no longer pertinent. It's that easy.

Speaking of chain, *agunah*, Hebrew for "anchored" or "chained," is a term for a Jewish woman who is chained to her marriage until her husband manumits her on the official, meaning that without a get, a woman cannot break the bonds of marriage and thus cannot remarry, even if her man abandoned her or is presumed dead.

CHARITY: Jews and *Tzedakah*

While one unfortunate Jewish stereotype is the age-old image of Cheapy the Jew, the truth is that Jewish law obligates the Chosen Tribe to donate money to charitable causes. This act of giving is called *tzedakah*, a Hebrew word meaning "righteousness." In fact, the Torah instructs Jews to fulfill the obligation of *tzedakah* by giving 10 percent of their income to the poor every third year (Deuteronomy 26:12), plus an additional unspecified offering following harvest reaping. (Leviticus 19:9-10) If you're not a reaper, this just means mo' money.

Some Talmudic rabbis and sages assert that *tzedakah* is the highest com-

mandment of all, the energy equivalent to all other commandments combined. Maimonides devoted some serious parchment in his Mishneh Torah to instructions regarding laws concerning gifts for the poor. Furthermore, Rabbi Yehoshua ben Korcha basically likens a person who doesn't fulfill the mitzvah of *tzedakah* to an oyster-po'boy-eating worshipper of idols. Finally, the liturgy of the High Holidays asserts that bad things cometh to those who have sinned, but *tefillah* (prayer), *teshuvah* (repentance), and *tzedakah* can reverse this judgment no matter how many Sundays have passed without calling your mother.

Finally, check this: In 2006, *Businessweek*'s list of the fifty most generous philanthropists included fifteen Jews. Pretty amazing when you figure that Jews, who make up only 2 percent of the American population, are 30 percent of America's biggest donors. In general, Jews rank pretty darn high on such lists. They also comprise more than half of the first fifty-seven billionaires to join the Bill Gates and Warren Buffet Giving Pledge, a group of megarich Americans who have vowed to give away more than half their assets before they die! Now, *that's* what I call generous!

Law & Order SV-Jew

Much like the adage "happy wife, happy life," the Torah's be-kosher-or-die-trying mandate applies to all facets of Jewish living, from the kitchen to the coffin and beyond. Indeed, the Lord God didst dictate to Moses His specific instructions for how to keep your mother happy, your soul healthy, and the Messiah on speed-dial: Eat no flesh from forbidden animals, lay off the blood, and marry a nice Jewish girl, and not only will your kitchen be kosher, but Jew(s) will too! While the Diaspora, Moses Mendelssohn, and the advent of shrimp cocktail didst veer a mess o' Yids from the law as it was writ and re-writ, one salient fact remains: You may not keep kosher, but you are what you eat.

CHAPTER 4

HOLY DAZE:
A Survival Guide to
the Jewish Holidays
(High or Otherwise)

They tried to kill us.
They failed. Let's eat!

—CLASSIC JEWISH JOKE

While many Jewish holidays commemorate tragic events in Jewish history (though some of those did have happy endings), other holidays are straight-up joyful. Still others are personal and reflective, a time to consider who you are and how to clean up your act before God takes your toys away for good. On the one hand, you have your Passover and your Purim and your Hanukah, all holidays that celebrate a triumphant vanquishing of the enemy but at great collective cost. On the other, you have your introspective holy days—holidays during which you can kick back, tune in, and get real about the week, the year, or your personal relationship with God, whether this relationship is deeply committed or you're still seeing other people.

For Reform Jews in the United States, most of whom are Jewish-minded rather than religious, holiday "observance" is casual and happens four or fewer times a year, that is to say, on Rosh Hashanah, Yom Kippur, Hanukah, and Passover. Indeed, said days and the foods consumed therein form the sum total of many a Jew's ritual observance, a pick-and-choose spiritual smorgasbord that's possibly two steps short of shrimp cocktail under the mistletoe. For religiously observant Jews—the Orthodox and most Jews living outside the Americas—knowing the history behind the holidays and maintaining strict ritual observance is an important way of showing one's devotion to God via prayer, study, and remembrance rather than an excuse to buy expensive handbags and overindulge in fried food.

But now that we are back to the food, with the exception of the hardcore fast days—more on those in a few—the majority of Jewish holidays center around certain symbolic foods and how to ingest as many of them as possible without falling off the bikini-ready bandwagon. So while dyspepsia is a badge of honor in most Jewish households during regular days, this injunction goes triple for the feast days, mostly because now not only do the foods actually mean something, but God literally commands us to eat them and multiply! It's like Jewish loaves and fishes for the kosher set; in other words, biblically sanctioned bagels, lox, and sex! Thanks, God!

DID JEW KNOW? Jewish holidays fall into three categories: biblical, rabbinic, and post-rabbinic. Biblical holidays are the ones that get a shout-out in the Bible, such as Passover, Shavuot, Sukkot, Rosh Hashanah, and Yom Kippur. Rabbinic holidays are those that developed during the rabbinic period: Shemini Atzeret, Simchat Torah, Hanukah, and Tisha B'Av. Post-rabbinic holidays commemorate significant events in Jewish history during the past 2,000 years: Yom Hashoah, Yom Ha'atzmaut, Yom Hazikaron, and Yom Yerushalayim. Tu Bishvat is also considered post-rabbinic.

When's the Party?

The Jewish day begins and ends at sunset, rather than midnight, so all Jewish holidays begin at sundown on the evening before the specified date. Jews infer this order from the wording of the story of creation in Genesis chapter 1: "And there was evening, and there was morning, one day." (Genesis 1:5) Another reason for this order is that it's easier to tell when the sun is officially down than when it is up. Before the sixteenth century—when clocks were invented—no one thought in terms of minutes, only in terms of day, night, and astrological patterns. The Jews were among the earliest peoples to use astronomy as a method of tracking elaborate patterns in the sky to tell time and organize it into a reliable calendar.

Time after Time: A Note on the Hebrew Calendar

In all countries outside of Israel, holidays are celebrated for an extra day beyond the biblical requirement. Here's why: The Jewish calendar is lunar, which means that each month begins with the new moon. As soon as the Sanhedrin (see page 118) caught a glimpse of the new moon, they sent messengers to inform people that the new month had begun. Now, this was all well and good for the party-time people who lived in the next village, but not so good for those who dwelt out of town. To remedy this glitch in the system, those in more remote locales went by the day count of the previous month (twenty-nine or thirty days) and celebrated the holiday on both days just to be safe.

Even after a more precise calendar came into play, all Jews maintained this ancestral practice except for Israelis, even when they are not in Israel, mostly because it was never the custom of their ancestors. The exception to this rule is Rosh Hashanah, because it occurs on the first day of the month, when all messengers had the day off for the new moon. Thus, even Israelis didn't know when it was officially the new moon. Meanwhile, Yom Kippur is celebrated for one day only, mostly because fasting for two whole days would be too much of a hardship for your average Jew who was used to gorging during the holiday season.

AND ON THE SEVENTH DAY, HE ATE TUNA SALAD: The Ritual of Shabbat

Shabbat is not only the oldest Jewish holiday, originating from Moses receiving the Ten Commandments on Mount Sinai, but it is also the only ritual observance mentioned in the Ten Commandments—"Remember the Sabbath Day, to keep it Holy." (Exodus 20:8) Indeed, most people unfamiliar with Shabbat focus on its oys rather than its joys, that is, seeing it as a time of restrictions rather than a time when Jews can at last set aside "weekday concerns" such as work or rush-hour traffic and devote themselves to higher pursuits like praying, eating, and, yes, *schtupping*. The Talmud enjoins that Shabbat is a wondrous gift that God gave to the Jewish people, and the Jew who fulfils its mitzvot is considered God's partner in creation.

> "More than Israel has kept Shabbat, Shabbat has kept Israel."
> —AHAD HA'AM

Though Shabbat commemorates God's creation of the world, the actual Shabbat ritual as we know it today didn't go official until Moses and the Tabernacle. Since Shabbat is so old and so important—more important than even Yom Kippur—it makes total sense that Jews celebrate it every single week. Of course, there's celebrate and then there's celebrate, but the Talmud says if all the Jews of the world would completely observe just one lousy, stinking Shabbat, the Messiah would immediately appear and redeem us for cash back and points.

Jewish Time-Out

Just as God managed to get some much-needed R & R after six long, hard days of working for the weekend and creating the world, Jews take a load off, too. According to the section of the Shulchan Aruch that deals with the laws of daily life and holiday behavior, Shabbat begins on Friday evening and continues until the appearance of three stars in the sky on Saturday night. During this period, all regular workday activities (see following) are suspended in favor of resting, eating,

DID JEW KNOW? A Shabbat elevator is one that is set to stop at every floor so no one has to press any buttons and thereby violate the Shabbat prohibition against using electricity. You'll find Shabbat elevators in hotels and hospitals in cities that have big Jewish populations, like New York, Buenos Aires, or any city in Israel.

going to synagogue, and spending time with family and friends. And it all starts with candles, Kiddush—the blessing over the wine—and *motzi*, the blessing over two loaves of challah. And did I mention eating?

A Candle in the Wind: The Shabbat Candles

Much like blood, fire was another powerful element in ancient life. It provides light, which was the very first thing God created, and is essential for heat, cooking, purifying, and ritual. For Jews, lighting the candles on Shabbat is a way to usher in the Sabbath and harness the symbolic potential of fire the way one might harness the power of prayer to connect with the divine.

It is a mitzvah for the woman of the house to light the Shabbat candles, mostly because it is a woman's privilege to bring light and goodness into their personal domain (the home) and thusly the larger world. (It also offers a chance to rectify the faux pas committed by Eve, who extinguished the light of God by tempting Adam to eat the forbidden fruit.)

Sanctified: The Kiddush Cup

Kiddush, literally "sanctification," is the prayer that the big daddy of the house recites over a cup of wine on Shabbat and other festivals. The Kiddush cup is a gold or silver cup that that is filled with wine and then lifted to symbolize the commandment both to remember the Sabbath and sanctify it.

Challah at You Late-ah!

Challah is a special loaf of braided bread that consists of six strands of dough woven together. Combined, the two loaves on the Shabbat table have twelve strands, symbolizing the Twelve Tribes of Israel. The two loaves of challah also represent the manna that God rained down on the Jewish people when they wandered for forty years in the desert after their exodus from Egypt. The manna didn't fall on Shabbat or holidays, since God was resting on those days; instead, a double portion would fall the day before.

The Thirty-Nine Prohibited Activities

The Talmud names thirty-nine kinds of work specifically prohibited from sundown Friday to sundown Saturday. These activities are forbidden because they represent

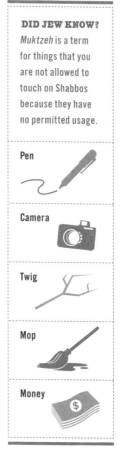

DID JEW KNOW?
Muktzeh is a term for things that you are not allowed to touch on Shabbos because they have no permitted usage.

Pen

Camera

Twig

Mop

Money

creativity or mastery over nature, which, during Shabbat, is best left to God. They are further divided into four categories of work that folks tended to do in olden times—making clothes, making food, building shelter, and making useful things (like leather) from animals.

Additionally, a slew of contemporary rabbis have added plenty of other modern no-no's to the list, such as riding in an elevator or playing video games. Clearly these rules are more stringently observed by Orthodox and some Conservative Jews, than by your average Reform Jew, who may only light some candles, make *motzi*, and Kiddush, if that. Some of the things you are allowed to do include walk, study, drink alcohol, pray, and make love. (Unless your love session involves any of the prohibited activities, such as shearing, winnowing, or hog-tying.)

Schtupping on Shabbos: It's a Double Mitzvah!

While Jews cannot create anything on Shabbos, they sure can procreate. The concept of *Oneg Shabbat*, the "joy of Shabbat," reminds people to slow down and feed the body, mind, and soul. So go ahead and rock a long nap, a good book, or some afternoon delight. In fact, sexual intimacy between a husband and wife is not

THAT TIME OF THE MONTH: ROSH CHODESH AND THE JEWISH INVENTION OF LADIES' NIGHT

Rosh Chodesh, literally "head of the month," is the first day of each new month and is considered a minor holiday. According to one interpretation, it was originally celebrated by all, but because of the golden calf incident, it became a ladies-only event: Freaked about how long Moses had been on Mount Sinai, the Israelites asked his older brother, Aaron, to make an idol (Exodus 32). Annoyed but ultimately giving in, Aaron told them to fetch the golden earrings from their wives, sons, and daughters. Apparently, the wives, reluctant to surrender their bling and to participate in the whole idol-worshipping debacle, said, "Hell no." The holiday was their reward.

only encouraged, it's also a commandment that comes directly from the Torah: "Be fruitful and multiply" (Genesis), and while you're at it, make sure the little woman enjoys herself (Exodus).

Gotta love the Jews.

Cholent: Who Eats It and Why

Cholent is a traditional Jewish beef stew that is prepared on Friday before sundown and left to simmer for twelve hours, after which it is eaten for Shabbos lunch. *Cholent* was developed centuries ago as a way to honor Jewish restrictions on cooking but still have a hearty, warm meal. Word to the wise: Some *cholents* take a century or more to digest!

The *Eruv:* Don't Call Me a Silly String!

Since it is not permitted to carry anything from the private domain to the public domain on Shabbat, rabbis in the modern age have had to look for workarounds, especially for people who live in cities. One loophole they found is called an *eruv:* a string that creates an enclosure around certain observant neighborhoods and within which it is permitted to carry certain items. Essentially, an *eruv* renders a neighborhood (a public domain) into a massive private domain and thus enables people to carry things like keys, medicines, strollers, or canes. Google Maps even has images of the neighborhoods around which there is an *eruv*, and most cities have an *eruv* hotline you can call either to report a felled *eruv* or verify that an *eruv* is intact. On some level, *eruvs* are a bizarre form of self-sabotage; who wants to actually carry things if they don't have to?

THE LIST

DO NOT: Plant, plow, reap, gather, thresh, winnow, sort, grind, sift, knead, cook, shear, scour, beat or comb wool, dye, spin, warp, make two loops, weave, separate two threads, tie, untie, sew, tear, trap, slaughter, flay, cure meat, smooth, score, cut, write, erase, build, demolish, extinguish a fire, ignite a fire (or use electricity), apply a finishing touch, carry/schlep, pay for anything.

DO: Pray, read, learn (as long as you don't write anything down and/or you're not reading electronically), imbibe, take a leisurely stroll, visit with friends and family, sleep, have marital relations, eat.

Shabbat Do's and Don'ts

OK IN GOD'S BOOK		NO CAN DO	
Walking		Mowing the lawn	
Praying		Making fire	
Studying		Shearing sheep	
Imbibing		Driving	
Making love		Trading	
Attending lectures		Surfing	

In other words, you can't take something that's in one form and divide it up into another for some use, thus creating a new form. So you can neither rip paper towels, nor water plants, nor shave your legs (as this would, depending on your level of hairiness, create a furrow).

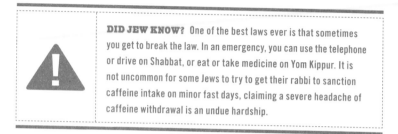

DID JEW KNOW? One of the best laws ever is that sometimes you get to break the law. In an emergency, you can use the telephone or drive on Shabbat, or eat or take medicine on Yom Kippur. It is not uncommon for some Jews to try to get their rabbi to sanction caffeine intake on minor fast days, claiming a severe headache of caffeine withdrawal is an undue hardship.

The Shabbos Goy, or Thank G-D for Those Gosh-Darned Gentile Neighbors

A Shabbos goy is a non-Jewish person who does all kinds of schtuff for observant Jews that they aren't permitted to do on Shabbat, such as turn on the light in the bathroom or move something that is considered *muktzeh*. Here's where it gets tricky: Technically, a Jew may not ask a non-Jew to perform Shabbat-prohibited work, though if a Shabbos goy should enter your home and unbeknownst to you turn on a light, it wouldn't be the worst crime. Famous Americans who once served as Shabbos goyim include Martin Scorsese, Colin Powell, and Mario Cuomo.

It's Over When It's Over: Havdalah

Just as candles are lit to welcome in Shabbat on Friday evenings, Havdalah (Hebrew for "separation") is a ceremony that marks the end of Shabbat and other holidays, distinguishing them from regular old weekdays. Here's how it goes down: The man of the house recites a blessing over a glass of wine, a box of spices, and a candle with multiple wicks. This ritual triad is meant to enable a person to experience the end of Shabbat with all five senses: taste the wine, smell the spices, see the flame of the candle, feel its warmth, and hear the blessings.

THE DAYS OF AWE:
Rosh Hashanah and Yom Kippur

The ten days that start with Rosh Hashanah, the Jewish New Year, and end with Yom Kippur, the Day of Atonement, are called the Days of Awe, or the High Holy Days. In case you were assuming that High Holy Days meant "high" or Days of Awe meant "awesome," think again. During this solemn time, Jews are instructed to examine their misdeeds so they can exact what Rabbi Joseph Telushkin calls "an ethical and religious reassessment of one's life" and get atoning before it's too late, i.e., before God decides who shall live and who shall die and who shall have to take the LSAT again.

Three rabbis are competing to determine whose synagogue
is the most liberal. One claims his shul has ashtrays
in the pews on Shabbat. The other claims his shul serves challah on
Passover. The third, however, outdoes them all by saying,
"Every year in September we put up a sign on the front door that
reads: CLOSED FOR THE HOLIDAYS."

—CLASSIC JEWISH JOKE

Here's how it works: Basically, the Great Equalizer has books in which He inscribes names of the naughty and nice. These books are open for revision during the Days of Awe, after which God seals the deal on Yom Kippur. Thus, sincere and soulful atoning during the crucial ten days can reverse a whole year's worth of transgressions, even if you're Bernie Madoff. So if you wanted to do a *select-all-delete* for some of the previous year's transgressions, the Days of Awe are the time to bring out the Jewish big guns: repentance, prayer, charity, boredom, and suffering. The High Holy Days are so important to a Jew's sense of identity that even the more secular Jews, who wouldn't know from the Kaddish if it hit them in the kishkes, make an appearance at temple, causing extra chairs to be brought from the basement to accommodate the sudden agglomeration of repentant Jewish behinds. In fact, most synagogues wisely use this time to hit up members of the congregation for a little gelt before they disappear until next Yom Kippur. And in case you thought tickets to the High Holy Days were free, think again. It's like flying somewhere during the holiday season—it costs more money, the airport is crowded, and you are likely to get stuck in a middle seat.

SUNDAY IS THE NEW SATURDAY

Until the third century, Christians also kept the Jewish Sabbath. In fact, it wasn't until the Jewish-Roman Wars that Sunday became de rigueur. Seems the Church, eager to distinguish their Sabbath from Shabbat, decided to make sure all good Christians worked on Saturday and rested on Sunday, lest they "judaize."

Another explanation for why Sunday became the new funday derives from a movement known as the cult of Sol Invictus, the Invincible Sun. This sun-worshipping cult became popular in the Roman Empire around the early part of the second century BCE, and its iconography, in which the sun symbolized Christ, then influenced early Christian liturgy. Indeed, even the orientation of the early churches was changed; instead of facing Jerusalem, the churches faced the rising sun in the east.

Rosh Hashanah: Jewish New Year

Forget auld lang syne. That's Gentile New Year. *Rosh Hashanah*, literally "head of the year," is auld, auld, auld lang syne: a two-day celebration in the form of the second-longest prayer service of the year. (The only longer one is on Yom Kippur.) Aside from ushering in the New Year, Rosh Hashanah also commemorates the anniversary of the creation of Adam and Eve and their sway over mankind's role in the world. Kind of like original sin for Jews, but with more food. The three important themes of the day:

- Sovereignty (of God as King of the Jew-niverse)
- Remembrance (remembering just whose Jew-niverse it is)
- Blowing the shofar (to remember)

Sounding the Blast: The Shofar

A shofar is a ram's horn that is summarily sounded one hundred times at specific intervals during the synagogue services on Rosh Hashanah. In fact, Rosh Hashanah is alternately called *Yom Teruah*, "the Day of the Blast." (Again, not *blast* as in "have a blast" but *blast* like blow your guts out trying to sound that thing.) Back in the day, the shofar blew to mark the start of a holiday or a war. The most famous example of the latter occurs in the book of Joshua, where the shofar was used as part of the battle plan that ultimately felled the city of Jericho.

The Jewish philosopher and physician Maimonides believed that the cry of the shofar is intended to wake up the soul and remind it to focus on repentance. Thus, it is a mitzvah to sound the shofar in shul on Rosh Hashanah according to a set series of four different blasts:

- Teki'ah: a long, unbroken blast
- Shevarim: a long blast divided into three segments
- Teruah: nine staccato blasts
- Tekiah Gedolah: a show-stopping, triple-long teki'ah

Take Me to the River: The Ritual of Tashlikh

Tashlikh, meaning "casting off," is a ritual performed on the afternoon of the first day of Rosh Hashanah. Congregants amass near a natural body of water, recite prayers, and then symbolically cast their sins into the water. Sometimes bread or small stones are used to symbolize both the casting off of sins as well as the idea of sin's impermanence in the eyes of a forgiving God. The practice derives from Micah 7:18-20: "You will cast all their sins into the depths of the sea."

So When Do We Eat?

After all the praying and the casting off of sins, a Jew gets hungry. Many Jews, even those less observant, gather for a giant family meal that usually includes apples and challah dipped in honey, to symbolize the hope of a sweet new year. Sometimes other foods are served, such as honey cake, or seasonal fruit, such as a pomegranate. In the Bible, the land of Israel is praised for its pomegranates, and not just because they are high in antioxidants. The pomegranate is a symbol of righteousness, due to the fact that its purported 613 seeds correspond to the same number of *mitzvot*, and eating these seeds symbolizes a Jew's wish that the coming year will hold as many *mitzvot*. Another Rosh Hashanah food tradition is the cooking and serving of fish heads, an ancient symbol of fertility that, while gross, also conveys the idea of the "head" of the year.

Yom Kippur: Jewish Lent

Yom Kippur, the Day of Atonement, is the holiest of holies and the complement/bookend of Rosh Hashanah. Jews observe this day and honor its themes of repentance and atonement with a twenty-five-hour session of fasting and prayer. According to the liturgy, Yom Kippur is when God seals every Jew's fate, so if there was ever a good time to fast, this is it. "But on the tenth day of the seventh month it is the Day of Atonement; there shall be a holy convocation for you and you shall afflict yourselves. You shall not do any work on this very day, for it is the Day of Atonement to provide you with Atonement before HaShem your God. For any who should not be afflicted on this day will be cut off from his people." (Leviticus 23:26-30)

> "I once wanted to become an atheist but I gave up. They have no holidays."
>
> —HENNY YOUNGMAN

For the most part, Jews spend the day at synagogue suffering from massive caffeine withdrawal and thinking about how hungry and thirsty they are. When they aren't focused on starvation and dehydration, they ask for forgiveness for wrongs done against God and other human beings, and make various confessions of guilt. Hopefully, after they have sat through the five prayers that comprise the Yom Kippur service, they forgive other people and are forgiven by God. Then, and only then, can they also forgive themselves.

Here are some of the ironclad rules of Yom Kippur observance.

- All of the rules that apply to Shabbat
- No eating or drinking
- No sex
- Praying
- No bathing, anointing, or washing
- No wearing of leather shoes

Forgive Me, Rabbi, for I Have Sinned: The Art of Jewish Confession

In case you were jealous of the free therapy that the confessional affords the Catholics, Yom Kippur affords you the opportunity to confess a total of ten times during the prayer service and never have to do it again, at least until the following year. So you might not get a football scholarship to Notre Dame, but Jew still get more bang for your buck by packing an entire year's worth of confessing into a single day.

Basically the confessional consists of broad categories under which specific personal sins or transgressions occur, for instance: spurning parents and teachers, associating with impurity, cheating, denying, lying, profaning the name of the Lord, evil inclinations and unclean lips, pride, tale baring, envy, confusion, contentiousness, provoking, rebelling, committing abomination, going astray, leading others astray, swearing falsely, speaking impurely, gossiping, gorging, scoffing, casting wanton looks, lusting, coveting, and demanding usurious interest. In other words, everything fun you haven't done since your twenties.

The Origin of the Scapegoat

As part of the Yom Kippur ritual during the biblical era, the high priest presented a ram and two goats for sacrifice. The ram was for a burnt offering, and the two goats were for a sin offering. He brought the two goats to the Tabernacle and cast lots for them, one for God and one for Azazel, a mysterious goat demon. The goat for God was summarily sacrificed but the goat for Azazel was used for an unusual ritual. The priest would confess over it the sins of the people, thus imbuing it with the wickedness of his tribe, and then hand it over to a man who would then release it into the wilderness.

> **DID JEW KNOW?**
> Since Hanukah and Purim are nonbiblical holidays, they are not considered *yom tov*, and so regular activities, like working or carrying, are allowed.

Yom Kippur and the American Pastime

Yom Kippur is a *yom tov,* a day when work is forbidden, like Shabbat only without the *cholent* and the sex—i.e., the thirty-nine prohibited activities must be observed, and then some. This is often plenty challenging for regular civilians, let alone famous athletes whose presence stands to make or break the big game. Some athletes who have observed Yom Kippur, even on game day:

In 1934, first baseman Hank Greenberg declined to play ball on Yom Kippur, causing *Detroit Free Press* columnist Edgar A. Guest to pen the following lines: "We shall miss him on the infield and shall miss him at the bat, but he's true to his religion and I honor him for that."

Hall of Fame pitcher Sandy Koufax opted out of pitching Game One of the 1965 World Series because it conflicted with Yom Kippur. When pitcher Don Drysdale, who was swapped in for Koufax, fared poorly, he reportedly told his manager, "I bet right now you wish I was Jewish, too."

SUKKOT: Jewish Camping

Sukkot is a biblical feast day that celebrates the harvest and thusly all other related forms of nature's transient, fertile, and abundant bounty. It is an eight-day event, though only the first two are considered *yom tov*. The Hebrew word *sukkot* is a plural form of *sukkah*, meaning "tabernacle" or "booth." Sukkot is also known as the Feast of the Tabernacles—*tabernacle* meaning the temporary but powerful port-a-shul used by the wanderers. The holiday recalls the transience and the devotion of the Jewish people during their forty-year wander in the desert. "For a seven-day period you shall live in booths. Every resident among the Israelites shall live in booths, in order that your [ensuing] generations should know that I had the children of Israel live in booths when I took them out of the land of Egypt." (Leviticus 23:42–43) Following this divine injunction, our weary band of desert schleppers erected tents, or booths, every time they arrived at a new and remote encampment.

Today, the sukkah is a temporary walled structure with a roof crafted from leaves or branches that is meant to recall those flimsy tents that lacked air-conditioning, insect repellent, or AeroBeds. As part of the Sukkot ritual, Jews eat their meals inside the sukkah, and some even go so far as to catch some zzz's in there. That's right: a Jew camping. An oxymoron if ever there was one!

Requirements for Your Sukkah

Choose any of the seven species of fruits and grains that the Hebrew Bible lists as indigenous products of Israel for your sukkah: grapes, wheat, barley, figs, pomegranates, olives, and dates. This fruit is hung from the roof of your sukkah and lends it a festive, fragrant air.

The Talmud instructs that the *sechach*, or roof, needs to be thick enough so that the shade inside the sukkah is greater than the sunlight. If the branches or greenery are not sufficient, they do not qualify as sechach.

The Jerusalem Talmud adds that, ideally, one should not place too many branches on top of the sukkah; you should be able to see the larger stars in the night sky through the branches. Rabbi Joseph Te'omim (1727–1792) explained that gazing at the heavens and seeing the stars would remind one of the majesty and awesomeness of the Creator. This idea is articulated by King David in Psalms 8:4–5: "When I see Your heavens, the work of Your fingers, the moon and stars that You have established, what is man that You should remember him, and the son of man that You should be mindful of him?"

SHEMINI ATZERET: Jewish Assembly

Though it is considered a festival in its own right, Shemini Atzeret, "the Eighth Day of Assembly," falls on the last day of Sukkot. As part of the Shemini Atzeret ritual, Jews who live outside of Israel leave the sukkah and eat their meals (climate-controlled and bug-free) in the house.

Be Happy, Damn It!

An essential part of Shemini Atzeret is the recitation of the prayer for rain. Also key is continuing to fulfill the obligations of *simcha*, "joy." In fact, as the celebration of abundance, Sukkot is known as "the Time of our Happiness," and this happiness is expected to extend through Shemini Atzeret.

DID JEW KNOW? Though Yom Kippur is a fast day and therefore by no means a rollicking good time, it is actually considered the happiest day of the year. Why? Because it is a day of forgiveness for all sins, big and small. Think of it as cleaning out the closet: It's a pain in the neck while you're doing it, and you are forced to confront the embarrassing stuff you used to wear, but afterward you feel so fresh and so clean.

SIMCHAT TORAH: Jewish Book Club

The second day of Shemini Atzeret is Simchat Torah, literally "Rejoicing in the Law." Simchat Torah marks the end of the annual cycle of Torah readings that take place during synagogue service throughout the year. At long last, Jews finish reading the last bit of Deuteronomy and immediately rip into the first verses of Genesis. Rabbi Joseph Telushkin points out that while the other happy holidays like Hanukah and Purim celebrate Jewish victories over enemies set on their destruction, Simchat Torah has only positive associations: joy at finishing the Torah and joy at the opportunity to study it again. As such, it is the only 100 percent happy holiday in the Jewish calendar.

We're Never Gonna Survive Unless We Get a Little Meshugge

The evening service of Simchat Torah features a dance around the circumference of the synagogue while prominent members of the synagogue march around holding Torahs. Then a second group picks up the Torahs and the dance continues. Following this bit of religiously inspired free cardio, the morning service can get crazy-pants. Congregants sometimes imbibe alcohol while the service is taking place and try to drown out the cantors' crooning with drunken, joyful melodies of their own.

HANUKAH: Jewish Christmas

Thanks to Adam Sandler, Macy's, and the Lubavitchers, everyone knows the "Eight Crazy Nights," even those folks who year after year insist on wishing you a "happy" Yom Kippur. Maybe it's the giant menorahs that are displayed prominently in front of various municipal buildings, courtesy of Chabad, or the blue and white decorations that festoon the local pharmacy, but everyone knows this is the time to get presents from Hanukah Harry and sing the dreidel song.

Hey, Jude: The Story of Hanukah

The Jewish holiday of *Hanukah*, a Hebrew word meaning "to dedicate," is a rabbinic holiday that commemorates the Jewish defeat of the Seleucidite Syrian Greeks in 165 BCE by a priestly family called the Maccabees. These Maccabees sought to defeat not merely the Greek occupiers but also their Jewish acolytes, the so-called "Jewish Hellenizers."

Though Hanukah is conspicuously missing from the Mishnah, it is given some serious coverage in rabbinic writings, particularly those of Maimonides. Here's the thing: nowhere in the writings on the Eight Crazy Nights does it say, "Thou must shop until thou drop." What happened was this: The increasing level of assimilation by Jews into Gentile society pitted Hanukah against Christmas, a central Christian holiday that drives the engine of modern Western consumerism. Inevitably, Jews turned up the heat on Hanukah in terms of shopping and giving.

So What's It About?

Hanukah commemorates the rededication of the Second Temple in Jerusalem. Back in the day, Syrian King Antiochus the IV overthrew Jerusalem, wrested the city from the Jews by means of force, and looted the Second Temple (see chapter 1.) To make matters worse, he erected an altar to Zeus in the temple, banned circumcision, and sacrificed pigs on the temple altar. As you can imagine, his actions provoked a massive rebellion. A righteous Jewish priest and his five sons led a revolt against Antiochus and won, due in no small part to the priest's number-three son, the great warrior Judah Maccabee, a.k.a., "Judah the Hammer." To the great joy of the Jews, Judah liberated, koshered, and rededicated the Temple.

Lighting Is Everything!

Here's where we get to the menorah: Though there are two different types of menorah, only one is lit during the eight nights of Hanukah. The Hanukah menorah, or *Hanukiah*, is a nine-branched candelabrum commemorating the great victory of the Jews against the Greeks. (The non-Hanukah menorah is of the seven-branched variety that was used in the desert tabernacle and both the First and Second Temple in Jerusalem and has become emblematic of both, as well as of the State of Israel.)

The menorah in the Temple was supposed to burn all night, every night, which required a hefty amount of olive oil. Unfortunately, after the Maccabees reclaimed and rededicated the Temple, there was only a small flask of oil left, enough to burn for just one day—yet, somehow, the oil lasted for eight days, just the right amount of time needed to make a fresh batch of oil. It was a Hanukah miracle!

The menorah consists of nine lights, one for each of the eight nights of the festival, and one for the *shamash*, which is generally taller or somehow distinguished from the other candles and is used to light the others. According to the Talmud, the lights of the menorah must be used only for meditation, not illumination; thus, the shamash is there in case you need a reading lamp. That said, the main purpose of the menorah is to publicize the miracle (which is why it is placed in a window).

Fried Food and Gambling: Hanukah Habits

During Hanukah it is customary to eat foods fried in extra-virgin olive oil to commemorate the miracle of that tiny amount of oil keeping the menorah aflame for eight days and nights. Some of these complex-carb yum-yums include latkes—

Dreidel How-To

Each player starts out with about fifteen coins, real or chocolate, and puts one piece in a communal pot. The first player spins the dreidel and either wins some gelt from the pot or hands over part of the stash.

THE RULES

ב	**Nun** If the dreidel lands on the letter *nun*, nothing happens and the next player spins.
ג	**Gimmel** If the dreidel lands on the letter *gimmel*, the player takes the contents of the pot.
ה	**Hey** If the dreidel lands on the letter *hey*, the player takes half the pot.
ש	**Shin** If the dreidel lands on the letter *shin*, the player puts one piece of gelt back in the pot.

DID JEW KNOW? The initial purpose of the dreidel game might have been to cover the fact that Jews were studying the Torah when the Greeks had outlawed the study of Jewish texts. The Jews would hide out in caves to study, and if the lookout spotted an incoming Greek, the Jews would stash their scrolls and pretend to be gambling.

potato pancakes—and *sufganiyot*, which are deep-fried, jam-filled donuts. These donuts not only symbolize the miracle of imminent quadruple bypass, but also the sweetness of the Hanukah festival.

After the menorah is lit and the deep-fat fryer suitably worked, Jewish children settle down to a rollicking game of dreidel. A dreidel is a four-sided top that features Hebrew letters on each of its four sides. The letters are an acronym for the sentence *Nes Gadol Haya Sham*—"a great miracle happened there."

PURIM: Jewish Halloween

Purim is a raucous one-day celebration that occurs one month before Passover and commemorates one of the greatest turnarounds in Jewish history. In about the fifth century BCE, ruler Xerxes I of Persia (presumed to be none other than King Achashverosh in Hebrew) was minding his own business when his vizier, an evil grouch named Haman, attempted to annihilate the Jews of ancient Persia (see chapter 1.) The Jews were saved by a heroic mensch named Mordechai and his hot cousin/wife Esther. To celebrate this banner moment, Jews are commanded to eat *hamantaschen*, which are triangle-shaped cookies filled with poppy seeds and/or prune or apricot jam, put on kooky costumes, and party like Gentiles.

The Whole Megillah

The book of Esther, or the Megillah, is the unwitting poster child for how intermarriage saves lives if you let it. In this tale, King Achashverosh marries Esther, the local beauty who also happens to be Jewish (though for obvious reasons, she keeps this info on the down low.) Meantime, her cousin Mordechai manages to uncover and foil a plot to assassinate the king.

Enter Haman, who also takes to walking around town wearing an idol on his neck and making people bow down to it. Mordechai refuses. Incensed, Haman obtains permission to kill all the Jews. *Purim* is the Persian word for "lottery," the system by which Haman planned to pick the date for his dastardly

DID JEW KNOW? Hadassah, the Women's Zionist Organization of America pioneered by Henrietta Szold, is named for Esther, the biblical heroine who grew a pair of matzo balls and saved her people. The original meeting of the group coincided with Purim, and so they decided to take the name Hadassah, Esther's and Henrietta's Hebrew name, in the hope that they would have the same luck as Esther in promoting the Zionist ideal.

genocidal plan. The king goes for Haman's idea, that is, until he learns that it was Mordechai who thwarted his prior assassination attempt.

In the end, Esther mans up and tells the king that she's a Jewess, and he reverses the decree against the Jews. Haman gets hanged on the very gallows he intended for Mordechai, and Mordechai gets promoted to prime minister.

What Happens on Purim Stays on Purim

Beyond drinking until you can no longer tell the difference between "blessed be Mordechai" and "cursed be Haman," Purim also includes a synagogue service featuring a reading of the Megillah. Whenever Haman's name gets mentioned, congregants shake noisemakers called groggers and yell "boo!" and get all kinds of participatory in order to drown out the sound of Haman's name. Most synagogues put on Purim Spiels, comedic or satirical plays that tell the story of Purim.

Another tradition that adds to the all-round party atmosphere of Purim is that everyone, adults and children, wears kooky costumes to the synagogue service to replicate the many disguises the Jews had to don to triumph against the wicked Haman. Traditionally, these costumes are Purim-inspired, as in characters from the Purim Story. In contrast to the overt miracles of the holidays of Hanukah and Passover, the miracle of Purim was disguised/submerged in a series of natural events, such as the way Esther initially concealed her Jewish identity. The Talmud also writes that just as the Jews were pretending to be serving other gods, God pretended that He was going to destroy the Jewish nation, which, of course, he saved instead. (Talmud Megillah 12a) That said, a fair number of girls go the Halloween route and show up as sexy Jewish kittens or naughty Jewish nurses. Another requirement of Purim is to donate money to charity and send *mishloach manot*, literally "the sending of portions," or gift baskets of food and drink, to friends. Sending *mishloach manot* is a mitzvah meant to make sure everyone has adequate snacks for the feast of Purim as well as to promote unity among the Jewish people, in case we ever have to band together again to fight an evil, Jew-hating king or protest a Mel Gibson movie.

The *mishloach manot* baskets must contain at least two kinds of ready-to-eat food, such as fresh or dried fruit, chocolate, nuts, candy, or hamentaschen. Depending on whom you ask, the shape of these cookies derives from shape of Haman's favorite headwear, his purse, or his ears.

PASSOVER: Jewish Easter

Passover, or Pesach, is all about Exodus, baby. It's about the mortar of slavery, a great leader, and the sweet taste of freedom. In case you need a refresher: After the Jews had been in Egypt for some time, there arose a pharaoh who knew not Joseph (pal to the previous pharaoh). He said, "These Jews. As usual, they're so pushy and greedy and proud. Let us make them slaves before they rise up against us."

To prevent an uprising, Pharaoh decreed that all Jewish boy babies should be murdered. And so a wise woman from the Tribe of Levi plopped her Jew-baby in a basket and floated it up the river, *stat*. The baby was found by Pharaoh's daughter, who kept him and called him Moses, meaning "pulled or drawn out."

Years later, Moses was minding his own business in Midian when a burning bush struck up a conversation with him, the gist of which was, "Get thy taut *tuchus* back to Egypt and save your people." So back Moses went. He demanded that Pharaoh let his people go, but to no avail, at least until God decided to expedite matters with the ten plagues.

Passed Over

While any of the plagues would ruin anyone's vacation, it was with the tenth plague, the slaying of the firstborn, that things got hairy. Since God instructed the Israelites to mark the doorposts of their houses with lamb's blood, the angel of death bypassed the Jewish homes and hit only the Egyptians, which was too terrible even for Pharaoh to endure, and so he decided to let the Jews go. This decision lasted about all of five minutes, but gave Moses the chance to lead the Israelites out of Egypt and ultimately into Canaan (but not without a few hair-raising Best Friends Fear Factor moments). Before Pharaoh decided to chase after them, the Jews made it to the edge of the desert, led by a pillar of clouds during the day and a pillar of fire by night.

"What do you call someone who derives pleasure from the bread of affliction? A matzochist."

—CLASSIC JEWISH JOKE

Next, as part of God's whole it's-for-your-own-good thing, He actually caused Pharaoh to pursue the Israelites with chariots. After which the Red Sea parted: God commanded Moses to hold his staff over the water and a strong wind divided the sea, allowing the Israelites to pass through. By the time the Egyptians appeared on the scene, panic had ensued. God clogged their chariot wheels, the water began to rise, the Egyptians were destroyed, and the Jews burst into song. (Possibly the biblical origin of Jews in musical theater, but more on that later.)

Next came schlepping around in the desert for forty long years, eating God's heavenly dandruff. The Israelites may have risked melanoma, but in the end they got the Ten Commandments, the Torah, and Charlton Heston.

Chametz: Let My People Go

Since the Jews had to peace out of Egypt while the going was good, they didn't have time to pack and wait for their bread to rise. They just grabbed some dough and ran. Thus the beloved matzo: the unleavened bread that is both the staple of the Passover holiday and the clogger of many a Jewish digestive system. In order to prepare for the holiday, Jews remove all traces of *chametz*, "leavened goods," from their homes and eat off special Passover plates for the duration of the holiday.

Seder Right Words, Eat Der Wrong Ones: The Passover Table

Like many Jewish victories, Passover is celebrated with a Seder, a joyous meal that has its own liturgy, rituals, and symbols. These rituals include drinking four glasses of wine, eating obscene amounts of matzo, and enacting various events of the Exodus story with symbolic foods and jolly songs. A special prayer book called the Haggadah recounts the story of Passover and explains its customs, such as reclining at the table, eating bitter herbs, and teaching Passover to the "four types" of children, especially the ones who have ADHD.

On the Seder table, there is a stack of three matzoth. During the fourth part of the Seder, the big-daddy leader will break the middle of these three pieces in two. The smaller piece goes right back to the matzo plate, and the larger piece, known as the *afikomen*, a Greek word for "dessert," is broken and subsequently hidden by either the Seder leader or by children who have stolen it. Either way, bargaining and bribing ensue until the *afikomen* is recovered. Since the Seder is not considered over until everyone at the table has eaten a piece of the *afikomen*, this transaction is actually very important and could, in some homes, lead to a new Prius. The Passover holiday is eight days long, but Seders are held only on the first two nights.

Elijah

Elijah was a prophet in the Northern Kingdom of Israel. Some of his superhuman feats of prophetic goodness include raising the dead, confronting the idol-worshipping King Ahab and his wife Jezebel, and defeating their god Ba'al. When Elijah's biblical story ends, a chariot of fire lifts him into the heavens.

DID JEW KNOW? The first time the word *Jew* appears in the Bible is in the book of Esther. The reference is to Mordechai from the Tribe of Benjamin, but he is called Jew because by the time of Mordechai, Judah has emerged as the dominant tribe. It is at this juncture that the Twelve Tribes came to be known as "Jewish."

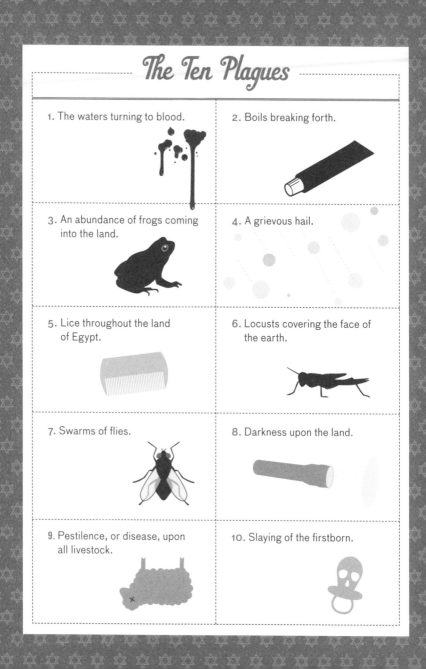

The Ten Plagues

1. The waters turning to blood.

2. Boils breaking forth.

3. An abundance of frogs coming into the land.

4. A grievous hail.

5. Lice throughout the land of Egypt.

6. Locusts covering the face of the earth.

7. Swarms of flies.

8. Darkness upon the land.

9. Pestilence, or disease, upon all livestock.

10. Slaying of the firstborn.

Elijah's name is invoked during Havdalah and in the Haggadah. Since he is the guardian of newborn boys, a chair is left empty for him at the Brit Milah. Also, a cup of wine is poured for him at the Passover Seder. Homeboy gets around. Also, his tongue is shaped like a straw, which is why you never actually see him pick up the cup.

SHAVUOT: Jewish Cheesecake Festival

Shavuot memorializes the day that God gave the Torah to the Israelites on Mount Sinai. It is also a harvest festival. Some Shavuot customs include the reading of the book of Ruth, all-night Torah study sessions, and mass consumption of dairy products. The book of Ruth describes the seasons of the barley and wheat harvests and recounts that Ruth, a convert, had a ceaseless longing to become a member of the Jewish people. "Wherever you go, I will go; wherever you live, I will live. Your people will be my people, and your God will be my God." (Ruth 1:16) Additionally, King David, Ruth's great-grandson, was born and died on Shavuot.

The artery-clogging dairyfest that is Shavuot finds its origin in a number of rabbinic sources. At that point in the history of Jewish gastronomy, kosher hadn't been invented yet (neither had lactose intolerance). Since the Torah had just been received, this new system was far from second nature. This is why the Jews chose to eat dairy by default: They didn't have proper kosher pots for eating *fleyshik* and so were limited to blintzes, cheesecake, cheese ravioli, and cheese kreplach.

Honey is a traditional Shavuot food; the Song of Songs compares the Torah to honey, "Like honey and milk, it lies under your tongue." (Song of Songs 4:11)

The numerical value of each letter of the word *chalav*, the Hebrew word for "milk," is forty. Thus the consumption of dairy foods on Shavuot corresponds to the forty days Moses spent on Mount Sinai learning the Torah from none other than the Teacher of Teachers.

Pulling an All-Nighter

Another custom of Shavuot is to stay up all night studying the Talmud, Mishnah, or Torah. As usual, since this is a Jewish custom, there are more than a few reasons why some Jews choose to burn the midnight oil: Apparently, the Jews all overslept that fateful morning, and God had to wake them up so he could teach them the Torah. Rabbinic sources suggest that Jews now rectify this mistake by staying up all night to study. The twenty-four hours of the day also correspond to the twenty-four books of the Hebrew Bible.

TISHA B'AV: Jewish Diet

The Fast of Tisha B'Av (the ninth of Av) commemorates the destruction of both the First Temple by the Babylonians and then the Second Temple by the Romans. Though these tragic events happened about 655 years apart, they occurred on the same day in the Hebrew calendar, the ninth of Av.

WHY THE NINTH OF AV OFFICIALLY BLOWS

- On the ninth of Av, 586 BCE: The Babylonians destroyed the First Temple.

- On the ninth of Av, 70 CE: The Romans destroyed the Second Temple.

- On the ninth of Av, 135 CE: The Romans destroyed the Betar Fortress, the final remaining Jewish fortress in the Bar Kochba Revolt.

- On the ninth of Av, 1290: The Jews were expelled from England.

- On the ninth of Av, 1492: The Spanish government issued the decree ordering the expulsion of the Jews from Spain.

- On the ninth of Av, 1914: Germany declared war on Russia, effectively kicking off the First World War.

The Seder Plate

The Passover Seder plate comprises an arrangement of six symbolic foods referenced and eaten during the Seder itself. The six foods are:

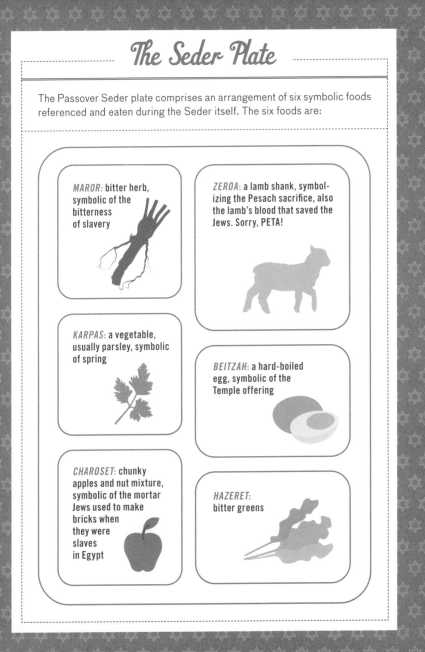

MAROR: bitter herb, symbolic of the bitterness of slavery

ZEROA: a lamb shank, symbolizing the Pesach sacrifice, also the lamb's blood that saved the Jews. Sorry, PETA!

KARPAS: a vegetable, usually parsley, symbolic of spring

BEITZAH: a hard-boiled egg, symbolic of the Temple offering

CHAROSET: chunky apples and nut mixture, symbolic of the mortar Jews used to make bricks when they were slaves in Egypt

HAZERET: bitter greens

Like its more famous predecessor Yom Kippur, Tisha B'Av is a day of complete fasting as well as other similar restrictions, such as no leather shoes, bathing, shaving, or sex. Also, study of the Torah is forbidden because the day is mournful and Torah is tiramisu for the heart. That said, it is permitted to read the more lugubrious books of the Hebrew Bible, such as Lamentations or Job and/or to study parts of the Talmud that discuss the destruction of the Temple(s). Observant practitioners may sit on low stools following the custom of mourners at shivah.

THE MINOR LEAGUES
Tu B'Shevat: Jewish Tree-Hugging Day

Judaism has two different New Years: Rosh Hashanah, the New Year for mankind, and Tu B'Shevat, the New Year for the Trees. Customs associated with this day include eating fruit that grows in Israel as well as planting young saplings.

On Tu B'Shevat some Sephardic Jews make a second Seder following the custom of sixteenth-century Kabbalists. Four cups of wine are drunk, verses that discuss the vegetation of Israel are read, and fruit of the seven species are eaten, specifically barley, wheat, grapes, figs, pomegranates, olives, and dates.

Lag Ba'Omer: Jewish Pyrotechnics

Rabbi Shimon Bar Yochai was a disciple of Rabbi Akiva, one of the preeminent contributors to the Mishnah and "the Head of all Sages." After the Romans murdered Rabbi Akiva, Bar Yochai criticized the Romans for their cruelty and was then forced to hide out in a mountain cave with his son for thirteen years. During this time, he wrote the Zohar: a commentary on the mystical aspects of the Torah that forms the basis of Kabbalah.

Bar Yochai died on the thirty-third day of the Omer, or Lag Ba'Omer. On the day of his passing, he revealed some seriously sublime and juicy kabbalistic secrets to his disciples. Legend has it that this revelation was accompanied by continual daylight until he completed his final teaching and died.

As a result, the custom of lighting bonfires is an essential element of Lag Ba'Omer, the anniversary of Bar Yochai's death—a day of celebration of the man and the spiritual light of his teachings.

The Fast of Gedaliah: Jewish Master Cleanse

The fast of Gedaliah is a minor fast day observed after the second day of Rosh Hashanah, which commemorates the assassination of Gedaliah. After Babylonian King Nebuchadnezzar conquered Jerusalem, he appointed Gedaliah as governor. Many Jews who had fled to other lands returned to Judah and life continued apace.

That is, until Baalis, another king, freaked out about the Judean presence and sent another Judean to kill Gedaliah.

Yommy, Yommy, Yommy: Newish Jewish Holidays

Just when you thought Jews couldn't get any more holidays, in 1948 the State of Israel went ahead and established four more! While the Reform, Reconstructionist, and Conservative movements have given these holidays the official green light, the Hasidim and the ultra-Orthodox view them as "secular innovations" and do not, I repeat, do not celebrate them.

- Yom HaShoah—Holocaust Remembrance Day
- Yom Yerushalayim—Jerusalem Day: Commemorates the 1967 reunification of Jerusalem and reestablishment of Jewish control of the Old City as a result of the Six-Day War
- Yom Hazikaron—Memorial Day: Day of remembrance for veterans, fallen soldiers, and civilian victims of terrorism
- Yom Ha'atzmaut—Israel Independence Day

Jews Have More Fun

No matter the category—biblical, rabbinic, or post-rabbinic—nor the tone—exuberant or depressing—the Jewish Holidays form the warp and weft of what it means to be a Jew: mournful, dyspeptic, and waiting for something that isn't going to happen. To the Jew whose sum total of hours logged in shul over the past year would be lucky to make it into the double digits, observance may well mean knowing where to get the most authentic matzo ball soup or, once in a great while, lighting candles on Shabbat, especially if those candles are the sexy-time candles by the bath tub. One of the many great aspects of being a Jew is that God not only wants you to get a little on the holidays, he made it a mitzvah! So go ahead, light a candle. *Ess a bissele.* Call your grandmother and wish her and everyone in Boca a happy Yom Kippur!

DID JEW KNOW? In the Hasidic community, *upsherin* is a watershed first haircut moment that marks a boy's entry into the world of *aleph-bet,* yarmulkes, and tzitzit. So that the Torah will be "sweet on the tongue," parents cover the letters of the Hebrew *aleph-bet* with honey, and the children lick the letters as they read them. Since Leviticus is the first book from which Orthodox children begin their learning, a parent or teacher might also cover the letters of the first part of Leviticus with honey, and the kids lick the honey off the words and read them. This custom is both to instruct that the word of God is sweet and to get kids to love the Torah at an early age instead of McDonald's.

CHAPTER 5

GOY VEY!
Conversion, Assimilation, and the Art of Spiritual Mixology

My wife is Catholic, I'm Jewish. We're raising our children to be sad.

—JON STEWART

A hundred years ago, the idea of intermarriage, conversion, or even the simple act of chitchatting with a goy might have seemed as impossible to a Jew in the Pale of Settlement as it did to Tevye in *Fiddler on the Roof*. Never mind what your friendly neighborhood Cossack might have thought about the whole enterprise. Meantime, neither could have imagined quite the level of secularization that would be prevalent in the New World by the late twentieth century. Indeed, if they did, both might have held hands and jumped head-schlong into the Black Sea.

Indeed, for today's Jews of North America, secularization—the movement away from strict adherence to Jewish law and toward a Jewish cultural identity— is either a righteous manifestation of long-awaited equality or, quite simply, the very death knell of Judaism. Even Moses Mendelssohn and all of his nonpracticing progeny could never quite have conceived the concept of cultural Judaism: the umbrella term for nonpracticing Jews who align themselves more with Larry David than King David and know more about where to get the best matzo ball soup than the biography of the great Jewish leader whose exit strategy led to said delicacy's origin.

To put it another way, for those Old World Yids for whom the whole melting-pot concept would have seemed unthinkable on its own, the current meltdown of the very pot itself would have made the fiddler fall off his roof and into the melted pot's residual puddle of Jew stew. The question is, after our stalwart fiddler toweled off, would he then have married a *sheygetz*, moved to Park Slope, Brooklyn, adopted a child from Ethiopia, and raised it as an agnostic Unitarian yogi?

A JEW IS A JEW IS A JEW, *NU?*

Before we go deeper into the various solutions, ablutions, and dilutions of Judaism, let's first get clear on what exactly makes a Jew a Jew and what, aside from belief in Christ or Mohammed, makes a Jew no longer a member of the Chosen Tribe.

DID JEW KNOW? Speaking of Chosen! Contrary to the implications of the Chosen Tribe's exclusive-sounding moniker, Judaism does not purport that Jews are innately superior to the rest of God's adoptees and bastard stepchildren. According to the Talmud tractate Avodah Zarah, God actually offered the Torah to everyone, but only the Jews were smart enough to know that when Daddy offers you something, you should just take it and follow it without question, especially if He's holding a mountain over your head.

Jew U: Who Is Officially Jewish (According to Rabbinic Judaism)

- Anyone whose parents are both Jewish.
- A person whose mother is Jewish, whether or not said person is actually raised as a Jew. For example: Madeleine Albright was raised Catholic and remained blissfully "unaware" of her Jewish ancestry till she was an adult. Doesn't matter! Still a Jew, Maddy! Still. A. Jew.
- A person who willingly converts to Judaism.
- Any Jew who involuntarily converts to another religion, as was the case with the conversos. Indeed, they and their matrilineal descendants are still considered Jewish. That said, even if the Jew willingly converts to another religion, Orthodox Judaism still considers the person Jewish, albeit a *schlimazel* and a heretic.

Who Is Officially Jewish (According to North American Reform and UK Liberal Movements)

- Anyone whose parents are both Jewish.
- A person with one Jewish parent and who claims Jewish identity.
- Anyone who converts to Judaism.

SO YOU WANNA BE A JEW?
A Survival Guide to Righteous Conversion

Depending on your take, the effort required for a Gentile to convert to Judaism (as opposed to anything but Judaism) serves a few different purposes:

1. To ensure that said Gentile's desire to convert is sincere and of their own accord and not just to piss off their parents, where a tattoo and a lesbian wedding might do the trick.
2. To ensure that this sincere desire doesn't have to do solely with nabbing a Jewish husband.
3. To ensure that even if the above were true, the main impetus of the conversion would be to live as a Jew, keep a Jewish household, and be fruitful and multiply according to the Halakhic definition, i.e., as much as humanly possible and with Jews only.

JUDGE JEW-DY: THE BEIT DIN AND THE SANHEDRIN

The *beit din* is the rabbinical court of Judaism that presides over various legal aspects of Orthodox (and some of Conservative) Jewish life, from property and family disputes, Jewish divorce (*get*), and kosher certification to all matters mourning, mohel, and *mikveh*.

No matter the reason, the conversion process is pretty darn labor-intensive and thus self-selective. For starters, according to the Shulchan Aruch, there are three absolute musts for any conversion to be considered valid:

- mitzvot—learning and adhering to the commandments
- *milah*—circumcision
- *mikveh*—ritual bathing

Keep in mind that, technically, all conversions are supposed to follow Orthodox guidelines, even if they are heading down a more liberal path. (**NOTE:** *Orthos do NOT accept any other conversion style than the deep cut.*) That said, due to the staggering amount of mitzvot prospective converts must learn and ultimately live, it's not unusual for most converts to end up considerably more religious than they originally intended, even if they are marrying someone who only goes to temple on Yom Kippur during leap years.

Study, Snip, Dip: The Conversion Trifecta

Christmas getting too darn expensive? Dyeing Easter eggs not doing it for you anymore? Whether you're bored and looking for a new, time-consuming hobby, simply love studying, or have been thinking about changing the look of your manly member, then it may be time to start Operation Conversion. It may seem overwhelming at first, but when you're walking up the aisle to "Sunrise, Sunset" and all your friends and relations are weeping with relief that you won't die a spinster, it will all seem worth it.

Mitzvot

The requirement of mitzvot essentially means that the convert to Orthodox Judaism must believe in God and the ultimate divinity of the Torah, plus accept all—that's right, *all*—613 commandments of the Torah with her/his whole mind and heart rather than solely for the purposes of a higher batting average when hitting on Jewish singles. The convert must also accept Judaism to the exclusion of all other religious faiths. Finally, the convert must raise all progeny as Jews, meaning Hebrew school, teen tours to Israel, and unlimited access to therapists.

REFORMATION NATION LITE

Reform Judaism in the United States often gives its wannabes a pass on the necessary prerequisites to conversion. In fact, in the late 1800s, the inner sanctum of the American Reform rabbis decided to admit all converts to the Jew Club regardless of "initiatory rite, ceremony or observance." In other words, forgo your Christmas ornaments and glazed ham, and voilà, you're a Hebrew.

Jew Boards

TEN JEW REVIEW PRACTICE QUESTIONS

Is this gonna be on the test? Here's the deal: If you want to convert to Judaism, you're gonna have to dedicate at least a year to studying and living a seriously Jewish life before even thinking about going in front of the *beit din*, especially the Orthodox *beit din*. What's more, just as most Americans probably couldn't pass the test to become a naturalized citizen of the United States, depending on the shul, most Jews wouldn't pass the Judaism test without some serious study time, even if they went to Hebrew school, and got bar/bat mitzvahed and confirmed. Many more sample questions as an well as an extensive suggested-reading list can be found at www.halakhicconversion.org.

1. How many *melachas* are forbidden on Shabbat?

2. Is the Hebrew calendar lunar or solar based?

3. What are the five things forbidden on Yom Kippur?

4. What are the two key Torah mitzvot performed on the first night of Pesach?

5. If a bee is not kosher, why is honey kosher?

6. Why is a *mechitza* essential to a synagogue?

7. What color undergarments does a woman wear during the *shiva nekiim*?

8. May one pass gas while wearing tefillin?

9. What is the name of the blessing one says after using the restroom?

10. What are the Jewish fast days?

ANSWERS

1. There are thirty-nine categories of activity that are expressly verboten on Shabbat.

2. **Both: lunisolar.** The Hebrew calendar is based on the rotation of Earth on its axis (day), the moon around Earth (month), Earth around the sun (year). Months correspond to a 29¾-day lunar cycle, but the year (which can be either twelve or thirteen months) corresponds to the solar cycle.

3. Eating/drinking, wearing leather footwear, bathing, anointing, *schtupping*.

4. Telling the story of Passover and eating matzo.

5. **The Mishnah** (see chapter 8) lays down the law that anything that hails from an animal that is not kosher is, well, not kosher, while the product of a kosher animal is considered kosher. Bees are flying bugs and thus are nonkosher in and of themselves, but their honey isn't actually a product of their little fuzzy bee bodies; it is only stored there.

6. The *mechitza*, or partition between the men's and women's section in shul, serves the purpose of keeping one from getting too distracted by members of the opposite sex whilst praying. Basically, the idea is that when you pray, you are uniting yourself with Big Poppa, and this holy union cannot be achieved when there is a third element involved. In other words, no threesomes. At least, not in shul.

7. During the *shiva nekii'm*, or seven clean/blood-free days, a woman must wear white underwear.

8. **Kinda, but only if involuntary.** According to RambaM's *Mishneh Torah*, if one passes gas voluntarily, this act is considered deprecating. If one passes gas unwittingly, he should wait until the gas subsides before returning to prayer. If possible, he should step back four cubits to expel the gas. After the air has cleared, one may utter the following *berachot*, or blessing: "Master of all the world, You created us with many orifices and ducts. Our shame and disgrace is apparent and known before You. Shame and disgrace during our life, worm-eaten and decaying in our death."

9. **The Asher Yatzar,** literally "He who has formed." It goes a little something like this: "Blessed are You, Adonai our God, King of the universe, who has formed man in wisdom and created in him many orifices and many cavities. It is obvious and known before Your throne of glory that if one of them ruptures or one of them is blocked, it would be impossible to survive and stand before You. Blessed are You that heals all flesh and does wonders."

10. Yom Kippur, Tisha B'Av, Ta'anit Esther, Shiva Asar B'Tamuz, Asarah B'Tevet, Tzom Gedaliah.

Formal conversion to Judaism stipulates that a Jewish court, or *beit din*, "house of judgment," comprising three learned men (or women, in the Reform and Conservative traditions), has to administer the oral exam that determines whether or not you are ready to be a Jew. In fact, should your test not go according to plan, the *beit din* also has the power to deny a conversion and send you right back to Christmas City, though this rarely happens.

Back in Temple times, the *Sanhedrin*, Greek for "sitting together," was the central court of seventy-one judges entrusted with the task of keeping the Oral Law and making sure everyone was doing right by Hashem. In the book of Numbers, God commands Moses to gather the very first Sanhedrin, consisting of Moses and seventy other luminaries, and bring them to the Tent of Meeting. After Moses's death, another great sage was appointed as leader, or *Rosh HaYeshiva*, literally "head of the sitting." The trickledown: Aside from the Sanhedrin, there were also smaller courts of twenty-three judges each who would deal with capital and other cases, and courts of three (the *beit din*) who mostly handled monetary matters or rituals such as conversion. These days, only those matters that can be resolved by the *beit din* are judged in religious courts.

MILAH, OR WHAT MAKES MY HOT DOG KOSHER?

Since most conversion procedures follow Orthodox guidelines, an adult male looking to convert to Judaism must have a Brit Milah, or ritual circumcision, performed by a qualified mohel. (See chapter 3.) That is, unless the poor guy lucks out with a nice Conservative or Reform rabbi who turns a blind eye and lets poor Peter keep his coat on. Additionally, since Judaism doesn't want you to die of a heart attack, if you're going Reform or Conservative, you can sometimes opt for a *hatafat dam brit*—a pact blood-dripping—in which you only have to lose a drop of blood from the head of your penis.

Q: I'm an adult male converting to Judaism, but I was circumcised as a baby. What should I do?

A: Same as above. Sorry, Steve.

Here's the dilly: If the aspirant be already of non-foreskinned status, then he still must undergo the *hatafat dam brit* as part of his conversion journey. The only exemptions from the extruded drop of blood are when someone has had three brothers die as a result of circumcision or when someone is a hemophiliac.

Hot Tub Time Machine: The *Mikveh*

Every Conservative and Orthodox convert (and a fair number of Reform ones, too), must also undergo full immersion in a ritual bath as the final part of his or her conversion. (See chapter 3.) The best part of this holy skinny-dip is when a member of the *beit din* pops their head in at the end to make sure our convert has immersed according to ritual specifications. **NOTE:** *When the* beit din *makes an appearance during a female conversion and all the rabbis are male, they take proper precautions to maintain the laws of* tzniut, *modesty.* Finally, after our convert has done the ol' double dip and recited the specified blessing, "Blessed are You, O Lord, our God, King of the universe, who has sanctified us with His commandments and commanded us regarding the immersion," he/she has successfully completed all necessary rituals and can now proudly phone home and say, "Mama, I'm a Jew!" There. Wasn't that easy?

Babe Ruth: The Original Righteous Convert

While she didn't have to undergo any of the formal conversion rituals, the biblical heroine Ruth is the Hebrew Bible's first ever non-Jew-to-Jew convert. Indeed, the book of Ruth has helped many a *maidel* to stay on the Jew path, even when it seemed like maybe it was a better deal to remain a Methodist. In case Jew need it, here's the *Reader's Digest* version of her inspiring story: Ruth and Orpah, two Moabite ladies from 'round the way, marry the sons of Naomi and Elimelech, an Israelite couple fleeing famine in their homeland. When Naomi's hubby and then his two sons die, Naomi decides the time is nigh to skedaddle back to Bethlehem and tells Ruth and Orpah to remain in their motherland and remarry.

DID JEW KNOW? In the late 1970s, Bob Dylan (born Robert Allen Zimmerman) then rock's most famous Yidl mitn fidl, reportedly became a born-again Christian and released two gospel albums. Since then, the iconoclast has rejoined the Jew Crew. In fact, he has supported the Chabad Lubavitch movement (see chapter 2), possibly even hitting the scrolls at one of Chabad's many yeshivas, and had his two sons, Samuel Isaac Abraham and Jakob Luke, bar mitzvah-ed.

After just a brief discussion of how arduous the decision to remain on Team Jew will be, Orpah decides to remain amongst her idol-worshipping people, while Ruth steadfastly remains loyal to her mother-in-law, no matter how many times Naomi attempts to turn her away. Finally, Ruth seals the deal with the following utterance: "Wherever you go, I will go; wherever you live, I will live. Your people will be my people, and your God will be my God. Where you die, I will die and there I will be buried." (Ruth 1:16–17) The upshot of the story: Naomi allows Ruth to return with her to Bethlehem, where Ruth scores a rich Jewish husband named Boaz.

Ruth's conversion is a banner choice on a couple of levels, the first being that long before Naomi and Elimelech arrived on the scene, Ruth had grown disgusted with the idol-worshipping ways of her people, especially their ritual of sacrificing cute little Moabite children to the pagan god Moloch. Another essential boon of Ruth's conversion is that instead of being some forgotten pagan princess, she will later go on to become the great-grandmother of none other than King David! According to Christian tradition, Ruth is also an ancestress of Jesus. Oh well, Jew can't have everything.

The Khazars: Thirteenth Tribe or Jewish Atlantis?

The Khazars were a powerful seminomadic people who established one of the largest nations of medieval Eurasia, occupying most of modern-day Russia, Ukraine, Crimea, and Turkey. At some point during the eighth or ninth century,

ASENETH: YET ANOTHER RIGHTEOUS BIBLICAL CONVERT WHO KNEW A GOOD THING WHEN SHE SAW IT

For those Jews who made the harrowing schlep from Canaan to the Promised Land and then found themselves slaves in Egypt, it might not seem like conversion to Judaism would be a recommended move. Tell that to Aseneth, the virgin daughter of a pagan priest (read: idolator) whom Pharaoh gave to Joseph, he of the Amazing Technicolor Dreamcoat. Sister up and went monotheistic and lassoed herself a hot Joey!

Khazar royalty and most of the aristocracy converted to Judaism, followed by part of the general population. There is much speculation regarding the wherefores of this move at a time when the rest of the world was busy doing, shall we say, quite the opposite.

Regardless of how many regular Khazars actually converted, there's one hugely contested theory that Ashkenazic Jews are descendants of the converted Khazars rather than the Israelites. This theory is popular among the sect known as Black Hebrews and Arabs whose identity is tied up in asserting the authenticity of their connection to Israel while downplaying that of other Jews.

What a *Shanda*: Jews for Jesus

Founded in the '70s, Jews for Jesus is an evangelical Christian organization whose members think of themselves as Jews, yet believe that the Messiah has come and gone, that he was none other than Jesus Christ, and that he was the product of virgin birth. The group also purports that God exists as the father, the son, and the Holy Ghost and that Israel exists as a covenant between God, Jew, and Gentile.

In 1993, The Supreme Court of Israel ruled that Jews who espouse Christian beliefs are not Jews and as such are not eligible for the automatic citizenship that Israel grants to all Jews, even those who now and again date shiksas or eat pork. The idea behind this seemingly draconian ban was that letting in people who are trying to get Jews to go goy is actually anathema to the whole purpose of Israel, and did we spend all those years irrigating the desert and then surviving the Nazis only to have to listen to Christmas carols?

Guess Jew's Coming to Dinner!

As a people who have been persecuted pretty much since they originated monotheism and whose numbers are teetering at about one quarter of 1 percent of the world's population, the Jews have strong opinions on intermarriage. For the Orthodox and Hasidim, most of whose lives are too insular to meet or mate outside the faith, intermarriage and its dilution of the tribe is considered nothing less than "the Second Silent Holocaust." The end; do not pass go, do not collect 200 shekels. What's more, this Hebrews-with-Shebrews-only injunction extends to the bedroom as well as the chuppah. In other words, if you want to knock the boots, they'd better be kosher, and you two had better be married to each other, or it's out of the kvestion.

Meantime, while Conservative rabbis might not necessarily all reject an interfaith partnership outright, they still hold out the hope that the Jewish side of the equation might rekindle an interest in their faith and the Gentile side might eventually be persuaded to convert and all offspring will be raised as Jews. Even Reform or Reconstructionist communities, by far the most accepting, do not view interfaith marriage as a cause for celebration. In fact, most Jews seeking to marry outside the faith would be hard-pressed to find a rabbi who would officiate their wedding, no matter the amount of money donated to the temple, that is, unless

QUICK-CHANGE ARTISTS: A SAMPLING OF STARS WHO CONVERTED TO JUDAISM

- **DREW BARRYMORE**: Drew's a Jew! She reportedly converted for art-dealing hubby Will Kopelman.

- **IVANKA TRUMP**: Converted to marry businessman Jared Kushner.

- **ISLA FISHER**: Converted to marry Ortho funny-mensch Sacha Baron Cohen.

- **LIZ TAYLOR**: Converted in 1959 after the death of her third husband Mike Todd.

- **ELIZABETH BANKS**: Converted to marry sportswriter/producer Max Handelman.

- **NELL CARTER**: Converted while married to her first husband, the son of Holocaust survivors.

- **ANNE MEARA**: Converted before she married Jerry Stiller. The two then spawned Ben Stiller.

- **MARILYN MONROE**: Converted to marry playwright Arthur Miller, continued to identify as Jewish after they divorced.

- **CONNIE CHUNG**: Converted to marry Maury Povich.

- **SAMMY DAVIS JR.**: Converted after surviving the near-fatal automobile accident that cost him his left eye.

the couple promised to give their children a Jewish education.

Simply put: No matter how observant or secular the community, the going idea is that Jewish numbers are dwindling, and if Seth Berkowitz marries Colleen Quinn, that's all she wrote. As the Good Book says, "A bird can love a fish, but where will they live, and what will happen to the motion of the ocean?"

No Can Jew:
God's View on Intermarriage

Speaking of the Good Book, although inter-faith love sessions do occur in le Bible, God's negative opinion on the whole intermarriage topic is pretty clear: "You shall not intermarry with them, [the seven nations of the land of Canaan]: do not give your daughters to their sons or take their daughters for your sons. For you will turn your children away from Me to worship other gods." (Deuteronomy 7:1–3) The one exception to this rule pertained to marriage with non-Jewish women who were taken as war booty, though even these women had to convert eventually.

In the post-exilic period, the realization that Jews were a chosen (read: holy) people crystallized, and the ban on Jews marrying Canaanites extended to Jews marrying all non-Jews in general—thus the rabbinic prohibition against intermarriage and the exclusion from the Nation of Israel of all who married outside the faith.

Assimilation: Bu-Jews, Hin-Jews, and the Hanukah Bush

In addition to the obvious perils and delights of intermarriage and the seductive power of Christmas trees, many blue-state Jews find respite from the doldrums of Western suffering with various Eastern practices whose

**THE UN-CHOSEN:
A SAMPLING OF JEWS
WHO LEFT THE FAITH**

- The Apostle PAUL

- False Messiah SABBATAI ZEVI (See chapter 1)

- British prime minister BENJAMIN DISRAELI

- Writer HEINRICH HEINE

- Composer GUSTAV MAHLER

- Austrian actor-director ERICH VON STROHEIM

- Politician ROBERT MOSES

- French philosopher and activist SIMONE WEIL

- YOUSSEF DARWISH, Egyptian labor lawyer, converted to Islam

- Jews for Jesus founder MOISHE ROSEN

- British singer MARIANNE FAITHFULL

- Folk singer ARLO GUTHRIE

- Serial killer DAVID BERKOWITZ

- BILLY JOEL, who had Jewish parents but mysteriously was raised Catholic

special brand of idolatry offers an exotic alternative to both traditional Judaism and traditional Jewish decor. Throw in the rampant secularizing of Jewish America and the billion-dollar industry that is yoga and meditation, and you've got a bunch of Jews who know more about Krishna and Siddhartha Gautama than they do about Hillel or the Vilna Gaon. In fact, Tibetan Buddhist master Chögyam Trungpa Rinpoche once said that so many of his students were Jews, they formed the Oy Vey school of Buddhism.

Of these Easternized Yids, many might hit an ashram with nary a thought about Judaism's absolute ban on idolatry despite it being one of the three laws that, along with premeditated murder and adultery/incest, a Jew must die before violating. So, what's a little yoga between friends? Answer: no big deal, as long as you don't chant or practice yoga in a studio that chants, features altars, or displays images of Hindu deities or Thai Buddhas.

The Dalai Lama: Coming Soon to a Seder Near Jew!

In 1995, the Religious Action Center of Reform Judaism of Washington, D.C., hosted a Seder for none other than Tibet's exiled Buddhist leader, the Dalai Lama. Rocking a black *kippah* along with his customary red and gold robes, His Holiness munched on his first matzo as he told the other attendees, "I think that right from the beginning, the Tibetans learned that we must copy some of the Jewish determination and the techniques they have used to keep their identity, their religious faith, their traditions under difficult circumstances." As the Seder concluded with its traditional "Next year in Jerusalem," the votive was echoed with a resounding new blessing: "Next year in Lhasa."

> "When the student is ready, the teacher appears."
> —THE BUDDHA

Kabbalah: A Tree (of Life) Grows in Hollywood

So What's Up With That Red String?

Way back in 1995, comedienne Sandra Bernhard stumbled on Kabbalah and told her famous friends, such as Roseanne Barr (Jewish) and Madonna (not Jewish), that the time was nigh to find a rabbi and get to studying. When the Material Girl started wearing a red string around her wrist, attending Shabbat services, and going by the Hebrew name Esther, other celebs jumped on the mystical bandwagon, and the next thing you know, Kabbalah was being touted as the next best thing since yogalates. This resurgence was linked in part to Rabbi Phillip Berg's controversial Kabbalah Centre in New York City. By 2009, the Kabbalah Centre's assets totaled more than $260 million. That's a heck of a lot of red string bracelets and magical water!

Other celebs spotted red-stringing it included: Michael Jackson, Elizabeth Taylor, Rosie O'Donnell, Paris and Nicky Hilton, Lindsay Lohan, Gwyneth Paltrow, Mariah Carey, Nicole Richie, Charlize Theron, Victoria Beckham, Naomi Campbell, Goldie Hawn, Lucy Liu, Britney Spears, Reese Witherspoon, Mick Jagger, Sienna Miller, Alex Rodriguez, and Anthony Kiedis.

HIN-JEW

A Hin-Jew is a person of half-Jewish and half-Hindu descent, which is to say, someone who always disappoints his/her parents regardless of how many times he or she reincarnates. Hin-Jew is also a term for an assimilated Jew who discovers yoga and changes her name from Karen Goldberg to Shakti-Bhakti Goldberg. This phenomenon is also known as being Yogish. Some Yogish superstars include:

- **DIANE BLOOMFIELD**, a yoga teacher who canonized Torah Yoga: an experience of Jewish wisdom through Iyengar yoga instruction interwoven with the study of traditional and mystical Jewish texts.

- **DAVID BEN-GURION**, Israel's first prime minister, was both a yogi and a student of Buddhist meditation.

- **KRISHNA DAS**, born Jeffrey Kagel, on Long Island, a Jew who took a trip to India and came back a *bhakti yogi*— someone whose practice involves call-and-response devotional chanting, otherwise known as *kirtan*.

- **ALLEN GINSBERG**, American poet and iconoclast who extolled Buddhist and Hindu spirituality and teachings, especially when they involved psychedelic drugs.

- Ram Dass, né Dr. Richard Alpert, ex–Harvard professor, spiritual teacher and author of *Be Here Now*. In 1967, Alpert traveled to India, where he met Hindu guru Neem Karoli Baba, who subsequently dubbed Alpert "Ram Dass"—"servant of Lord Rama."

- **JAI UTTAL**, born Douglas Uttal, world music yoga-lebrity and *kirtan* rock star.

DID JEW KNOW? Kabbalah's red string has multiple meanings: a talisman to ward off the "evil eye"; an amulet for spiritual blessing; and a mini replica of the red string that ostensibly girt the Tomb of Rachel, wife of Jacob. Some rabbis say the red thread recalls Rachel's modest selflessness while reminding us to fulfill the mitzvah of *tzedakah*, charity. Others say that the red string is not Jewish in origin.

But will I go insane if I take a continuing-ed Kabbalah class at my local community college? Maybe. The reason being that only God understands the mysteries. Thus, some subjects of the Kabbalah can make one go insane, especially if not adequately prepared. Also, if Jews manage to unlock the mystery and all that power escapes, it could fall into the wrong hands and then Xenu would be king of the world and there would only be Tom Cruise movies. That said, there are some aspects of Kabbalah that are accessible to mere mortals dabbling in the discipline:

- The five senses are able to access only about 1 percent of reality without the wisdom of Kabbalah. The other 99 percent comes from Kabbalah study, and provides the essential context without which we will never understand the 1 percent.

- It's all about light: Everyone has direct access to the Light, but sometimes *klippot*, literally "peels" or "shells," get in the way of receiving pure spirit. Studying Kabbalah is divine Liquid Drāno strong enough to cut through even the most stubborn *klippot*, yet still gentle on your pipes.

- It's also about trees, specifically the Tree of Life, both a symbol of the path to God and a map of all creation.

- You and your emotions are your own worst enemy. In other words, the woman in front of you at Starbucks who takes twenty minutes to decide whether or not to get her latte with whip is not Satan, your ego is. If you do not restrict your ego, you limit your limitless potential to experience the divine light of Frappucinos.

- Astrology, as in the Zodiac, is true. And Jewish! Not only is it proto-astronomy, it is a way of interpreting the vault of heaven and unlocking the mysteries from on high.

- Wasted sperm are abandoned souls that become demons. So deposit wisely, otherwise it's Jewish *Dawn of the Dead*.

While Tevye might never have rolled out a yoga mat for all the unlimited class cards in Anatevka, one thing's for certain: Homeboy definitely would have viewed the complete elimination of all boundaries between Jew and Gentile as bad for the Covenant. True, the Jews' precarious position in the world did force them to stick together and, on some level, made them more Jewish, but whether or not *tsuris* or insular living keeps people Jewish remains to be seen. Indeed, if Tevye, Golda, or, for that matter, Britney Spears could talk, they might ask where, exactly, does all this watering down and mixing up leave the so-called People of the Book? Are they still the People of the Book even though, technically, they either live their lives pretty much bookless or according to such a mishmash of books, traditions, and practices that only a New Agey Comp. Religion prof could relate? And if a bird can in fact love a fish, will their children be birds or fish, where will they live, and will there be decent lox?

CHAPTER 6

JEW BETTER WORK:
How Jews Put
the *J* Back in Job

*Which is the merchant here,
and which is the Jew?*

—THE MERCHANT OF VENICE, ACT IV, SC I

Though the Jews didn't invent cities per se, they may as well have. Ditto the shtetl—a small Jewish town/village typically found in pre–World War II Russia and Eastern Europe. While both cities and shtetlach existed long before Abraham made the immortal schlep from Ur to Canaan, if it weren't for Jews, neither would have caught on as they did. Look at it this way: Throughout history, Jews have been relegated to living in ghettos, settlements, or shtetls; they've also often been barred from most forms of gainful, "respectable" employment. These restrictions forced many Jews to put the shtetl to the metal, thereby redefining the world economy from the time of Uruk (among the world's first early Bronze Age cities, economies, and writing systems) to modern-day New York City.

Diamonds Are a Jew's Best Friend

As anyone lucky enough to have a relative in the business will tell you, when it's time to buy the rock for your beloved, go big, go high quality, and, above all, go Jewish! Here's why: Until paper money came into general use in Europe in the seventeenth century, the general currency was gold and silver coins and gemstones. Due to a high theft rate, this form of exchange was both risky and schleppy, a situation to which the Jews had been accustomed since before the Diaspora. While this familiarity may not have directly led to the Jews' success in the diamond trade, it sure helped.

Here's how it all went down: After Vasco da Gama's infamous boat ride to India in 1498, a direct diamond-trading route was established between India and Portugal that then carried over to the Netherlands. While the Jews of Eastern Europe were busy becoming skilled laborers, peddlers, and craftsmen, the Portuguese crypto-Sephardim opened diamond-cutting and -polishing houses and established themselves as essential players in a growth industry.

"Why did God invent the goyim? Somebody's gotta pay retail."
—CLASSIC JEWISH JOKE

Fast-forward to the 1600s, when now-wealthy Jewish diamond-cutters and traders in the Netherlands financed the Dutch East India Company. Next, the Brits discovered mines in Brazil and birthed the British East India Company, eventually moving the diamond center from Amsterdam to jolly ol' England. Yet again the Jews followed and established themselves as key players, wisely selling the stones to the Gentile nobility via Jewish purchasing and trading agents otherwise known as Court Jews.

Court Jews Versus Port Jews: Lenders and Vendors

Even though they arrived as refugees from the Inquisition, Port Jews played an essential role in the maritime and modern trade economy of the seventeenth and eighteenth centuries. Since the port towns were more liberal environments due to the influx of various types of people and folkways, Jewish traders were able to do business openly and subsequently flourish. Also helpful: their Diaspora connections in other port cities and marked expertise in mercantilism, peddling, and, as we mentioned before, schlepping. As a result, the Sephardim in Brazil and Amsterdam helped shape and grow transatlantic trade.

Court Jews, on the other hand, is a term applied to Jewish banker types who emerged during the medieval era as the financiers and moneylenders to the nobility of Europe (more on this in a moment). In return for this service, Court Jews enjoyed both serious wealth and some of the status and social privileges of the Christian world. In other words, social position rather than Inquisition.

So, How Did the Orthos Manage to Become Diamond Dealers?

As Hasidism managed to wend its black-hatted way westward at the outset of the nineteenth century, the small Hasidic communities of Antwerp and London got into the ice-hocking business, and the trend stuck. When vast diamond reserves were discovered in South Africa at the end of the nineteenth century, a group of Orthodox dealers formed "the syndicate," a gang o' high-rollin' Heebs who pooled their resources to soak up the glut in the diamond market so *bubbe's* engagement ring would be worth more than two pebbles and a stick of gum.

Trader Jews

In the later seventeenth and early eighteenth centuries, as Europe became more affluent, its rulers and nobles became obsessed with increasing revenue. As a result, some countries, including France, Germany, and the Netherlands,

DID JEW KNOW? Glückel of Hameln (1646–1724) was a Jewish businesswoman, merchant, and prolific diarist who meticulously chronicled daily life in the German Jewish ghetto. She traded jewelry, lent money, kept books, ran a sock factory, and conducted trade from Amsterdam to Paris, enjoying an unprecedented position of power for a woman at the time, let alone a Jewish woman. When Glückel's first husband was asked on his deathbed if he wanted to leave final instructions for his wife, he reportedly replied, "My wife, she knows everything. Let her do as she has done until now." Glückel bore fourteen children, twelve of whom married into Europe's most prominent Jewish families. Some dames have all the Glückel!

became more "tolerant" of their Jews, mostly because they were actually helping to buoy and grow both international and local economies, and who wouldn't want that?

Since Jews were denied the right to own land, restricted in terms of occupation, and subject to sudden dislocation, they had to acquire professions that were not dependent on land ownership but instead relied upon intellect, international savvy, and street smarts. Thus, certain classes of Jews became default pioneers in the professional worlds of trading and finance.

Indeed, two loose groups had emerged by the eighteenth century: the Jewish peddlers and the considerably more successful Jewish merchants, bankers, and business leaders. In Germany, Jews were even granted exemption from certain taxes, that is, as long as they continued to make trade connections for the Gentile elite and help them continue to schtuff their coffers.

Again, the restrictions on what Jews were actually allowed to trade—gold, jewels, and pawned items—proved a boon, helping the Tribe move from the pawnshop to peddling to the world of retail, where some eventually became affluent importers and exporters.

A Price above Rubens: Jews and Money Lending

Back in the Middle Ages, the charging of interest on loans was a major no-no for members of the Catholic church. Thing was, as the Reformation reared its WASPy head and economic systems continued to evolve, the papacy decided interest should be paid on certain risky investments. Once Europe started using paper money, the days of I-lend-you-six-gold-ingots-for-your-six-goats were long gone, and the European economy changed forever. Also, surplus capital became more important as the economy became less and less agrarian, which created a new demand for money lending. Enter the Jews, a people unfettered by the specific Christian prohibition against usury and therefore uniquely suited to this novel form of financial transaction, without which there would be no trade, industry, or commerce.

Mo' Money, Mo' Problems

The one catch in what was otherwise a win-win—Jews serving as financial intermediaries and lending money with interest and thereby keeping European trade economies afloat—was that even though the Church and the nobility of Europe approved of Jew-sury, it still remained illegal and thus Jews could be prosecuted, a move that came in handy if a Jew started getting too powerful and needed to have his assets seized. Also, let's say a king borrowed money from a Jew and didn't have enough money to make good on his debts. His solution could be to kill the Jew or exile him.

Shylock and Barabas: *The Merchant of Venice* and *The Jew of Malta*

Shakespeare's play *The Merchant of Venice* concerns a grouchy and loathsome moneylender, Shylock, who seeks vengeance on a Jew-hating Christian merchant who has defaulted on a loan. The price: oh, just a pound of flesh, give or take.

> I am a Jew. Hath not a Jew eyes? ... If you prick us, do we not bleed?
> If you tickle us, do we not laugh? If you poison us, do we not die?
> And if you wrong us, shall we not revenge?
>
> —*THE MERCHANT OF VENICE*

Here are some little-known factoids about the play and how it fits into global anti-Semitism:

- For starters, there were at most 200 Jews in Elizabethan England when Shakespeare was writing. Why? They had all been banished under the Edict of Expulsion in 1289 and were persona non grata until Oliver Cromwell invited them back after the revolution. So, it's unlikely Shakespeare or any of his cronies ever met an actual Jew they didn't like.
- Regardless of their minuscule numbers in England, Jews were accused of kidnapping children on Easter and/or drinking Christian blood on Passover.

Meanwhile, in 1594, Queen Elizabeth's personal physician, Rodrigo López, a converso of Portugese origin, was convicted of plotting to poison the queen and was summarily executed. The López trial and execution may have inspired Christopher Marlowe's play *The Jew of Malta* (1589), which then perhaps inspired Shakespeare. Marlowe's play features a merchant named Barabas, who is depicted as having more wealth at his disposal than all of Malta put together. When a Christian governor seizes his money, Barabas goes on a vengeance-seeking killing spree that makes Shylock's agonized carping seem warm and fuzzy in comparison.

> **DID JEW KNOW?** Barabas was originally the name of a notorious Jewish criminal who lucked out due to Jerusalem's custom that allowed none other than Pontius Pilate to release one prisoner from his/her death sentence based on the roar of the crowd. Sadly, this did not go as well for Jesus as it did for Barabas, whom the crowd o' Jews voted off the cross. For any Christian audience in the Renaissance, a character carrying that name would have to be the worst kind of murderer.

The Lure of Shekels: From the Rothschilds to Goldman Sachs

By the time the Industrial Revolution transformed Europe's economies, the need for capital to finance the various mills and factories had made money-lending acceptable (and legal), and great Jewish banking families, such as the Rothschilds and the Warburgs, achieved power and prominence. Indeed, these and other German Jewish families founded the investment-banking firms that became the modus operandi of world finance—as opposed to commercial banks upon whose coffers the world economy had previously relied. Let's not forget the fact that the Jews were actually forced to focus on developing the investment-banking system due to their full-on exclusion from the commercial banking sector. Thus, one could argue that it's actually the goyim who are to blame for the "Jewish monopoly" on banking rather than the so-called greed-mongers looking to succeed and excel in the first country to let them do so in the history of history.

Ponder this: Since steam, coal, and improved textile production suddenly made it easier for the world to produce goods more quickly, effectively, and cheaply, it also became essential to continue to keep this whole mechanized operation afloat via an elaborate system of phantom money, otherwise known as the misunderstood monolith of investment banking and capital formation. Rather than bore Jew with an explanation of what investment banking actually is or its history in terms of financing the entire global economy—take that, Occupy Wall Street—let's instead focus on the family that made both real money and faux dough as we know it famous: the Rothschilds.

Let's agree to agree, whether or not peeps secretly wanted to marry one of them, the majority of non-Jews viewed the Rothschilds as highfalutin', hook-nosed, greedy Christ-killers who controlled the world economy, facilitated the assassinations of more than a few U.S. presidents (including Lincoln), and/or quite possibly started the War of 1812! While these overwrought conspiracy theories may or may not continue to hold sway over current

> **DID JEW KNOW?**
> The Yom Kippur liturgy does describe demanding any form of usurious interest as a transgression, but only if a Jew charges this interest to another Jew. Since the Jews were moneylenders to Gentiles only, God let them off on a technicality.

> **DID JEW KNOW?**
> Hitler was a huge fan of *The Merchant of Venice*, natch. Since Shylock was the embodiment of so many greedy Jew stereotypes, Nazi propaganda often featured images of Shylock!

Meet My Millionaires!

A SAMPLING OF THE TRIBE'S MOST (IN)FAMOUS FINANCIAL HEAVY HITTERS AND QUITTERS

Firm & Founders	Origins
Kuhn, Loeb, and Co., 1867–1977 Abraham Kuhn and Solomon Loeb	Dry-goods merchants from Cincinnati who started an influential investment bank that merged with Lehman Brothers in 1977.
M.M. Warburg, 1798–present; **Warburg Pincus,** 1938–present Moses Marcus Warburg; Eric Warburg	Originally from Italy, the family established itself in Germany in the 1500s; descendants set up banks in London and New York.
Goldman Sachs, 1869 Marcus Goldman; Samuel Sachs	German-born Marcus Goldman established the investment banking, securities, and investment-management firm in 1869 and was joined by son-in-law Samuel Sachs in 1882. The firm joined the New York Stock Exchange in 1896.
Lehman Brothers, 1850 Henry and Emanuel Lehman	Bavarian dry-goods merchants who set up shop in sweet home Alabama, where they capitalized on cotton's market value; these commodities traders later settled in New York, where they established their world-renowned firm in 1855.
Lazard Ltd. Formerly Lazard Frères & Co., 1848 Alexandre Lazard and Elie Lazard	The brothers Lazard immigrated from Lorraine, France, to New Orleans, Louisiana, where they opened up a dry-goods biz, went très international in 1852, and focused exclusively on money matters in 1876.

Fun Fact

Jacob Schiff, son of a Rothschild broker in Frankfurt, joined the firm, married a Loeb, and financed the Pennsylvania Railroad and the Louisville and Nashville Railroad.

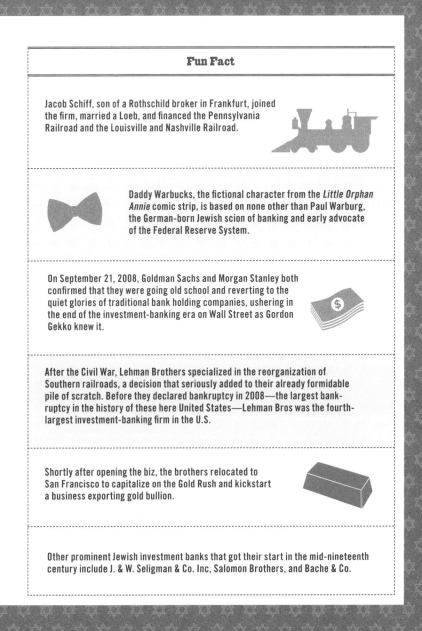

Daddy Warbucks, the fictional character from the *Little Orphan Annie* comic strip, is based on none other than Paul Warburg, the German-born Jewish scion of banking and early advocate of the Federal Reserve System.

On September 21, 2008, Goldman Sachs and Morgan Stanley both confirmed that they were going old school and reverting to the quiet glories of traditional bank holding companies, ushering in the end of the investment-banking era on Wall Street as Gordon Gekko knew it.

After the Civil War, Lehman Brothers specialized in the reorganization of Southern railroads, a decision that seriously added to their already formidable pile of scratch. Before they declared bankruptcy in 2008—the largest bankruptcy in the history of these here United States—Lehman Bros was the fourth-largest investment-banking firm in the U.S.

Shortly after opening the biz, the brothers relocated to San Francisco to capitalize on the Gold Rush and kickstart a business exporting gold bullion.

Other prominent Jewish investment banks that got their start in the mid-nineteenth century include J. & W. Seligman & Co. Inc, Salomon Brothers, and Bache & Co.

anti-Semitic factions bent on blaming the Jews for the so-called evils of Wall Street, at the time the Rothschilds rose to prominence, the timbre of Europe was still one of rampant paranoia about Jews and money regardless of the fact that banking was now technically fair game to both Jew and Gentile alike.

Mayer Rothschild: Gold Metal Usury

Born in the *Judengasse*, or "Jew's alley," of Frankfurt, Mayer Rothschild (1744–1812) built his financial business there and placed each of his five sons at the helm of a different branch in five major European financial centers. He also shrewdly kept the fortune in the family via arranged marriages between first or second cousins. Historian Paul Johnson observes that unlike the earlier Court Jews who were vulnerable to violence, anti-Semitism, and theft, the Rothschilds were immune to attack because their assets were "circulating through the world as stocks, bonds and debts." During the nineteenth century, the family had the largest private fortune in world history. As time went on, this wealth declined substantially due to its division among literally hundreds of descendents. So, in case you were wanting to drink egg creams on Easy Street, better to bank on Mark Zuckerberg: less history, better stock options.

Isaac Moses and Haym Salomon: Patriotic Peepaws of New-World Banking

When the Revolutionary War began in 1775, America's Jews numbered about 2,000 (out of a population of approximately two million). Yet this humble handful o' Yids valiantly upheld the patriot position, lent money to the war effort, and helped rebuild what would soon become the one and only nation to grant full rights to Jews, setting a standard that other countries soon followed. Meanwhile, as America was struggling to cast off the yoke of the British in the name of freedom, two Jews were instrumental in funding the war effort and providing materials and monies for postwar cleanup. These Jews were Isaac Moses and Haym Salomon. This is their story.

DID JEW KNOW? Luis de Santángel was the baptized Sephardic financial adviser to King Ferdinand and Queen Isabella of Spain. It was his crypto dough that covered much of Columbus' infamous voyage to America. Believe it or not, de Santángel convinced the king and queen that a Christian-ized Asia would make the risky and expensive voyage worthwhile, then proceeded to finance Columbus' expedition, preventing Isabella from having to sell the crown jewels. In 1497, King Ferdinand exempted de Santángel and his family from the Inquisition, but alas, not before his cousin was beheaded.

Isaac Moses was a merchant who hightailed it over to the rebel city of Philadelphia while the Brits were busy occupying the Big Apple. In the Liberty City, Moses became one of early America's most successful merchant shippers. After the war, his firm Moses & Sons became brokers, bankers, retailers, wholesalers, and traders in commodities such as foods, furs, liquor, cotton, and jewelry—basically anything that would stand still for a price tag.

Haym Salomon was one of the most important Jews of the Revolutionary War era. A Spanish and Portuguese Jew from Poland who immigrated to the colonies during the American Revolution, he quickly became a banker and sympathizer with the patriot cause. In fact, Salomon was ordered by George Washington himself to destroy British warehouses but was caught and condemned to execution in 1776. Thankfully, Salomon spoke ten languages, so the practical Brits decided to take him on as a translator. Arrested again in 1778, Salomon was again sentenced to death, but he managed to escape, this time to Philly where he revived his former broker biz and floated loans to the government—sans fees!—and subsequently paid the salaries of none other than Thomas Jefferson, James Madison, and James Monroe when the U.S. Treasury's gelt had done near run dry.

From Pushcarts to the Department Store: A Whole Jew World

Before we get into the enchanted microcosm of the department store, a word on peddling and the Tribe: Though by no means solely a Jewish occupation, Jewish peddlers had been trooping around Europe as early as the Middle Ages. By the time of the first wave of Jewish immigrants to North America in the nineteenth century, peddling had become a starting point for many young Jews. Arriving in the New World, these young men put in their years selling secondhand clothing, pots, rags, or whatever else was in de pan. After these newly arrived Yids learned English and accumulated capital, they moved on to phase two: dry goods and department stores. In fact, most of the great Jewish department store tycoons began their careers as peddlers, as did a large number of other Jewish businessmen (and women).

There are a number of reasons why the Jews achieved such a high level of success in retail. For starters, since Jews had been excluded from other professions that were reserved for Christians, as well as from owning land, they had more experience with travel and commercial enterprise than their goyishe brethren. They also developed a knack for recognizing niche markets, creating new products, and ultimately promoting new ways of selling everything all under one roof, i.e., that world of wonder otherwise known as the department store, which would one day become the shopping mall.

From Skid Row to Saks Fifth Avenue

While Jews didn't invent the department store per se, these modern shopping meccas owe much to Jewish retail genius. Indeed, the department store sought to eliminate shlepping from shopping, even reducing the stress of having to figure out what to buy with their elegant and seductive window displays that would, come Christmas, become an ostentatious celebration of all things Saint Nick.

On another level, you could say that the history of the North American department store, specifically the New York flagship versions thereof, was linked to the history of the Jews in the New World, especially the German Jewish immigrants who arrived on America's shores in the wake of the Civil War and built glamorous and imposing structures in which they sold everything from intimates to home furnishings. Some of the greatest Jewish-owned and -operated department stores include Altmans, Gimbels, Kaufmann's, S. Klein, Lazarus, I. Magnin, Mays, Bloomingdale's, Abraham & Straus, Bergdorf Goodman, Neiman Marcus, Hecht's, and Filene's.

Jews and the Invention of the Great American Pastime: The Shopping Mall

Victor Gruen (1903–1980) was an Austrian architect who was the pioneering designer and promoter of that great North American juggernaut, the shopping mall. In 1954, Gruen developed the Northland Center near Detroit, then the largest shopping center in America, featuring one hundred shops and its own road system. Next came the Southdale Center near Minneapolis—the first enclosed center on any real scale and the first ever modern shopping mall, complete with department stores and other shops circumnavigating a huge covered court where one could sit under the potted palms and munch tasty snacks. In other words, Jews also invented the food court! *Nu*, who else?

HELLO, GORGEOUS:
Jews and the Beauty Industry

While Judaism is not conceptually opposed to cosmetics, Jewish custom doesn't support caking it on for the purposes of vamping it up and tramping it out. In fact, two stories in the Hebrew Bible espouse the notion that sometimes less is more. In one, Esther rejects her spa treatments before she is presented to Ahasuerus. Meantime, when Jezebel gets gussied up in finery and heavy eye makeup before her death, it's implied that too much makeup is for prostitutes, rather than nice Jewish girls.

> "A woman who doesn't wear lipstick feels undressed in public. Unless she works on a farm. "
> —MAX FACTOR

But the biblical style council didn't stop many a Jew from helping to found this booming biz. While German Jews were busy establishing investment-banking firms, other Ashkenazi revolutionaries were busy making sure they looked good doing it. In fact, of the five great cosmetic industry pioneers, Max Factor, Estée Lauder, Helena Rubinstein, Charles Revson (Revlon), and Elizabeth Arden, only the last was not Jewish.

The Factor Factor:
How a Polish Jew Invented Mass-Market Beauty

Born Maksymilian Faktorowicz in Poland circa 1872, Max was the ur-progenitor extraordinaire of modern makeup as we know it. One of ten children, Max began his career at age nine as an apprentice to a pharmacist and wig maker. It was in the pharmacy that he acquired the skill at mixing his various potions. He soon opened up a shop in Moscow selling wigs, cream, and rouge. Among his customers was a theater company that performed for Russian nobles; next thing you know, Max has a gig making up the makeup for the Imperial Russian Grand Opera.

DID JEW KNOW? The biggest Max Factor makeup order ever was for the Charlton Heston film *Ben-Hur*. The company provided 600 gallons (2,271 litres) of "light olive makeup" to make sure the extras in the States had the same olive complexions as the extras filming in Italy.

MADE UP BY MAX FACTOR

- false eyelashes
- eyebrow pencil
- lip gloss
- foundation
- waterproof mascara
- liquid nail enamel
- smear-proof lipstick

Cut to 1908, when Max, now Max Factor (courtesy of the Ellis Island administrators), moved to Los Angeles, where he began creating makeup specifically for screen actors that wouldn't crack, cake, or fall off in chunks in the middle of a close-up. Soon, movie stars such as Joan Crawford, Bette Davis, and Jean Harlow were running as fast as their famous gams would carry them to Max's makeup studio to sample his "flexible greasepaint," the first makeup created for film, as well as his line of human-hair wigs. He founded his company in 1909.

When the Hollywood stars began clamoring to wear their Factor faces offscreen as well as on, Max went back into the lab to create makeup that would wear well in natural lighting and not make everyone look like Gloria Swanson in *Sunset Boulevard.* Soon, regular janes got nutty to glam it up like their favorite stars and, in the 1920s, Max Factor introduced a line of everyday cosmetics to the general public. Forget electricity, trains, or even the Industrial Revolution! Before Big Daddy Max popularized the word *makeup*, few women used cosmetics, but ever since Max invented beauty in a tube for the mass-market audience, most ladies feel naked going to the store without their face on.

Mass-Market Makeup: The Jewish Kings and Queens of Pretty Paint

Helena Rubinstein and the Pseudoscience of Corrective Skincare

Chaya "Helena" Rubinstein (1870–1965) was a Polish-born skincare magnate whose brilliant idea of correcting "problem skin" made her one of America's richest women.

When Rubinstein docked in Australia in 1902, she had no money, little English, and a suitcase stuffed with jars of magic beauty cream. Within a few years, she managed to parlay that notorious suitcase into a luxurious cosmetics salon where she "prescribed" beauty treatments for problem skin types summarily diagnosed by one of her elegant beauty technicians. Rubinstein opened more salons in London, Paris, and New York. She also revolutionized the use of pseudoscience in marketing, wearing a lab coat in her advertisements even though, technically, her only training had been a brief tour of European skincare facilities.

> "There are no ugly women, only lazy ones."
> –HELENA RUBINSTEIN

In 1928, Rubinstein sold the American business to none other than Lehman Brothers for $7.3 million. After the Depression, she bought back the now-worthless stock and turned the boat around by establishing salons in cities throughout the United States, including a spa on New York's fashionable Fifth Avenue, where she commissioned Salvador Dalí to design a powder compact and paint her portrait. Not bad for a Jewish girl who came to the New World with nothing but a suitcase of questionable cream.

Estée Lauder

Estée Lauder was born Josephine Esther Mentzer in Corona, Queens, circa 1906. One of nine children, she got her retail experience from helping out at her father's hardware store, where she dreamed of becoming a famous actress while working among the various nuts and screws.

After high school, Estée joined her uncle's beauty-product business, where she learned how to mix creams and administer rejuvenating facial massages. Soon she married Joseph Lauter (the spelling was later changed) and subsequently created the Estée Lauder Company in 1935.

By 1948, Lauder was selling her creams at Saks Fifth Avenue, where her innovative personalized selling approach convinced customers that a real beauty regimen should comprise multiple products. She also gave samples to her various celebrity friends, such as Princess Grace of Monaco, so that they might act as Lauder ambassadors. In 1953, she introduced Youth Dew, a fragrance-cum–bath oil that ladies poured copiously into their bathwater instead of delicately daub-

> "The most beautiful face in the world? It's yours."
> –ESTÉE LAUDER

ing behind each ear; she moved 150 million bottles by 1984. Meantime, when her loyal customers returned for a refill, Lauder's sales gals seductively proffered free samples of other Lauder products, not only getting customers to use more cosmetic items, but also shaping and perfecting the now-infamous department store perfume bombardment and sample barrage.

Her innovative sales techniques combined with her nonstop work ethic made Lauder the richest self-made woman in the world as well as the only woman to be included in *Time* magazine's 1998 list of the Twenty Most Influential Business

DID JEW KNOW? When Estée Lauder was born, her parents originally wanted to name her Esty, after her mother's favorite aunt, but when it was time to write out the birth certificate, her parents went with Esther but called her Esty at home. When her father, a Czechoslovak Jew, pronounced Esty, it sounded like Estée due to his thick accent.

Geniuses of the Twentieth Century. Additionally, Lauder was also counted among the most philanthropic people on the planet. In fact, the Lauder Company's charitable contributions are monies earmarked for the construction of playgrounds in New York's Central Park, the restoration of Versailles, and upward of $131 million to New York's Whitney Museum—one of the largest single donations ever made to a museum.

Charles Revson

Charles Revson (1906–1975), a Yid from Somerville, Massachusetts, grew up in a cold-water flat in Manchester, New Hampshire. At twenty-five years old, after being turned down for a promotion at a now-forgotten cosmetics company, Revson started his own company (with his brother and a friend) and called it Revlon, Inc. In 1932, he made his fortune selling nail polish in a vast array of colors, and later took said fortune to the next level with matching lipsticks. The company took off from there, adding fragrances,

> "In the factory we make cosmetics; in the drugstore we sell hope."
> —CHARLES REVSON

including the eponymous "Charlie." Known for his irascible personality, Revson remained chairman of Revlon until his death in 1975. Revson fun fact: One of the cosmetic billionaire's lady friends was none other than singer Eartha Kitt! Not bad for the son of a humble cigar roller!

I CAN'T GET IT FOR YOU WHOLESALE:
Jews and the Ready-to-Wear Gentile Aesthetic

While Jews have been peddling rags and other schmatta since their days in the shtetl, they've come a long way from red tents and red thread. Just as their fellow immigrant brethren adopted new-world names, customs, and mannerisms, newly minted American Jews sought to look, live, talk, and taste American. On the one hand, the Hasidim clung pertinaciously to styles that hadn't changed since Satu

Mare, while on the other hand, their secularized cousins longed to shed their old-world appearance and embrace the style of (more or less) the first land to welcome them. Yet, what, exactly, was the style of a land made almost entirely of immigrants? Who could redress this dilemma and dress a nation of people trying to appear as if they were possibly members of the Daughters of the American Revolution? The Jews—specifically the Jewish designers, merchandisers, and retailers responsible for outfitting America according to the way they thought America was supposed to look.

That said, it wasn't just their own people whom the Jews dressed for success, though this was the demographic where they began. It was also every other kind of non-Jew from Catholic to Methodist and everything in between. In other words, American Jews not only helped put American fashion on the map, but they also taught Gentile America how to dress like Gentiles. Jews basically canonized the now-

classic and oft-copied American WASP aesthetic—Shetland sweaters, riding boots, tartans, plaids, and denim—with the effortless ease of someone whose family had been in the United States for generations rather than ten minutes.

Levi Strauss

A Jew from Buttenheim, Bavaria, Levi Strauss invented and popularized the blue jean, originally an emblem of utilitarian practicality and the promise of the freedom of the American West. Founded in 1853, Levi Strauss & Co. began as a dry-goods supply company for miners in San Francisco during the gold rush, an era that provided the four thousand or so Jews who wended their way west with prodigious opportunities to fulfill the miners' constant demand for boots, clothes, and other supplies.

Consequently, in 1872, Jacob Davis, a Latvian tailor who had settled in Nevada, started making men's work pants that used metal rivets for greater durability. He came to Strauss for assistance financing this endeavor, and the two decided to work together. In 1873, Davis and Strauss received the patent on the process of riveting pants, and the original 501 Jean was born. In 1936, Levi Strauss & Co. added the red tab attached to the right rear pocket so that the brand could be readily identified at ten paces. Both the rivets and the red tab still exist today.

Ralph Lauren

Ralph Lauren, born Ralph Lifschitz, may not be the only Jewboy in town who tapped into the urban appetite for equestrian Americana, but he sure made some major bucks doing it. Originally a designer of neckties, which he branded under the name Polo and sold at Bloomingdale's starting in 1967, Lauren debuted a line of classically tailored women's suits in 1970, a surprising move in an era of flashiness and couture edge that also birthed the sweat suit as leisure wear. As the '70s became the preppy, ostentatious '80s, Lauren took a page from American high society (or rather, what an indoorsy Jewish boy from the Bronx thought of as high society), a plaid-heavy dream of polo matches, fresh-faced women, pearl necklaces, and golden retrievers, and made it into a multibillion-dollar business whose haute WASP logo, an equestrian holding his polo mallet aloft, is now as American as bagels and lox.

Where most designers aim for new, new, new, Lauren's signature look is at once as familiar and traditional as it is effortless. As architecture critic and writer Paul Goldberger would say, "Lauren may be the first designer who has transformed the world by not doing anything new at all." Indeed, Lauren took Americana to a whole new level by elevating timeless classics such as the navy blazer and the velvet headband to iconic status. He made them the staples in a look that said "tea sandwiches and brandy snifters" more than it said "borscht and Manischewitz." Suddenly, actual WASPs began sporting Lauren's signature pieces as though they and their ancestors had been wearing them their whole lives, and the world went JASP.

A DEEP BOW TO THE MODERNS: OTHER JEWS WHO UTILIZE ERSATZ WASPERY TO TURN HEADS AND CREATE BUZZ

To say that American Jews were the sole creators of the WASP look is like saying the Jewish writers and producers of early television shows defined how the Gentile America thought and lived—it's true, but there's a lot more to it: Jewish designers defined the Gentile aesthetic that made goyim want to run out and buy the clothes that Jewish guys and gals imagined WASPs wore while the Jewish guys and gals were lighting Shabbos candles in their parents' apartments in the Bronx and Queens. Behold some of the greats who keep Mary and Chad (or Darnell and Shalonda) wanting to dress like a Lifschitz: Donna Karan, Isaac Mizrahi, Zac Posen, Michael Kors, Kenneth Cole, Marc Jacobs, Diane von Furstenberg, Tommy Hilfiger, Elie Tahari, Stella McCartney (Jewish mother!)

Calvin Klein

Another great Jewish denizen of the Bronx, Calvin Klein turned dungarees into kiddie porn and tighty-whities into a national event. Additionally, his name became synonymous with the understated, urban, and distinctly American elegance that made Paris and Milan sit up and take notice. Klein was initially recognized in the late '60s for his suits and coats but soon came to be known for his sophisticated sportswear. His looks have encompassed the sensual freedom of the cocaine-addled disco era, the designer-soaked '80s, and the edgy '90s anorexic-meets-heroin-chic aesthetic that made model Kate Moss a household name.

Klein's first collection, a line of youthful yet simple and sophisticated coats and dresses, premiered at erstwhile department store Bonwit Teller. Klein was also responsible for ushering in the era of designer jeans by putting his name on the back pocket of his for-fashion-purposes-only denims and making a fourteen-year-old Brooke Shields infamous for the "Nothing comes between me and my Calvins" campaign. In the 1990s, Klein elevated underwear to a whole new level with his massive billboards of a deeply ab-alicious Marky Mark wearing naught but his Calvins. What Jewish girl wouldn't want a piece of that?

Counter Culture

On some level, the seemingly schleppy/shady worlds of usury, mercantilism, gemstones, and dry goods demonstrate how the ever-resourceful Chosen Tribe turned a world of anti-Semitism into opportunity and the act of gilding the lily into gelt. Look at it this way: Jews were a nomadic population for whom mercantilism almost seemed a default setting. As the world continued to cast them out, they just packed up their ever-accumulating pile of fabrics, furnishings, spices, and bling and set forth for the next port city, thereby turning old-world know-how into new-world merchandise and making everyone look better doing it. Where others might have taken one look at yet another Gentile mob, turned *tuchus*, and thrown in the *tallit*, the Jews just turned their eyes toward Hashem and proclaimed, "Oh good, more customers!"

CHAPTER 7

SPEAK LOUDLY AND CARRY A BIG SCHTICK: Jews in the Entertainment Industry

Give the public what they want, and they'll come out for it.

—HARRY COHN

Fact: The American dream existed long before the Jews hit Hollywood. It's just that until the Jews got into the act, nobody knew what they were dreaming. What's more, as soon as they ditched the Old World, the Jews set about the task of defining and immortalizing the land they loved in every possible entertainment medium, from stage to screen to computer screen. Here's how: While some Yiddles were hitting it big on Tin Pan Alley and the Great White Way, others smelled opportunity in moving pictures and headed west to stake their claim on the hills of the American imagination. In fact, from the moment the Jews got their *tuchuses* to Tinseltown, pretty much every Tom, Dick, and Harry's idea of what it meant to be American was informed by people who had been on these shores for barely more than a generation.

The Geniuses of the Studio System

Near the end of the nineteenth century, Thomas Edison (not a Jew) invented the Kinetoscope, "an early motion-picture exhibition device" through which a viewer could watch a series of sequential images run over a light source, otherwise known as a "movie." However, while the invention and its patent were Edison's, the innovations that followed mostly belonged to a bunch of streetwise Ashkenazi immigrants who took Edison's magic box of light and built an empire that put the American dream on the map. This empire was called Hollywood.

HARRY COHN (1891–1958)

A one-time streetcar conductor and vaudevillian, Harry Cohn started the company that became Columbia Pictures Corporation with his brother in 1919. Initially, Columbia was a low-budget "corned beef and cabbage" studio, until 1934, when Frank Capra's comedy *It Happened One Night* became the first film to win an Oscar "grand slam" of Best Picture, Best Actress, Best Actor, Best Director, and Best Screenplay. Other Cohn classics include *Mr. Smith Goes to Washington, The Jolson Story, From Here to Eternity, On the Waterfront*, and *The Bridge on the River Kwai.*

While the curmudgeonly Cohn prospered as a producer, let's just say this monstrous mogul never won mensch of the month. Known for his hardline management style—he kept a picture of Mussolini on his desk—and some hardcore casting-couch misfires, Cohn's practice was to scoop big-name actors such as Lloyd Bridges and Rita Hayworth from other, more expensive studios and bring them on for one-picture deals.

Speaking of Rita Hayworth, Cohn was rumored to have tried to get Hollywood's greatest beauty face-up on the casting couch, an attempt that Hayworth summarily nixed. Other Hollywood hotties who rejected the chance of a late-night pas de deux with Cohn's *schvantz* included Kim Novak and Joan Crawford. In fact, when Mommy Dearest allegedly felt the presence of Harry's Tom, Dick and Harry, she

famously retorted, "Keep it in your pants, Harry. I'm having lunch with Joan and the boys [Cohn's wife and kids] tomorrow."

A foul-mouthed taskmaster while he lived, Cohn's legacy was that of a man who made more movies than friends. At Cohn's famously well-attended funeral, Red Skelton was quoted as saying, "It proves what Harry always said: Give the public what they want, and they'll come out for it."

CARL LAEMMLE (1867–1939)

The progenitor of Universal Pictures, German-born Laemmle arrived on U.S. shores in 1884. After working in Chicago as a bookkeeper, he began buying movie theaters, known as nickelodeons (for the five-cent admission price), eventually expanding his efforts into film distribution. Later he fought the Motion Picture Patents Company, which was trying to exercise a monopoly on film technology, by forming the Independent Motion Picture Company and hightailing it to Hollywood, a nothing kind of town rife with great weather and a plethora of fabulous outdoor locations on which to shoot moving pictures. In 1912, he joined a group of other early-film businessmen to combat what he referred to as the "film octopus" and founded what would become Universal Pictures, where, over the course of his career, he produced more than 400 films, including *The Hunchback of Notre Dame*, *Uncle Tom's Cabin*, *Showboat*, and *The Phantom of the Opera*.

THE BIOGRAPH GOIL

In order to generate public interest in the lovely Miss Florence Lawrence, Laemmle spread a rumor that she had died in a streetcar accident, then subverted his own rumor by saying she was fine, thank you very much, and would be starring in one of his upcoming movies. In other woids, a Jew invented buzz!

Of the great founding fathers of Hollywood, Laemmle was considered the most easygoing. For starters, he was among the first to give actors screen credit and thus created one of the first named movie stars: Florence Lawrence, previously known as "the Biograph Girl." What's more, on the lot, Laemmle's studs, starlets, and grips often referred to him as Uncle Carl, due to his avuncular persona and his penchant for nepotism—at one point he allegedly employed seventy relatives, not to mention his son, Carl Jr., who eventually took over as head of the studio. Regarding Laemmle's habit of keeping it all in the *mishpochah*, poet Ogden Nash penned the couplet: "Uncle Carl Laemmle/Has a very large faemmle." He was also the first mogul to let outsiders tour the lot, ultimately giving rise to a very lucrative if tacky tourist juggernaut.

In the 1930s, Laemmle, who had maintained strong ties with his European roots, arranged for and financially sponsored the emigration of hundreds of Jews from his hometown of Laupheim, Germany, to America, thus saving them from certain death at the hands of the Nazis.

WILLIAM FOX (1879–1952)

Born in Hungary, Wilhelm Fried (his name was changed at Ellis Island) immigrated to America with his parents when he was still an infant. As a young man, he tried his luck first as a newsboy and then in the garment industry before buying his first nickelodeon, which he soon built into a successful chain. Sensing opportunity in the land where dreams are made, he began producing movies and, in 1915, moved to California and founded the Fox Film Corporation.

In 1927, Fox—also known as "the Man Who Forgot to Sleep" for his hard-working hustle—purchased the rights for sound technology and called it the Fox Movietone sound-on-sound system, a sound-recording method that became the industry standard along with Fox Movietone News reels. A sample of Fox's filmography: *Seventh Heaven, Mother Knows Best, A Girl in Every Port, A Connecticut Yankee*, and *Me and My Gal*.

A series of unfortunate events, including a failed attempt to take over the Loews Corporation, a bad car accident, and the stock market crash of 1929, culminated in Fox losing control of the studio and filing for bankruptcy. To add insult to injury, at his bankruptcy hearing in 1936, Fox foolishly attempted to bribe the judge, an act of perjury for which he was sentenced to six months in prison. After his sad stint in the clink, Fox retired from the film business and slipped into obscurity. When he died in 1952, not a single Hollywood producer attended his funeral. Regardless of the fact that Fox died the forefather that film forgot, his name lives on in both 20th Century Fox and Fox Broadcasting Company.

SAMUEL GOLDWYN (1879–1974)

Known for his ruthless ambition, anger-management problem, head for public-ity, and unintentionally hilarious "Goldwynisms," movie mogul Samuel Goldwyn became Hollywood's preeminent "independent" producer—mostly because none of his partners could tolerate him for more than ten minutes.

Born Schmuel Gelbfisz into a Hasidic family in Warsaw, Samuel (then known as Samuel Goldfish) left his hometown on foot and, in 1899, wended his way to Gloversville, New York, where he became a successful glove salesman. In 1913, after moving to Manhattan and marrying the sister of theatrical producer Jesse Lasky, our intrepid glover joined forces with Lasky and none other than Cecil B. DeMille and convinced the two to produce films. The company's first film, *The Squaw Man,* was among the first moving pictures shot in Hollywood. Later, the core of that company would become Paramount Pictures.

In 1916, having changed his name to Samuel Goldwyn, Uncle Sam started Goldwyn Pictures, which eventually became Metro-Goldwyn-Mayer (MGM), a company from which he was ultimately ousted. That said, his eponymous company's roaring-lion trademark became one of Hollywood's most recognizable icons.

Regardless of Goldwyn's infamous inability to play well with others, it was as an independent producer that Goldwyn really made his mark. Due in part to Goldwyn's understanding that what the public wanted was a happy ending, combined with his talent for hiring great writers for his films—Dorothy Parker, Lillian Hellman, and Ben Hecht, to name a few—Goldwyn became one of the Jewish Mafia's most successful independent movie producers. Some great Goldwyn pictures include *Arrowsmith, Dodsworth, Stella Dallas, Dead End, Wuthering Heights, The Little Foxes, The Best Years of Our Lives,* and *The Pride of the Yankees.*

Along with his knack for understanding (and producing) what the public wanted, Goldwyn was also famous for his malapropisms, or "Goldwynisms," sayings that were made all the more laughable because of his heavy Eastern European accent. Some of these Goldwynisms include:

- "A verbal contract isn't worth the paper it's written on."
- "You can include me out."
- "Our comedies are not to be laughed at."
- "Let's have some new clichés."
- "Anybody who goes to see a psychiatrist should have his head examined."

Mayer was head of MGM and the spirit daddy of the "star system," which named, created, developed, protected, and, on more than one occasion, destroyed stars. In fact, one of the studio's taglines was "more stars than there are in the heavens."

Born Lazar Meir in 1884, the man who would be Louis B. Mayer and his family ditched Minsk and ended up in New Brunswick, Canada, where Mayer's father started a scrap-metal business. In 1904, Mayer split for Boston, married his first wife, and renovated a burlesque theater. In a clever publicity stunt, Goldwyn overcame the dubious reputation of this theater of ill repute by debuting a religious film at the theater's reopening. Subsequent successful endeavors on the road to Tinseltown included Mayer paying D. W. Griffith twenty-five grand to obtain exclusive rights to *Birth of a Nation,* and a stint as a talent agent.

As head honcho of MGM, Mayer built the most financially successful movie studio on planet Earth and the sole studio to pay dividends through the Great Depression. He was also the first American ever to earn a million-dollar salary. As yet another movie mogul with strong opinions and a driving ambition, Mayer may have influenced people, but he had a hard time making and keeping friends. A ruthless negotiator, he was known for trying to lowball his stars and allegedly blackmailed Clark Gable. While he gave Judy Garland away on her wedding day to director Vincente Minnelli, he also participated in the Hollywood machine that kept Judy doped up on speed to keep her weight down and her spirits high.

Although Mayer and production chief Irving Thalberg initially saw eye-to-eye, their relationship eventually disintegrated over differences of taste: Mayer liked crowd-pleasers—*nu*, what producer doesn't?—while Thalberg leaned toward the literary. Thus Mayer canned Thalberg in favor of independent producer David O. Selznick. While MGM produced a slew of successful films—*Anna Christie; The Divorcee; Billy the Kid; Tarzan the Ape Man; Babes in Arms; Goodbye, Mr. Chips; On the Town; Gone With the Wind; The Wizard of Oz;* and the highly lucrative Andy Hardy movies—by 1951 the company had gone three years without a major Academy Award, and Mayer found himself fired from the position he had held for twenty-seven long and prosperous years. He subsequently went Garbo and retired from the public eye.

Sons of a Polish cobbler, Harry and Sam were born in Poland, and baby Jack entered the world in London, Ontario, Canada. Their first foray into the motion picture business was in Youngstown, Ohio, with the purchase of a Kinetoscope, a venture that led to the opening of movie houses. Fun fact: Their first makeshift movie house was furnished with chairs borrowed from a nearby undertaker. In 1917, after doing business with Carl Laemmle, the brothers set up shop in California.

Although brother Jack's career was the longest of all the Hollywood moguls, spanning forty-five years give or take, Sam and Harry were also instrumental in Warner Bros.' success. In 1926, Harry visited Western Electric's Bell Laboratories to check out their synchronized sound technology and maybe partner with them. A glitch in this plan was the anti-Semitism of the bigwigs at Western Bell—that is, until brother Sam convinced said Jew-hating honchos to sign with Warner Bros. after his wife Lina wore a gold cross at a company dinner! Unfortunately, Sam died just before the premiere of the first-ever full-length talkie in Hollywood history, *The Jazz Singer*, a volcanically successful Warner Bros. picture starring Al Jolson.

After the Wall Street crash of 1929, as the rest of America was waiting on the breadlines, the studio continued to distinguish itself with such unflinching and criti-cally acclaimed dramas as *Little Caesar* starring Edward G. Robinson, *The Public Enemy* starring song-and-dance man James Cagney, and *I Am a Fugitive from a Chain Gang* with Paul Muni.

Warner Bros. also debuted some new stars with names like Porky, Bugs, and Daffy. These animated characters, despite their success, were often viewed as the studio's forgotten stepchildren. As Jack Warner once said, "I don't even know where the hell the cartoon studio is."

ADOLPH ZUKOR (1873–1976)

Born in Hungary, Paramount founder Adolph Zukor (then Adolph Cukor) immigrated to the United States in 1889 and got his start in an upholstery shop in New York City before going on to become a successful furrier. In fact, according to film historian Neal Gabler, unlike the rest of his Hollywood competitors, Zukor "lived like a wealthy young burger and certainly earned the income of one." He later bought Abraham & Straus heir Lawrence Abraham's sprawling manse in Rockland County, New York.

In 1902, Zukor's cousin Max Goldstein asked him for a loan to expand a chain of theaters to feature moving pictures—a banner idea, considering the reigning novelty of the day was electric light! Zukor gave Goldstein the dough and became a partner in the company along with the likes of Marcus Loew. Next, he partnered with co-producer Jesse Lasky to found the Famous Players–Lasky Corporation, which then evolved into Paramount Pictures. The first Jew on the block to utilize a single company for production, distribution, and exhibition of motion pictures, Zukor served as president of Paramount until 1959. He died at the age of 103 in Los Angeles.

Some Paramount golden greats from the Zukor era include Cecil B. DeMille's *The Ten Commandments*, *Tom Sawyer*, *Dr. Jekyll and Mr. Hyde*, *Shanghai Express*, *A Farewell to Arms*, Bob Hope and Bing Crosby's "Road" movies, *Going My Way*, *The Lost Weekend*, *The Heiress*, *Sunset Boulevard*, *A Place in the Sun*, *The Greatest Show on Earth*, *Shane*, *Roman Holiday*, and *To Catch a Thief*.

Jewy the Jew: How the Jews De-Jew-ified Hollywood

Though America was the first country to give Jews full rights as citizens, it did not give them an all-access pass to its white-shoe firms, restricted country clubs, and top universities. What the Jewish Hollywood moguls wanted, and indeed what they created, was a club where Jews could not only belong, but also succeed, play golf, and possibly score a hot shiksa wife. Since they didn't want their Hollywood lifestyles to replicate any kind of old-world Jewish experience, they founded and socialized at the Hillcrest Country Club—a social club modeled on its tony, restrictive WASP-exclusive predecessors. They also set out to make films that were as American looking and sounding as, well, America. At least, the America of their dreams. And so in dreaming the dream, they dreamed of a land where the Jews lived like goyim and the goyim strove to become the Jewish definition of what it meant to be a goy.

Red Is So NOT My Color: The Ballad of Joe McCarthy and the Blacklisted Jews' Blues

Tinseltown, 1947: As Cold War tensions and Stalin's ruthless program of totalitarianism righteously fueled America's disdain of anything red, the country's previous habit of dressing to the left in the '30s gave way to full-on fear of communist subterfuge. Meantime a de facto group called the House Un-American Activities Committee (HUAC) went crazy crackers about the purported communist influence in Hollywood. As a result, scores of screenwriters, directors, and actors were called before HUAC and asked to reveal any "affiliations" with the Communist Party as well as disclose the names of friends whose sympathies were possibly

BABES IN GOYLAND

Original Name	De-Jew-ified Hollywood name	Claim to Fame
Max Aronson	BRONCO BILLY ANDERSON	First cowboy movie star
Theodosia Goodman	THEDA BARA	Film's first femme fatale
Bernard Schwartz	TONY CURTIS	The Jew who donned a dress to smooch Monroe
Issur Danielovitch	KIRK DOUGLAS	"I am Spartacus."
Betty Joan Perske	LAUREN BACALL	The Jewish beauty who snagged Bogie
Muni Weisenfreund	PAUL MUNI	The original Scarface
Laszlo Lowenstein	PETER LORRE	The man who Jew too much
Julius Garfinkle	JOHN GARFIELD	"I Was a Sucker for a Left Hook"
Jack Kubelsky	JACK BENNY	America's favorite tightwad
Melvyn Kaminsk	MEL BROOKS	Your Jew of Jews
Mendel Berlinger	MILTON BERLE	Hollywood's biggest *schvantz*
Danny Kaminski	DANNY KAYE	Song and dance ham
Børge Rosenbaum	VICTOR BORGE	The clown prince of Denmark
Emanuel Goldenberg	EDWARD G. ROBINSON	The Jewish tough

suspect. Those who refused to cooperate were summarily blacklisted. Some continued to work by writing under a pseudonym or borrowing the names of nonblacklisted colleagues. Others became shoe salesmen.

As time went on, Cold War hawk Senator Joe McCarthy became the face of what many have called a witch hunt. His whole trip—that there were communists and/or Soviet spies in the federal government—ultimately led to lost jobs for those who spoke out against him, including various left-wing artists, academics, and politicos, many of whom were Jews. Though McCarthy was unable to substantiate his accusations and the Senate was ultimately forced to censure him, this period remains one of the more paranoid, and possibly anti-Semitic, periods of U.S. history.

In 1947, HUAC held a series of hearings regarding possible communist influence in Hollywood. After refusing to answer questions to the tune of "Are you now, or have you ever been, a member of the Communist Party?" ten Hollywood screenwriters, called the Hollywood Ten, refused to testify and were convicted of contempt, blacklisted, and imprisoned for up to a year. Of these ten, six—Alvah Bessie, Lester Cole, John Howard Lawson, Herbert Biberman, Samuel Ornitz, and Albert Maltz—were Jews.

> "Been called a Pinko Commie tool, got through it stinko by my pool."
> —STEPHEN SONDHEIM

Ultimately, up to 320 actors, directors, and screenwriters were officially blacklisted. Unless they changed thier names, fewer than 10 percent managed to rebuild careers in the entertainment industry. The Red Channels list, a pamphlet that published the identities of screen artists with alleged communist ties, included the names of such Jewish luminaries as Edward G. Robinson, John Garfield, Dorothy Parker, Aaron Copland, Lillian Hellman, Leonard Bernstein, Stella Adler, Phillip Loeb, Arthur Miller, and Zero Mostel, a.k.a. Tevye himself!

Schmuck You: The Chosen People and the Porn Industry

Speaking of a big, throbbing red menace to society, nothing says Jewish like the wonderful world of pornography. Porn is actually older than the oldest profession, second only to usury and perhaps more lucrative, and is considered more transgressive than prostitution, even when it's for Gentiles only. Which, you may recall, is also how the Jews got around the illegality of demanding usurious interest.

Let's consider: If the Pentateuch lists the following acts as illicit and therefore verboten: adultery, fornication, homosexuality, and sexual intercourse with close relatives, is it considered wrong if Gentiles are doing all the illegal *schtupping* and a Jew is filming it? Answer: Yes and no! But don't take my word for it. Instead, examine, if you will, the myriad of skintellectuals whose hard work helps keep marriage—and the Internet—alive!

Hide Your Eyes (Not Your Salami): Jewish Laws on Watching Dirty Movies

Believe it or not, according to generally accepted interpretation, porn is prohibited by the biblical injunction against "being led astray by your eyes." (Numbers 15:39) Clearly, this verse is not solely about pornographic content as much as a command against looking at things that might lead one to transgress, such as Gina Gershon or a pastrami sandwich. That said, even the Orthodox don't view desire as sinful, only the act of ejaculating anywhere other than your wife's vagina. In other words, even couples who cannot conceive are still supposed to *schtup*. So though it would seem that pornography is innocent in that it's a private act between a man and his Internet connection, it's technically a major no-no. Sorry, Schlomo.

A little shot o' history: In the late nineteenth century through the start of World War II, many distributors of erotic books and other "flagitious materials" were German Jews. In the years following World War II, America's most successful purveyor of smut was one Rueben Sturman, "the Jewish Walt Disney of Porn." Basically, Sturman was responsible for peddling and circulating a large majority of the pornographic material available in the United States up to and through the 1970s. He also innovated the peep-show booth by making it into a dark chamber, where instead of watching a live gal, the peeper watches a screen showing X-rated videos. Yet another world-changing Jewish innovation! Sturman was convicted of tax evasion and died in prison in 1997. Hopefully, they let him use a computer!

> "You cannot blame porn. When I was young, I used to masturbate to *Gilligan's Island*."
> —RON JEREMY

Screw You: Al Goldstein, *Screw* Magazine, and Freedom of the Putz

While Hugh Hefner and Larry Flynt begat the free porn revolution, nobody brought it home like Al Goldstein and his skin mag *Screw*. Like Flynt before him, Goldstein won a series of obscenity cases regarding the publication of lewd and rude materials, including a famous 1977 case in which Alabama governor George Wallace sued Goldstein and *Screw* for printing that the governor learned to "do sex" from reading the magazine! The two parties went soft and settled.

An Empire of Their Moan: How the Jews Invented the Porn Industry

Unsurprisingly, production of dirty motion pictures happened pretty much ten minutes after moving pictures were invented—one of the earliest pioneers was a French "director" by the name of Albert Kirchner, whose seven-minute 1896 film *Le Coucher de la Mariée* shows a bathroom striptease.

Cut to the permissive 1970s, where singles bars, peep shows, and porn theaters made mincemeat of the American male until video and the Internet brought Pee-Wee back into his playhaus. While most examples of Jewish studio Sin-ema feature all-American looking ladies—read: shiksas and their look-alikes—more than a few show distinctly Jewish-looking men getting their *schtup* on with these all-American lovelies, a seemingly winning combo. As usual, Jews manned the helm of this stalwart and lucrative salami and rode it hard all the way to the bank.

Kosher Pickle: How a Special-Ed Schlepper Went All the Way

> "The only reason that Jews are in pornography is that we think Christ sucks."
>
> —AL GOLDSTEIN

Once upon a time a hirsute homunculus from Flushing, Queens, by the name of Ron Jeremy—nickname: the Hedgehog—was ranked number one in *Adult Video News*' top fifty Hebrew superstuds of all time. Why? Having appeared in more than 2,000 adult films and directed some 280, he is listed in the *Guinness Book of World Records* for "Most Appearances in Adult Films." But what really makes the Hebrew Hedgehog a hero is that not only is he the chubby guy who gets to hook up with unlimited hotties, but he gets paid to do it!

Vivid Video and the Jew-dio System

As the VCR and later the DVD player brought porn away from the world of trench coats, a Jew named Steven Hirsch, "the Donald Trump of Porno," appeared on the scene. Hirsch's father had been none other than Sturman's stockbroker, and Hirsch used that little bit of nepotistic good luck to build Vivid Entertainment Group, a porn empire that would give Harry Cohn a serious hard . . . attack. In fact, Vivid neatly parallels the all-too-Jewish motion picture studio system of the 1930s and 1940s in which studios had exclusive contracts with various stars whom they would mold, milk, and toss off. Sidenote: Vivid was the first house on the naughty block to introduce celebrity sex tapes.

Big Daddy Is Watching Jew!

As it became easier and cheaper for stars to make their own films, many adult film stars and auteurs went the way of their ancestors and struck out for the land of

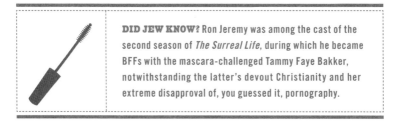

DID JEW KNOW? Ron Jeremy was among the cast of the second season of *The Surreal Life*, during which he became BFFs with the mascara-challenged Tammy Faye Bakker, notwithstanding the latter's devout Christianity and her extreme disapproval of, you guessed it, pornography.

Canaan looking for freedom, prosperity, and a way to get more bang for their buck. These are their stories.

Joe Francis: How a Nice Jewish Boy Became a (Kosher) Chicken Hawk

Joe Francis (1973–): A film producer best known as the creator of Girls Gone Wild, a video franchise that involves camera crews at party locations, such as Mardi Gras or spring break, filming consenting coeds as they shake what their *mamalehs* gave 'em. In the first two years of its existence, Girls Gone Wild made twenty million dollars. In 2008, four young ladies sued Girls Gone Wild for filming them while underage. Ultimately, an all-female jury found in Joe Francis' favor.

Joe Francis fun fact: In 2005, Girls Gone Wild donated 100 percent of the proceeds of their Mardi Gras DVDs to the Red Cross to help victims of Hurricane Katrina. Vat a nice boychik!

Seymore Butts: Porn's First Mama's Boy

Adam Glasser, a.k.a. Seymore Butts (1964–), is a director and on-camera talent who has produced a plethora of films in the world of gonzo porn. Born in the Bronx, Glasser adopted the nom-de-poon Seymore Butts and began producing his own line of Yiddy viddies in the '90s. In 2003, Glasser's life and nefarious career were the subject of *Family Business*, a reality program on the Showtime network. Appearing with Seymore were his mother and his sixty-year-old cousin Stevie, both of whom help Butts run his massive *tuchus* empire. Smart Jew that he is, Glasser used *Family Business* as a platform to publicize an Internet telethon to raise money for various freedom of speech causes. Vat a nice boychik!

> "The only thing we don't have a god for is premature ejaculation . . . but I hear that it's coming quickly."
>
> —MEL BROOKS

JEW HAVE TO BELIEVE WE ARE MAGIC: Jewish Magicians and the Occult

----

While the Torah is none too keen on witchcraft (and by association, magic), it's downright silent on the subject of grown men in moustaches and tight pants padlocking themselves into Porta-Potties in front of a live studio audience. In other words, there exist certain types of acceptable magic/illusions, but any Jew who attempts to subvert nature via the occult is going against the will of God, and God's willy is for professional use only. Behold the daring magicians who put the "ooh" in illusion and the "aah" in God.

Harry Houdini (1874–1926)

A Budapest-born American escape artist who became the most famous performer of the early twentieth century. His repertoire included escaping from police chains, ropes slung from skyscrapers, and straitjackets underwater. **SHIKSAPPEAL:** At nineteen, Houdini married a shiksa with whom he stayed for life, though the couple lived with his mother.

David Copperfield (1956–)

A New Jersey–born illusionist whom *Forbes* named "the most commercially successful magician in history" due to Copperfield having grossed more than three billion dollars, more than any other solo entertainer in history. **SHIKSAPPEAL:** Copperfield was once engaged to model Claudia Schiffer.

David Blaine (1973–)

A Puerto Rican Jewish endurance artist who has broken several world records for feats that any wise Jewish boy worth his weight in Talmud tractates would do best to avoid, such as "Buried Alive," in which Blaine was entombed in an underground box for seven days, "Frozen in Time," in which he was encased in a block of ice for about sixty-three hours, and "Vertigo," for which Blaine stood, unharnessed, atop a 100-foot (30.5-metre) pillar for thirty-five hours. **SHIKSAPPEAL:** Blaine has canoodled with the likes of Madonna, Daryl Hannah, and Fiona Apple.

RIDING CHAI: How the Jewish Voice Shaped and Defined American Comedy

---

If pondering the role of the Jews in porn wasn't proof enough, let me reiterate: Jews did not invent sex. Ditto comedy. But they sure as heck revolutionized both. In fact, it's pretty much redundant to say "Jewish humor." But let's just go ahead and say it anyway: Jewish humor! Hot Jew! *Gazuntite!*

The question is, what exactly defines Jewish humor? Is it gallows humor, that special combination of Eastern European accented pathos and bathos? Schleppers' neurotic lament? The subtle-to-not-so-subtle mocking of our forever friend and foe, the Gentile? Mother-in-law jokes?

Whatever the definition, vaudeville, the Borscht Belt, variety shows, sketch comedy, and even the great (if currently anemic) American sitcom all have Jewish roots, stars, and staff writers. While Milton Berle, Sid Caesar, George Burns, and Jack Benny defined and perfected comic timing, the great Jewish writers, especially those of early television—Mel Brooks, Carl Reiner, Neil Simon, and Woody Allen—set the standard for timeless comedy. What's more, these great Jew-rus of comedy paved the way for such legendary and ultimately Jewish watershed shows as *Saturday Night Live, SCTV, Seinfeld,* and *Curb Your Enthusiasm.*

Though women did perform in Yiddish theater, some troupes began as all-male-all-the-time, with men playing the female roles, especially the comic ones. This drag tradition may have been the precursor to the belief that pee-pee means funny and woo-woo means pencil sharpener of love. That said, Molly Picon, a Yiddish theater and film star most known for her 1936 tour-de-force *Yidl Mitn Fidl*, was one of comedy's pioneering female *badkhens*, as was Sophie Tucker, a.k.a. "the Last of the Red Hot Mamas."

From the Catskills to California: How the Borscht Belt Went From Lo Pro to High Ho and the West Was Won

The Borscht Belt, Jewish Alps, and Solomon County are all terms for the once-popular, now-defunct Jewish summer-resort communities that dotted the Catskill Mountains in upstate New York. These hotels, bungalow colonies, and camps were where the middle-class Jews of New York City went for weeks at a time to sun, nosh, kibbitz, nosh, cha-cha, and nosh some more with other Jews, especially in the Belt's grand heyday from the 1940s to the 1960s. Well-known resorts of the Jewish Alps include the Concord, Grossinger's, Kutscher's, the Nevele, Lansman's, and the Pines Resort.

Much like its fabulous and considerably more degenerate cousin Las Vegas, the Borscht Belt also featured various types of Jewish entertainment, from famous funnymen to up-and-coming acts getting their schticks wet on the Jew Circuit. So, *nu*? How about a little kosher chicken à la king followed by two pareve desserts "just to taste" and a live performance by one of these kings and queens of comedy:

Joey Adams, Bea Arthur, Jack Benny, Milton Berle, Joey Bishop, Mel Blanc, Fanny Brice, Mel Brooks, Lenny Bruce, Red Buttons, Sid Caesar, Eddie Cantor, Rodney Dangerfield, Phyllis Diller, Fyvush Finkel, Shecky Greene, Buddy Hackett, George Jessel, Danny Kaye, Alan King, Harvey Korman, Jerry Lewis, Jackie Mason, Zero Mostel, Molly Picon, Charlotte Rae, Carl Reiner, Don Rickles, Joan Rivers, Soupy Sales, Phil Silvers, Jerry Stiller, the Three Stooges, Henny Youngman.

Without Jew I'm Nothing: From the Jewish Alps to the Small Screen

Since the Borscht Belt audience was entirely Jewish—including the waiters—the comedians (and comediennes) were able to Jew it up in a way that they couldn't in front of a more mainstream (that is, Gentile) audience. The delivery was therefore openly and unapologetically *Yiddishkeit* and served to establish what, in a sublimated form, would become the Jewish roots of the entertainment industry, especially on the small screen.

With the advent of television in the late '40s, Jews yet again saw opportunity— one where a Catskills comedian might find a wider audience and earn a shekel or six. And so again, the Jews adapted their schmact to jibe with the requirements of this new situation and ran with it. Call it what you will—the greatest kosher cash cow of all time or the idiot box—but TV quickly became yet another industry in which the Jews could continue to mine and shape the American dream.

THE JEW TUBE: Vaudeville from the Comfort of Your Living Room

Before 1947, the number of North American homes with television sets fell somewhere in the thousands. These days, even though the Internet accounts for most, ahem, "viewing," the typical U.S. household contains an average of 2.98 television sets. You know whom we have to thank for this? A handful of mostly Jewish scientists/inventors and a Jewish vaudevillian in a dress—Milton Berle.

Jewish Turkeys and Kosher Hams: How a Jewish Man in a Dress Became One of the First Big Stars of the Little Screen

The budgeters of most programs from the golden age of television took a page from history's other great form of entertainment: prostitution. Both preferred their

---

THE RED TENEMENT: YIDDISH THEATER AND WHO WEARS THE FUNNYPANTS

For anyone who watches summer blockbusters, it may not come as a surprise that the word *badkhen*, Yiddish for "jester" or "clown," has no feminine equivalent. Maybe because it's not just Jews who invented Hollywood, it's Jewish *men*, many of whom needed to win the ladies with laughter rather than looks. Meantime, the reverse expectation was true for the ladies. Or as Joan Rivers once retorted to Johnny Carson when he suggested that men could be attracted to intelligence, "Oh please, Johnny. No man has ever put a hand up a woman's dress looking for a library card."

talent easy, fast, live, and, above all, cheap. In the early days of what we think of as television, vaudeville-inspired variety shows became the norm; there was a minimum of sets, not to mention a bushel of vaudevillians who honed their act on the radio and/or were willing to work for bupkes. Enter Mendel Berlinger, also known as Uncle Miltie.

Though Hollywood pooh-poohed the small screen and radio actors thought it a passing fancy, Milton Berle knew a good thing when he saw it. Already a veteran performer—he had appeared in silent films as a kid—Berle skyrocketed to fame in the late 1940s with his TV variety show *Texaco Star Theater.* Subsequently, he came to be known as "Mr. Television." Meantime, TV should've been called a Box o' Berle, because Uncle Miltie's show is credited with taking television sales to the next level. When he first went live, fewer than 500,000 sets had been sold nationwide, but when Berle went off the air in 1956, that number had reached nearly thirty million. Jew do the math!

> "Humor is just another defense against the universe."
>
> —MEL BROOKS

Shalom, Ladies and Germs!

In June 1948, Berle first hosted *Texaco Star Theater.* The show was an immediate and enormous hit. Slapstick bits, relentless jokes, and broad comedy (including Berle in drag) became the trademarks of his raucous television persona. By the 1949–50 season, the three top-rated TV shows were all variety shows: *Texaco Star Theater,* Ed Sullivan's *Toast of the Town*, and *Arthur Godfrey's Talent Scouts.* Within a short span of time, many entertainers, such as Dinah Shore and Perry Como, were headlining their own successful variety series. All thanks to Mr. Television!

As Berle's ratings began to fall, Texaco pulled its sponsorship and Buick stepped up, renaming the show *The Buick-Berle Show.* In 1956, the show was again retitled, this time as *The Milton Berle Show.* Ratings did not improve (regardless of the fact that the show had hosted two of Elvis Presley's earliest TV appearances), and Miltie finally called uncle after one full season. Though he would later play to packed houses in Las Vegas, in 1960 Mr. Television was hosting a show called *Jackpot Bowling*, in which he was forced to

DID JEW KNOW?

A pre-cursor to the Borscht Belt, the "Jewish Rialto," a strip of Yiddish theaters on lower Second Avenue in New York City, made Jewish household names of actors Jacob Adler of *Der Yidisher Kenig Lear* and Boris Thomashefsky of *Yiddish Hamlet.* P.S.: Actress and acting teacher Stella Adler was Jacob Adler's daughter.

deliver jokes between frames as contestants stroked, cranked, and tweened their way to victory.

The Tabernacle of American Comedy: *Your Show of Shows* and Its Legacy

While Milton Berle was being filmed wearing a dress in front of a live studio audience, a young saxophone-playing Jewish comedian by the name of Sid Caesar was starring in a series of revues in the Pocono Mountains. In 1949, NBC approached Caesar to adapt his popular and Borscht Belt-y comedy revue for television.

The show, *Admiral Broadway Revue*, which costarred a rubber-faced comedienne named Imogene Coca, ran for only eighteen weeks, but from its wake emerged *Your Show of Shows* (1950–1954). In addition to immortalizing the variety format, *Your Show of Shows* also made comic legends of its talented crew of performers including Coca, Howard Morris, Bill Hayes, and Carl Reiner. Unlike the raucous, cross-dressing antics of its predecessor *Texaco Star Theater,* *Your Show of Shows* ran the gamut from sight gags to satire and is considered the progenitor of all other sketch comedy shows that followed, including *Saturday Night Live.* Basically anything and everything became fodder for parody by Caesar and his esteemed rebbes of pantomime, timing, and schtick, including popular movies, silent movies, foreign films, and Caesar's various sketches as "the Professor."

> "When I was a kid, I was breast-fed by my father."
> –RODNEY DANGERFIELD

Your Show of Shows was also the kooky foster father of what would soon become the TV sitcom. To paraphrase Caesar himself, the show took what could have been simple broad comedy and made it believable and dramatic—add the requisite family setting, and Jew essentially have the formula for a successful sitcom. One recurring sketch featured Caesar and Coca as a married couple, the Hickenloopers, whose constant and humorous bickering informed such infamous married foils as Alice and Ralph Cramden on *The Honeymooners* and Lucy and Ricky on *I Love Lucy.* Additionally, Carl Reiner has said that the writers' room antics of *Your Show of Shows* formed the inspiration for *The Dick Van Dyke Show.*

Finally, while it never directly addressed Jewish topics, *Your Show of Shows* was nonetheless distinctly Jewish. Consider its staff writers: Mel Brooks, Neil Simon, Danny Simon, Mel Tolkin, and Carl Reiner—the great *machers* of comedy who made America laugh its *tuchus* off while secretly imbuing the show with hidden Jewish-isms, such as Caesar's Japanese character Taka Meshuga.

Wholly Holy: Jewish TV Shows

While it could be argued that technically everything is a Jewish TV show, a few shows feature wholly Jewish characters, politics and situations. For instance:

- *The Goldbergs* (radio: debuted 1929; TV: debuted 1949): A dramatic sitcom featuring the home life of a Jewish family in the Bronx. Gertrude Berg starred as Molly Goldberg, Jewish matriarch extraordinaire.

- *Rhoda* (debuted 1974): A spinoff of *The Mary Tyler Moore Show* starring Valerie Harper as Rhoda Morgenstern, a Jewish professional window-dresser with moxie to spare. Rhoda's wedding (to a goy!) was the second-most watched episode of all-time at that time, surpassed only by Little Ricky's birth on *I Love Lucy.*

- *Seinfeld* (debuted 1989): A sitcom about New Yorkers kibitzing and kvetching about "nothing." Some plotlines that dealt specifically with Judaism included circumcision and a high-strung mohel, the anti-dentite, Jerry and his girlfriend caught making out at a showing of *Schindler's List*, a gossiping rabbi, and an episode called "Shiksappeal" in which Elaine discovers Jewish men like her because she is not Jewish.

- *The Nanny* (debuted 1993): A sitcom starring Fran Drescher as Fran Fine, a Jewish door-to-door makeup saleswoman from Queens who becomes the nanny to three fancy-schmancy Gentile-spawn from Manhattan.

- *Curb Your Enthusiasm* (debuted 2000): Larry David, co-creator of *Seinfeld*, presents a Jew's-eye-view of life in the shtetl of Los Angeles. Each episode features Talmudic exegeses as David confronts and expounds on the minutia of various societal rules and questions of modern ethics that would give the Vilna Gaon a run for his money. Except instead of debating when it's permissible to wear *shatnez*—a blend of wool and linen that Jewish law prohibits wearing—it's whether or not you can use a prop nail from *The Passion of the Christ* to affix a mezuzah to the doorpost of thy gates, or what happens when you invite a sex offender to Seder.

DID JEW KNOW? Other successful Jewish vaudevillians of early television include Jack Benny, George Burns, Bert Lahr, Groucho Marx, and the Chosen Tribe's own Sammy Davis Jr.

From Allen Funt to Andy Cohen: Jews Invent . . . Reality?

Back in the golden age of television, a Jew named Allen Funt broke free of the soundstage to take his hidden camera to the streets, offices, and shops of the United States and film a series of unsuspecting schnooks in a ridiculous, embarrassing, or unusual situations. The show was *Candid Camera*—the very first reality show to hit the airwaves.

The show's roots go back to 1947, when Funt created a radio program called *Candid Microphone*. Funt's concept then transferred to television, where it ran on and off as a show or a series of specials though the 1980s. The premise, secretly filming regular folk managing absurd situations, became known for its now-infamous reveal: the sudden nightmarish announcement of the catchphrase, "Smile, you're on Candid Camera!"

Reality Killed the Radio Star: The Real Voild

Back in 1992, a Jew named Jonathan Murray and a Gentile named Mary-Ellis Bunim were trying to develop a soap opera for MTV. When that project proved too costly for a network still devoted to music videos, they came up with the idea of an "unscripted" soap, and *The Real World* franchise was born. Granted, Bunim/Murray's idea was inspired by the documentary *An American Family*—a 1973 proto-reality show created by Craig Gilbert (possibly Jewish)—but one salient fact remains: Just as Louis B. Mayer and his cronies saw the vast potential of light on a wall (and Milton Berle the potential of a Jew in a dress), so too did Jonathan Murray and his partner recognize the potential of unscripted, if managed, entertainment.

BEYOND THE BORSCHT BELT: LENNY BRUCE

Lenny Bruce (1925–1966) was a comedian, social critic, and legendary iconoclast whose profanity-laced commentary on such topics as sex, politics, and religion challenged social norms and led to his blacklisting at nearly every comedy club in North America. In 1961, Bruce was arrested onstage at the Jazz Workshop in San Francisco after using the word *c**ksucker*. His 1964 conviction in an obscenity trial was posthumously pardoned by Governor George E. Pataki in 2003—thirty-seven years after Bruce died of a drug overdose.

Twenty-plus years later, *The Real World* aired its twenty-eighth season, and entire networks are devoted almost exclusively to reality TV. Other life-affirming Bunim/Murray productions include *The Bad Girls Club, Keeping Up With the Kardashians, Project Runway, The Simple Life, The Challenge*, and *Road Rules*.

Are Those Real? How the Real(ish) Housewives Pumped up the Boob Tube

Once upon a time, a nice Jewish boy from Saint Louis named Andy Cohen had an epiphany: *Nu*, if America loved their housewives desperate, then maybe if they were real, America vould put a ring on it. And so, our Promethean Levite gathered a gaggle of Louboutin-ed lady-freunds from Orange County, California, and filmed them having it all—houses, husbands, Botox, and Birkins—and then hung the whole mess out to dry on Bravo. The initial result: *The Real Housewives of Orange County*—the show that begat the volcanically popular Real Housewives franchise of which Cohen remains both patriarch and executive producer.

After it became apparent that the Nation of Housewives had a larger audience than God, Cohen parlayed his reality coup into a live, late-night, low-budget talk show called *Watch What Happens Live*. At about 1.2 million viewers, (more than Conan or Chelsea Handler), *WWHL* features celebrity and/or Bravolebrity guests sucking down artisanal cocktails and dishing dirt on other Bravolebrities. While Cohen is not the first or only Jewish talk show host in town, he is the first openly gay host of a late-night talk show filmed on American soil.

A point of interest: *WWHL* includes a weekly segment called "Mazel of the Week."

SINGSPIEL NO MORE: Jews and the American Musical

With the exception of Hollywood and Uncle Miltie's underpants, no other art form offered the Jews a chance to create their own Gentile utopia quite like the American musical. Musical theater presented yet another world where the Jews could *singspiel* their stories of otherness and acculturation while still projecting mass appeal. Indeed, the golden age of the Broadway musical (1940–1960) mostly featured stories of spunky, earnest outsiders fitting in and making good—an optimistic vision of acceptance and assimilation in which the girls are pretty, the endings are happy, and the stakes are (secretly) kosher.

DID JEW KNOW?
Both Woody Allen and Larry Gelbart (of *M*A*S*H* fame) penned gags for Sid Caesar's television shows and specials.

In the Beginning: Origins of Musical Theater

Some backstory: The Puritans' view of theater as sinful left yet another void for Jews to create more than something from less than nothing. In fact, the Puritans' kibosh on anything having to do with plays meant that Jews could enter the field and thrive in it with relatively few restrictions. What's more, the early presence of other landsmen in the biz enabled all Jews with a Czech in their book and a song in their heart to come on along and make their mark on the Great White Way.

The All-Time Greats: Jewish Composers Who Made the World Sing and Dance

From about 1925 to 1955, while the world dealt with the likes of the Depression, Hitler, Stalin, and the Cold War, a group of Jewish writers and composers were busy creating a uniquely American art form that would express not only the immigrant Jew's desire for acceptance but also define what it meant to be American. In other words, the Jews may not have invented baseball, Oklahoma, or apple pie, but they sure as heck wrote great musical numbers about all of 'em!

Irving Berlin: How a Jewish Songster Taught America the Meaning of Patriotism (and Easter)

Born Israel Baline, Irving Berlin (1888–1989) is considered one of the brightest and most influential stars in the firmament of North American songwriters. The son of a Russian cantor who spent his early childhood evading Cossacks until he immigrated with his family in 1893 to New York's Lower East Side, Berlin spent his early childhood in dire poverty. After his father died, Berlin and his sisters were forced to work menial jobs to support the family's already meager

existence. One day, Berlin realized that not only was he bringing home less kosher bacon than his brother and sisters, but also that he had no practical skills to speak of save an ability to sing that he had inherited from his father. Reenergized, Berlin took to the streets of the Bowery and the Lower East Side, standing in front of saloons and singing his *Yiddishkeit* guts out. It was during this period that Berlin, exposed to ragtime music, realized that what the new-world audience wanted was simple, sincere tunes with heartfelt punch. This was confirmed when an Irish saloon owner, after hearing Berlin sing George Cohan's "Yankee Doodle Boy," called Berlin "Yiddish Yankee Doodle."

> "After Moses, the next great Jewish genius was Irving Berlin. He took the blood out of Easter and made it about fashion. And he took Christ out of Christmas and made it about snow."
> —PHILIP ROTH

Though untrained as a musician and able to play in only one key, Berlin wrote both the music and lyrics to all his hit songs, first as a composer on Tin Pan Alley, then for Broadway, and finally for the movies. His first world-famous song, "Alexander's Ragtime Band," was written in 1911 and launched its own dance craze as well as Berlin's career as the ur-songwriter whose music and lyrics continue to capture the hearts and minds of a nation, even those poor and possibly anti-Semitic souls who claim to hate musical theater.

DID JEW KNOW? Over the course of his decades-schlong career, Milton Berle became as well-known for the size of his salami as he was for his im-pecker-ble comedic timing. Once, while funnymen Berle and his ol' pal Phil Silvers found themselves taking a leak together, Silvers took one look at Berle's prodigious package and reportedly said, "You'd better feed that thing, or it's liable to turn on you!" What's more, even after Uncle Miltie's passing in 2002, his member continued to be firmly planted in both the minds and hearts of Hollywood. Seems that during his memorial service, a comedian friend of Berle's announced, "On May first and May second, his penis will be buried."

After Berlin began working on Broadway (via producer Jesse Lasky), he wrote the scores for no fewer than nineteen Broadway musicals, including *This Is the Army* (a show he wrote for the war effort during World War II), *Annie Get Your Gun*, and *Call Me Madam* (both shows starring Ethel Merman) and eighteen films, including *Top Hat, Easter Parade, Holiday Inn*, and *This Is the Army* (the latter co-starring Ronald Reagan).

In case Jew think Berlin only wrote for musical theater, which, at the time, was also popular music, Berlin also penned the greatly beloved and enduring classic of American patriotism, "God Bless America," the "unofficial national anthem of 1938." The phrase "God bless America" was apparently inspired by Berlin's own mother, who often uttered it as Berlin was growing up on the Lower East Side, poor but happy and Cossack-free.

George Gershwin: I Loves Jew, Porgy

Born Jacob Gershowitz (1898–1937) in Brooklyn, Gershwin began his musical career at age fifteen, when he worked as a song-plugger on Tin Pan Alley. While his first song earned him the sum total of five dollars, one of his next efforts, "Swanee," was popularized by none other than Al Jolson and sold more than a million copies. In 1924, Gershwin began collaborating with his older brother, lyricist Ira Gershwin, a fruitful partnership that birthed many a successful musical, including *Funny Face, Girl Crazy, Strike Up the Band*, and *Oh, Kay!*

Though George continued to write popular music, he also began to make inroads as an orchestral composer with his jazz-influenced compositions

Irving Berlin GREATEST HITS

"Oh, How I Hate to Get Up in the Morning"

"A Pretty Girl Is like a Melody"

"Blue Skies"

"Puttin' on the Ritz"

"Easter Parade"

"Cheek to Cheek"

"Heat Wave"

"How Deep Is the Ocean?"

"Let's Face the Music and Dance"

"There's No Business Like Show Business"

"You're Just in Love"

"White Christmas" (one of the most recorded songs in history)

"Rhapsody in Blue" and "An American in Paris." On some level, Gershwin was the Jerome Robbins of the world of classical music—an innovator whose work influenced and evolved the form yet continued to baffle the more serious critics. That said, his musical *Of Thee I Sing* was both a major hit and a Pulitzer Prize winner, and in 1935, Gershwin debuted *Porgy and Bess*, a folk opera now recognized as one of the great masterworks of American opera. **NOTE:** *Change Porgy's and Bess's names to Pinchas and Ruth, and change Catfish Row to a shtetl in Poland, and you've got the world's first Jewish opera.*

The Gershwin brothers would later go to Hollywood, where they wrote the scores for several Fred Astaire classics, including *Shall We Dance*, featuring such hits as "They Can't Take That Away From Me" and "Let's Call the Whole Thing Off."

George Gershwin died of a brain tumor at the age of thirty-eight.

George and Ira Gershwin's

GREATEST HITS

"Someone to Watch Over Me"

"S'Wonderful"

"Embraceable You"

"But Not for Me"

"I Got Rhythm"

"Strike Up the Band"

"Love Is Here to Stay"

"Summertime"

Getting to Know Jew: How Rodgers and Hammerstein Taught America to Love Asia and Oklahoma

Partners Oscar Hammerstein II (1895–1960) and Richard Rodgers (1902–1979) were an influential and innovative musical duo who collaborated on some of the quintessential masterworks of the musical theater canon: *Carousel, The King and I, Flower Drum Song, South Pacific*, and *The Sound of Music*. In addition to the output of their fruitful partnership, the pair also kicked the genre of musical theater up a notch, expanding the form beyond *Show Boat*, Hammerstein's previous collaboration with Jerome Kern (also Jewish).

While Rodgers and Hammerstein didn't compose works with identifiably "Jewish" plots such as, say, Curly McLain's bar mitzvah, the pair had a penchant for complicated characters who existed on the fringes of society (Billy Bigelow and Bloody Mary) or experienced various states of otherness (Anna and her king, Emile and Nellie, and even Mei Li and Wang Ta of *Flower Drum Song*). Indeed, their depictions of Asian culture in three major musicals speaks to the Jewish immigrant experience as well as to what is gained or lost in the process of assimilation

Rodgers and Hammerstein's

GREATEST HITS

"Oh, What a Beautiful Morning"

"The Surrey With the Fringe on Top"

"Oklahoma!"

"Some Enchanted Evening"

"A Wonderful Guy"

"Shall We Dance"

"My Favorite Things"

"Edelweiss"

for anyone from another culture.

Some historians of musical theater suggest that Rodgers and Hammerstein's handling of otherness was the precursor to edgier musicals such as *West Side Story* and the entire oeuvre of Stephen Sondheim. In fact, Rodgers and Hammerstein had been encouraged to remove the song "You've Got to Be Carefully Taught" from the score of *South Pacific*, but the pair, knowing all too well the blight of anti-Semitism, stuck to their guns and kept the song. Ultimately, the musical won nine Tony Awards, three Oscar noms, and a Pulitzer Prize. Score!

While we're on the subject, Rodgers and Hammerstein won thirty-four Tony Awards, fifteen Academy awards, and two Grammy awards. Not half bad for a law school dropout and a kid from Queens!

Hart to Hart: Richard Rodgers, Lorenz Hart, and the Lyrics of Suffering

Before Richard Rodgers paired his mad skills with the likes of Oscar Hammerstein, he had been in a fruitful if challenging partnership with Lorenz Hart, with whom he collaborated until the latter's death in 1943.

The R&H songbook belongs to a time when musicals were like American-cheese sandwiches, all form but no substance, i.e., fluffy songs held together by a book that existed solely to provide some verbal vamping between numbers

---

CAN WE TAWK: JEWISH TALK SHOW HOSTS

Bill Maher, Larry King, Jon Stewart, Chelsea Handler (Jewish father, Mormon mother, raised Reform), Dennis Prager, Jerry Springer, Maury Povich, Geraldo Rivera, Dinah Shore, Howard Stern, Joan Rivers, and Katie Couric (!).

"There's a Small Hotel"

"Where or When"

"My Funny Valentine"

"The Lady Is a Tramp"

"Bewitched, Bothered, and Bewildered"

> "The city's dreams
> can never spoil the dreams
> of a boy and goil."
> —LORENZ HART

before the dancing gals with the glorious gams took the stage. This duo understood the power of story and strove to take the form from its usual soupy leitmotifs and June/moon/spoon rhyme scheme, which Hart—who knew from melancholia, believe Jew me—managed to carry off with the aplomb of a person whose ancestors were desert-wandering nomads.

A bachelor who lived with his *mammele*, Hart suffered from alcoholism and would sometimes disappear for long stretches on alcohol-fueled binges, from which he would eventually emerge to rejoin Rodgers. Unable to find peace with his homosexuality and trapped between haunted mania and deep depression, Hart began to disappear for longer stretches, and the two writers argued, eventually making it impossible for Rodgers to continue their collaboration. The two split in 1943, just before Hart's death. Cause: pneumonia from exposure following an extreme alcohol binge.

Included among Rodgers and Hart's hit Broadway shows are *A Connecticut Yankee, Babes in Arms, The Boys from Syracuse,* and *Pal Joey.*

Frank Loesser: The Jew-ifying of Damon Runyon

Anything but lesser, Frank Loesser was born to a family of musical Jews in New York City. A college dropout who tried various jobs before he became a nightclub singer/pianist, Loesser sold his first lyric in 1931. After paying his dues on Tin Pan Alley, Loesser worked as a lyricist for Paramount Pictures in Hollywood, cranking out hit after hit until World War II, when he enlisted in the Air Force and left the land of freedom to stand up and sing for his country.

During the war, Loesser's special duty was to provide lyrics for camp shows,

> "Throw 'em a fake
> and a finagle,
> they'll never know
> you're just a bagel."
> —FRED EBB

including the 1942 hit "Praise the Lord and Pass the Ammunition," a patriotic ditty that became a hit with civilians and noncivilians alike. In fact, legend has it that the U.S. government imposed a limit on how many times the song could be played on the

As the Good Book Says

POP QUIZ ON *FIDDLER ON THE ROOF*

Fiddler on the Roof was the first musical to have the distinction of surpassing 3,000 performances and the only musical to be solely about Jews. What's more, it was the longest-running Broadway musical until *Grease* showed up on the scene and Danny and Sandy surpassed Tzeitel and Motel. *Fiddler* fun fact: While the movie version of *Fiddler on the Roof* became an instant Jewish classic, it was also directed by a Jew-y sounding non-Jew by the name of Norman Jewison.

1. On what Yiddish author's work is the story of *Fiddler on the Roof* based, and what is the name of the short story?

2. Who wrote the music and lyrics?

3. What are the names of Tevye and Golde's five daughters?

4. What is the name of the butcher to whom Tzeitel had previously been promised in marriage?

5. What is the name of said butcher's pearl-obsessed late wife?

6. Which daughter elopes with a *sheygetz*?

7. Finish the following lyrics:

    a. May you be like Ruth and like Esther, may you be_____?

    b. Life has a way of confusing us,_____

    c. Seedlings turn overnight to_____, blossoming even as_____

    d. Lord who made the lion and the lamb,_____.
       Would it spoil some vast eternal plan, if_____?

ANSWERS

1. Sholem Aleichem, *Tevye the Milkman and Other Tales*

2. Jerry Bock, Sheldon Harnick, and Joseph Stein

3. Tzeitel, Hodel, Chava, Shprintze, and Bielke

4. Lazar Wolf

5. Fruma-Sarah

6. Chava

7. a. Deserving of praise
   b. Blessing and bruising us
   c. Sunflowers...we gaze
   d. You decreed I should be what I am...
     I were a wealthy man

radio so the public wouldn't tire of it. Additionally, many musical-theater scholars note that Jewish composers of the WWII era displayed unparalleled patriotism in their music, put their careers on hold to enlist, and wrote the songs that kept the Allies teary-eyed and clutching their pearls.

After the war, Loesser returned to New York, where Cy Feuer (another Jew) asked him to write the music and lyrics to *Where's Charley,* an adaptation of the play *Charley's Aunt.* Following the success of *Where's Charley,* Loesser established himself as a double-threat songwriter who went on to write the music and lyrics for such golden Broadway greats as *Guys and Dolls, The Most Happy Fella*, and *How to Succeed in Business Without Really Trying.*

But let's talk G-D: Based on the stories of Damon Runyon, *Guys and Dolls* (for which Loesser won a Tony) encompassed the slyly Jewish vernacular of a bunch of mobsters and misfits trying like hell to make good on being bad. The players are an amalgam of "New York" characters whose colorful "Runyon-ese" takes on the vital timbre of Yiddish—a language spoken by outsiders and understood by an insular few who long for a *bissele* piece of American pie. Again, the subject matter isn't necessarily overtly Jewish, but the same themes prevail: outsiders struggling to assimilate and capitalize on the American dream, the battle between secular and sacred worlds, and the glories of overindulging on Lindy's cheesecake. Don't mind me! I'll just pick!

DID JEW KNOW?

Famous musical Jews with cantors for fathers: Al Jolson, Irving Berlin, Harold Arlen.

Leonard Bernstein: East Side, West Side, All Around the Town

Leonard Bernstein (1918–1990): A revered composer and conductor and possibly the greatest musical

"Lonely Town"

"The Best of All Possible Worlds"

"New York, New York"

"Conga"

"Ohio"

"Glitter and Be Gay"

"America"

"Maria"

"Tonight"

"Somewhere"

polymath, like, ever, Bernstein was also one of the first U.S.-born conductors to receive worldwide accolades for his additions to the musical theater canon and the *lingua symphonia.* Bernstein's name and fame stem from his years spent as music director of the New York Philharmonic as well as the composition of some of the world's best-known and nuanced operettas and musicals: *On the Town, Wonderful Town, Candide* (book by Lillian Hellman), and *West Side Story.*

A composer whose work fused myriad elements from jazz to Stravinsky, Bernstein was comfortable communicating in any patois. *West Side Story*, arguably one of the all-time great works of musical theater, not only bridged the gap between popular and more "formal" or classical music, but also communicated musically the richness and difficulty of immigrant life. As North American Jews continued to assimilate and Yiddish was further relegated to trace elements, the mournful yet ironic minor-key quality of the mother tongue wended its way into Bernstein's compositions, both literally (his symphony *Kaddish* and the ballet *Dybbuk*) and subtly (*Fancy Free* and *West Side Story*).

LEONARD BERNSTEIN COMING SOON TO A SHUL NEAR JEW

According to the composer's daughter Jamie Bernstein, the Bernsteins were not regular shul-goers; in fact, Mama Bernstein was a Catholic who converted, but father Leonard had a special place in his heart for "Kol Nidre." "My father would always go shul hopping that night," Jamie says, "or as he explained it, 'a little bit of Kol Nidre here and a little bit there.' Together with my brother they would visit a handful of synagogues around New York. . . .You can only imagine the faces of the *chazans* when they spotted Leonard Bernstein in the congregation. They must have been trembling in their *tallit.*"

Chappy Challah-days!

Identify which of the following beloved Christmas ditties were composed by Jews:

1. "Rockin' Around the Christmas Tree"

2. "White Christmas"

3. "Baby, It's Cold Outside"

4. "Let It Snow"

5. "A Holly Jolly Christmas"

6. "The Christmas Song"

7. "Silver Bells"

8. "Rudolph the Red-Nosed Reindeer"

9. "It's the Most Wonderful Time of the Year"

10. "Santa Baby"

Bonus round: "Do They Know It's Christmas?"

ANSWERS

1. J—Johnny Marks

2. J—Irving Berlin

3. J—Frank Loesser

4. J—Sammy Cahn and Jule Styne

5. J—Johnny Marks

6. J—Mel Torme

7. J—Jay Livingston and Ray Evans

8. J—Johnny Marks

9. J—George Wyle and Eddie Pola

10. J—Joan Javitz and Phillip Springer

Bonus round: J—Bob Geldof and Midge Ure

Harold Arlen: The Jew That Got Away

Born Hyman Arluck, Harold Arlen (1905–1986) was a nice Jewish son-of-a-cantor hailing from Buffalo who composed, along with some of the bestest lyricists of all time, many of the most glittering gold standards of the '30s and '40s. Most notable is "Somewhere Over the Rainbow" and other essential tunes from *The Wizard of Oz*, the movie that made Judy Garland, then just sweet sixteen, one of the most recognizable (and bankable) voices of the era and that inextricably linked her to that song for all time. Between 1930 and 1960, Arlen also composed or co-composed a number of Broadway musicals.

Harold Arlen's
GREATEST HITS

"Somewhere Over the Rainbow"

"Get Happy"

"Stormy Weather"

"Let's Fall in Love"

$\bigcirc$

"The Man That Got Away"

"Come Rain or Come Shine"

"That Old Black Magic"

"Down With Love"

"It's Only a Paper Moon"

"I've Got the World on a String"

In 1929, as the world was toppling over the precipice of the Great Depression, Arlen composed his first big hit, "Get Happy," an up-tempo number that launched his career and found its greatest performance decades later when Judy Garland, Ethel Merman, and Barbra Streisand belted it together on *The Judy Garland Show* in 1963. Speaking of Judy, Arlen also composed another of Judy's signature songs, the world-weary, late-night overdose-on-Vicodin weepfest otherwise known as "The Man That Got Away." A song that bookended the hopeful innocence of "Somewhere Over the Rainbow" as though to remind us what a haunted Jew never forgets: Life is suffering, and then you die alone in your parents' basement.

Kander and Ebb: Look for the Jewish Lining

John Kander (1927–) and Fred Ebb (1928–2004): As two of the great later collaborators of the musical-theater canon, Kander and Ebb captured the disenchantment of the 1960s with their sundry scores of isolation and inner turmoil, such as *Cabaret, Chicago, Kiss of the Spider Woman, Zorba, Woman of the Year, The Rink*, and *Steel Pier*. Though they are mostly known for their stage musicals, the pair also scored a number of hit films, including Martin Scorsese's *New York, New York,* containing the world-renowned, eponymous theme song.

Cabaret, the pair's Tony- and Grammy- and Academy Award–winning musical, depicts a highly uneasy Weimar Germany and focuses on two stories of marginalized groups soon to be decimated by the Nazis: homosexuals and, of course, Jews. In other words, just a fun, fluffy comedy. Only, in *Cabaret,* the world is far seedier, and the Jewish story, save that of Fräulein Schneider and Herr Schultz, considerably more diffuse.

Like those of many of their other Jewish predecessors, Kander and Ebb's shows portray outsiders forced to re-create their own worlds amongst a forlorn and forgotten few. Whether performers in a cabaret, cellmates, or the owner of a dilapidated roller rink, these characters feel neither at home in the world they created nor a particular attachment for the world they left behind, a world that, for all intents and purposes, abandoned and betrayed them. True, these musicals, as in many works from the disenfranchised 1970s on, aren't what my mother would call jolly, but what they lack in happy endings, they make up for in Chita Rivera and Liza Minnelli. And it doesn't get more Jewish than that!

Kander and Ebb's
GREATEST HITS
"Cabaret"
"Willkommen"
"Don't Tell Mama"
"Life Is"

"All That Jazz"
"Chicago"
"How Lucky Can You Get"
"It Only Hurts When I Laugh"
"Liza's Here"
"New York, New York"
"Steel Pier"

Bobby-Baby-Bobby-*Bubbe*:
Stephen Sondheim and the Disenchantment of the '70s Jew

Stephen Sondheim (1930–) is another Tony-, Academy-, and Grammy Award–winning composer and lyricist whose work addresses (and sings to) the long-suffering Jewish wretch in each of us. A lyricist with a tremendous range in terms of nuance and tone—note that Oscar Hammerstein was his mentor—Sondheim expressed the dissatisfaction and dashed hopes of the 1970s in a way that was both truthful and droll. More than simply gallows humor, his work respects the richness of life without being overly maudlin, unless, of course, ironically.

His additions to the musical-theater canon include *A Funny Thing Happened on the Way to the Forum, Company, Follies, Sweeney Todd, A Little Night Music, Sunday in the Park With George, Into the Woods*, and *Assassins*. Additionally, he wrote the lyrics for the likes of such Broadway legends as *Gypsy* and *West Side Story*. In other woids, with the exception of Mr. Cole Porter (not a Jew), there's not a Yid on Hashem's green earth who can bust a rhyme like Stephen Joshua Sondheim.

Where Kander and Ebb's work definitively left behind the happy ending in favor of the sardonic and tragic—um, Jew-ier?—Sondheim redefined the dramatic idea of the sad beginning peppered with life's fleeting moments of happiness, however haunted. This style gives the whole Jewish composer posse a run for its money in terms of commentary on the tragically bizarre moments that comprise this Jewish thing called life, no matter how WASPy a character's name initially appears. In other words, don't kid yourself, Chad! They're all Jewish!

Holy Schtick

Let's face it, Jews have had a highly successful 3,000-year history of storytelling. Indeed, when the Jews left the Old World for the New, they were able not only to reinvent their story but also to invent the way non-Jews define themselves vis-à-vis certain Jews' fantasy-version of Gentile life. The Tribe did this by placing Jewish music, humor, and even *schmeckles* at the forefront of the world's imagination and making the goyim think they'd thought of it. Kinda makes Jew wonder—maybe it's not that Jews invented the entertainment industry as much as they created a way of telling their story over and over again until at last they got a standing O instead of being chased out of town by inquisitors or Cossacks. *Nu*, what else could they do? As the great Jewish mystic Ron Jeremy once said, "It's gonna be weird to cut off the thing that's paid my bills all these years. I hope I can keep it as a souvenir."

CHAPTER 8

THE PEOPLE OF THE BOOK:
Jewish Lit from the Bible to Superman

Conquered people tend to be witty.

—SAUL BELLOW

While a list of Jews in sports may well add up to the smallest tome in the world—
neck and neck, say, with Jewish presidents or Jewish shark fishermen—the list
of Jews who've contributed to world literature is longer than the Talmud and
twice as sexy. In other words, Jews: They can't throw 'em or catch 'em, but they
sure can write 'em! For people who comprise about 2 percent of the world's
population, Jews sure make up a disproportionate number of its influential philosophers, authors, and thinkers, especially when you stop to consider that they
mostly did all that thinking and writing while either fleeing, surviving, hiding, or
all of the above.

This all may have started when Moses came down from Mount Sinai with the
Ten Commandments and a divine imperative to be God's law-bearer, social secretary, and stenographer. According to both the Jewish and Christian tradition,
the book to end all books found its earliest form through the mighty pen of none
other than Uncle Mo.

There is some debate about exactly how Moses managed to crank out the entire
Torah. Some hold that God revealed it to Moses in a forty-day cram session and that
Moses wrote it down immediately after he returned to flat ground. Others believe
that the Torah was delivered scroll by scroll and inscribed at a more leisurely pace
over forty or so years. Whatever the case, the idea is that Moses received the Torah
from God, right up until the last eight verses of Deuteronomy, which describe his
death and burial. Again, there are various hypotheses of who wrote this last bit:
Moses himself, prophetically; Joshua; or even the Big Man Himself.

Shortly after Moses left his body, it turned out there was still more to be said,
and so other learned Jews jumped on the literary bandwagon and started writing
their collective *tuchuses* off. End result: the Hebrew Bible known as the *Tanakh*—the
single-most influential and enduring best-seller save *The Da Vinci Code*! As if
that weren't enough of a literary tour de force, over the next however many centuries, the groupies of a certain Joshua Ben Nasri (and *their* groupies) wrote the
sequel: the New Testament. This strange and impressive document continued to be
tinkered with until the fourth century CE, when the Bible, as in the Old Testament—
what the goyim call the Hebrew Bible—and the New Testament were canonized,
forever pitting Jew against Gentile and making Charlton Heston a household name.

DID JEW KNOW? *The People of the Book* is a term used by Muslims to describe
non-Muslim faiths that have a revealed scripture: Jews, Christians, and Sabians. For
instance, the Torah was received from God on Mount Sinai rather than "made up and
written down" by some old white guys drinking kosher wine in a tent. This is why it is a
perennial best-seller: you can't argue with God!

Regardless of whether or not most people have actually read the thing cover to cover, no other Western work has had quite the impact or made it into as many hotel rooms. That said, there are some other works with equally long-lasting juju for the Jew-Jews. Read on and see for yourself!

I WRITE THE BOOKS THAT MAKE THE WHOLE WORLD SING: A Jew-ser-Friendly Guide to Judaism's Top Texts

The Tanakh

TaNaKh is an acronym used to represent the entirety of the Hebrew Bible, as in the collection of historical and legal writings, or "books," up to and through Chronicles. The acronym is formed from the Hebrew letters for Torah (teaching), Nevi'im (prophets), and Ketuvim (writings). While it's difficult to pinpoint an exact date of origin for this illustrious tome—there's actually a midrash that states that the Torah was written as a blueprint for all of creation prior to the creation of the world—most biblical scholars agree that the written books were a product of the Babylonian exile that were then formalized, or "sealed," somewhere in the neighborhood of 422 BCE, though the dates scholars give can vary based on each specific book. One thing is certain: In their earliest oral form, these stories are older than the Egyptian Book of the Dead. And that's wicked old.

The Old Versus New Testament Rotisserie Bible Game!

The Holy Bowl! Collect cards and assemble a dream team of your favorite heroes and heroines to wipe out the Romans and survive the Rapture. Lions sold separately.

A DID JEW KNOW AT-A-GLANCE GLOSSARY OF BIBLICAL TERMS

New Testament—Christian scriptures that focus on the events of the first century BCE.

Old Testament—Solely a Christian category, the Old Testament contains the Hebrew Bible plus some additional books thrown in for good measure.

Pentateuch—The first five books of the Bible; the Torah.

Septuagint—Second-century-BCE Greek translation of the Hebrew Bible.

Vulgate—Fourth-century-CE Latin translation of the Hebrew Bible.

DAVID

BOOK(S) OF THE BIBLE: Books of Samuel; Chronicles; Psalms

The attractive and musically gifted super-king of Israel. "Now he [David] was ruddy, and with beautiful eyes, and goodly to look upon." (1 Samuel 16:12-13)

POWERS: Plays a mean harp. Writes psalms. Slingshot expert.

LOGLINE: I'm king of the world!

****

TOR-IFIC! Old Testament Trading Cards!

ESTHER

BOOK(S) OF THE BIBLE: Esther

The Jewish orphan who made good through intermarriage as the hottie-patottie queen of Persian king Ahasuerus.

POWERS: Able to enslave Gentiles to her will, the whole Megillah.

LOGLINE: Intermarriage saves!

JOSEPH

BOOK(S) OF THE BIBLE: Genesis

This Jewish Beau Brummel had the foresight to store grain during a time of Egyptian abundance.

POWERS: Stellar planning skills. Solid family man. Great with Pharaohs.

LOGLINE: Not just a poor-man's *Fiddler!*

****

NOAH

BOOK(S) OF THE BIBLE: Genesis

The only good guy in town.

POWERS: Animal husbandry. Building with gofer wood. Navigating in a hurricane.

LOGLINE: Come aboard, we're expecting you.

DANIEL

BOOK(S) OF THE BIBLE: Daniel

Though he was taken into Babylonian captivity as a young man, this Old Testament hero stuck to his guns and became a prominent figure in the court, regardless of the fact that he didn't convert.

POWERS: Lion taming. Dream interpretation. Code breaking.

LOGLINE: I was right about the Romans!!!

****

JOB

BOOK(S) OF THE BIBLE: Job

A righteous and prosperous man whom God tests at Satan's urging to see how righteous he really is. Tests include killing his ten children, burning his sheep, and giving him seriously itchy boils.

POWERS: Stamina. Endurance. Loyalty.

LOGLINE: Takes a licking but keeps on itching!

****

JUDITH

BOOK(S) OF THE BIBLE: Apocrypha

The widowed beauty who saves her people from destruction by slaying the Assyrian general Holofernes. She sneaks into his tent, gets homeboy drunk, decapitates him, and exits the scene with his head in her purse.

POWERS: Major courage. Spy skillz. Beauty. Wiles. Great at a dinner party.

LOGLINE: Keeping kosher can save your life!

****

THE NEW JEW REVIEW: New Testament Trading Cards

★ PAUL OF TARSUS ★

BOOK(S) OF THE BIBLE: Pauline Epistles; Acts

The eczema-ridden, grouchy disciple-on-a-donkey who forever altered the course of Western history, not to mention the style of dress for Jewish genitals everywhere.

SIDEKICK: Timothy.

POWERS: Expert rider of donkeys. Great letter writer.

LOGLINE: I may not be Jesus, but I'm great at weddings.

★ MARY MAGDALENE ★

BOOK(S) OF THE BIBLE: Gospels

A carrot-topped foot fetishist with a possible sex addiction. In love with Jesus and is his bestest female disciple—but can possibly be yours, too, for a stick of gum and two shekels.

POWERS: Seductive looks. Unerring devotion. Fabulous pedicures.

LOGLINE: I may not be Esther, but I'm the queen of the Ho-ra.

★ JESUS H. CHRIST ★

BOOK(S) OF THE BIBLE: The Gospel(s) According to Matthew, Mark, Luke and John; The Acts of the Apostles; Pauline Epistles.

The original long-haired liberal and feminist. Tall, thin, 13 percent body fat, eight-pack. Perpetually thirty-three years old. Healer of lepers, pardoner of prostitutes. Died for your sins but always hangs around.

POWERS: Gift of gab. People person. Spins a good yarn. Great at parties (can turn water into wine).

LOGLINE: Sometimes it helps to have a father in the business.

THE ★ VIRGIN MARY ★

BOOK(S) OF THE BIBLE: Gospels; Acts of the Apostles; Revelation

Beatific girl next door who never got over the death of her son.

POWERS: Talks to angels. Expert donkey rider. Can reproduce asexually.

LOGLINE: God is my boyfriend.

★ JOHN THE BAPTIST ★

BOOK(S) OF THE BIBLE: Gospels

This house-of-bricks apostle knows how to stay out of trouble and put pen to papyrus. Though his mother is an exotic dancer (opportunity for requisite strip club scenes), he is a close personal friend and cousin of Jesus.

POWERS: Quickie converter (a plus for times of Inquisition). Great swimmer. Gift of prophesy.

LOGLINE: Elijah is so ninth century BCE.

★ JUDAS ★ "Thirty Pieces of Silverblatt" ISCARIOT

BOOK(S) OF THE BIBLE: Gospels; Acts of the Apostles

The notorious betrayer of Jesus and therefore the worst thing that happened to the Jews, but the best thing that happened to Mel Gibson.

POWERS: Speaks softly and carries a big purse. Kiss of death.

LOGLINE: I'll never tell.

The Dead Sea Scrolls

One fine day in 1946, a Bedouin shepherd was wandering on the northwest shore of what was then British Mandate Palestine (the West Bank), when he fell into a cave. Seriously. Lo and behold, in this cave, now known as the Qumran site, this accidental spelunker found, or rather fell upon, what looked to be seven ye olde scrolls stored in ye olde jars. These ancient scrolls, as well as others later discovered in caves nearby, consisted of manuscripts or fragments from every book of the Hebrew Bible except Esther and are now known as the Dead Sea Scrolls. Among other scrolls that were discovered around the same site were "extra-biblical documents," including the books of Enoch and Jubilees, as well as assorted manuscripts containing commentary, devotional poetry, and even astrology. The manuscripts, written in Greek, Hebrew, and Aramaic, have been dated to various points somewhere between 408 and 318 BCE!

This discovery of the Dead Sea Scrolls was significant on many levels, and not just because it's mad cool to stumble on ancient books in a cave. The scrolls give us a clearer understanding of how the Bible as we know it was actually transcribed over time. Before our klutzy caver, the oldest extant manuscripts of the Bible were Masoretic texts from about the tenth century CE. However, these biblical manuscripts from Qumran provide a much older cross section—more than a millennium—and vary remarkably little in terms of language and content, proving the age-old accuracy of the biblical tradition.

Though the authorship of the Dead Sea Scrolls remains in dispute, the most touted theory is that the Essenes, a Jewish sect from the time of the Second Temple, wrote them, hid them at some point between 66 and 68 CE during the Jewish Revolt, and then split the scene to look for greener and safer pastures. After this abrupt departure, the site of Qumran was destroyed and the scrolls were seemingly lost forever to the forces of nature and anti-Semitism. Makes Jew wonder what else is out there.

But Wait, You Also Get the Mishnah!

When the Jews received the Written Torah on Mount Sinai, there was a second part of this amazing package: a conglomeration of ideas and instruction called the Oral Torah—an oral explanation for how the Written Torah should be understood and carried out. This Oral Torah was passed down from generation to generation via the Sanhedrin (see chapter 5), until the destruction of the Temple, when the Sanhedrin was scattered and/or forced to go lo pro.

And so a rabbi by the name of Judah HaNasi grew neurotic at the idea that without a central authority, the dissemination of laws and teachings would be more willy-nilly than absolute, causing the Oral Law to be forgotten. And so he did what any smart, indoorsy Jew picked last for dodgeball would do: He wrote a best-selling book. In this case, the book was a written version of the Oral Torah.

Naturally, this was a massive undertaking but, undaunted, Rabbi Judah HaNasi began the task of editing, organizing, and explaining traditions and interpretations that had previously only been composed and decanted orally. The end result was the Mishnah: a definitive and esoteric written version of the oral law completed circa 190–200 CE. **NOTE:** *The word* mishnah *means "repeating," an essential component of how the Mishnah is taught, retaught, and learned among both scholars and students.*

The Mishnah is divided into six major segments that are then subdivided into sixty-three tractates with a whopping total of 525 chapters. These six segments are as follows:

- *Zeraim,* or "seeds" — agricultural laws
- *Moed,* or "holiday"— holidays and their ritual observance
- *Nashim,* or "women"— issues between men and women, or who wears the proverbial pants in this relationship
- *Nezikin,* or "damages"— criminal and civil law
- *Kodshim,* or "holy things"— the laws of the Temple
- *Taharot,* or "pure things"—the laws of purity and impurity

The Talmud

After the completion of the Mishnah, there followed many centuries of various hardships for the Jews, including increased religious persecution. Thus, many

---

HE CALLED: A WORD ON THE TORAH

In the wild and woolly world of rabbinic literature, the word *Torah* denotes the first five books of Moses, or the Pentateuch. These books are named from words that appear in the first few verses and say something about the book as a whole: *Bereshit* ("the beginning," Genesis), *Shemot* ("names," Exodus), *Vakira* ("He called," Leviticus), *Bamidbar* ("in the desert," Numbers) and *Devarim* ("words," Deuteronomy).

fled the scene for Babylon. Since the Jews were now decentralized over many lands and lacking one authoritative body, it became clear that the Mishnah alone could no longer suffice to convey the Oral Law, especially because the bulk of the Mishnah was written for hardcore scholars.

Next thing you know, a bunch of rabbis began conducting a series of fireside chats on the Mishnah and wrote down the core of said chats, the product of which formed the Gemara, meaning "tradition" in Aramaic and "completion" in Hebrew. The combo platter of the Mishnah and the Gemara became the Babylonian Talmud—the central text of rabbinic Judaism. NOTE: *The word* talmud *means "learning or instruction."*

The Talmud comprises arguments about things that may or may not have an immediately understandable, practical purpose, rather than the basics, such as "don't eat pork" or, for that matter, "don't pork thy neighbor's wife." (Those topics were already a given.)

In other words, in the Talmud, one finds long back-and-forth dialectics on legal reasoning, and legal rulings on *all* areas of Jewish law, including temple rituals and sacrifices, stories about sages, stories about biblical characters often based on verses from the Bible, homiletic interpretation of biblical verses, ethical teachings, and even medical advice. Believe it or not, there's even a part of the Talmud that discusses the penis sizes of various rabbis!

Rather than splitting hairs, the intention of these teensy-weensy arguments (and giant rabbinic schlongs) was ultimately to arrive at an understanding of Judaism's less tangible, ultimate reality: There's one God. You ain't it. Get used to it.

Midrash

Midrash is not a text in itself, but rather a method of interpreting texts. The two main texts that employ this method are the Talmud and the Midrash Rabbah—a collection of midrashic works.

Basically there are two types: Midrash Aggadah and Midrash Halakha. Midrash Aggadah is a method of analysis that attempts to explain or understand the ethics, decisions, events, and nuances of biblical narratives. The Hebrew word *aggadah* means "telling" or "story." (Think Haggadah, the liturgy of the Passover Seder that tells the story of the Exodus.) While Midrash Aggadah focuses on biblical characters to convey Jewish values and the nature of the Jewish soul, Midrash Halakha attempts to explain Jewish laws via the clarification of biblical texts—for example, how you lay tefillin rather than how you shall not lay thy neighbor's wife.

Shulchan Aruch

In rather stark contrast to its blabby Uncle Talmud, the *Shulchan Aruch* (circa 1563) codifies laws in current practice (as opposed to laws that pertain, say, to the Temple and how to worship there). Its author, Rabbi Yosef Karo of Safed (Israel), a Sephardic Jew and a Kabbalist, composed the Shulchan Aruch in four parts to break down the specifics of laws pertaining to the Sabbath and other holidays, kashrut, usury, tzedakah, Brit Milah, menstruation, *mikveh*, illness, death, marital relations, and property. *Shulchan aruch* means the "set table."

Zohar She Blows

The Zohar is the quintessential guidebook of Kabbalah, or Jewish mysticism, or why Ashton Kutcher and Demi Moore once dressed up like pigs for Purim.

While Kabbalah itself originates from oral teachings dating to the time of Abraham, the Zohar is a later mystical commentary on the Torah that grapples with the nature of the Godhead and the entire known and unknown universe as a form of tripped-out soul science. Since these topics are so confounding, many rabbis believe that Kabbalah study is intended only for the elite few who have already attained high levels of learning and spiritual mastery—which is to say, they've read the entire revealed Torah and/or seen all or part of Madonna's Drowned World Tour.

Though it is attributed to the great first-century scholar Simeon bar Yochai, the Zohar was also possibly addended in the thirteenth century by Spanish rabbi and Kabbalist Moses de León.

BUT WAIT, THERE'S MORE!

Somewhat before the composition of the Babylonian Talmud (sealed circa 550 CE), another group of rabbis in the Holy Land held similar discussions that became the Jerusalem Talmud (sealed circa 350 BCE). Generally speaking, when yeshiva *buchers* say "the Talmud," they are referring to the Babylonian Talmud, which is longer—about 6,200 pages!—less cryptic, and thus considered more authoritative than its somewhat forgotten older cousin.

You Can't Rashi Greatness

Since most of the books above don't come with users' manuals, various important rabbinic commentators have written books on the books of the People of the Book. These books are meant to both elucidate the ethics put forth by the rabbis who codified the Oral Torah, as well as add more books that need books to explain what they're talking about. Of all of these commentators, some of whom only a yeshiva *bucher* could love, none is more essential than Rabbi Shlomo Yitzhaki (1040–1105), a medieval French rabbi better known by the acronym *Rashi*.

A person of the book who loved nothing more than to read and write books about the books, Rashi was a winemaker by trade who was also the author of a comprehensive commentary on the Tanakh. His most irrefutable achievement, however, was his running commentary on the Babylonian Talmud, a paean to the simple pleasures of *peshat*—the literal, plain meaning of the text—and an indispensable tool for students attempting to unpack that eye-crossin' coda.

Great Minds Think Alike:
The Science of Jewish Philosophy

Western civ traces its roots back to two great cities: Athens and Jerusalem. As such, Jewish philosophers, as opposed to philosophers on Judaism, have also written their fair share of the books that make the whole world run out and buy CliffsNotes. In case you attended a liberal arts university without a core curriculum, behold an at-a-glance guide to but a few of their innumerable additions to intellectual history.

No Press Is Bad Press: Maimonides and the Perplexed

Moses Maimonides (1135–1204 CE) was one of the all-time great masochistic over achievers and perhaps the most important Jewish doctor-philosopher of the Middle Ages. Among other works, he wrote the Mishneh Torah, the authoritative fourteen-volume code of all of Jewish law, a commentary on the Mishnah, and *The Guide for the Perplexed*, a philosophical work that also had a far-reaching influence in the non-Jewish/secular sphere.

On top of his prolific writings, Maimonides was also the personal physician to the sultan of Egypt, a job that entailed treating his court and all the members of his sizable harem. In other words, Doctor-man was elbow deep in shiksa *schmundie* all day but still found time to come home and burn the midnight oil, a work ethic he maintained even while emigrating with his family from Spain to Israel to Egypt before God invented frequent flyer miles.

Maimonides' seminal *The Guide for the Perplexed* sought to find a meeting point between the Hebrew Bible and Aristotelian philosophy. After analyzing the ideas of the Torah, Maimonides turned on the industrial Vitamix of his mind and tossed in other seemingly radical ingredients such as Aristotelian logic, Muslim rationalism, and Jewish theology. While many Jews and even a few Gentiles recognized Maimonides' *Guide* as a masterwork, others thought it heretical and either burned it or tried to ban it. As usual, this only made more people want to read it.

Spinoza? I Hardly Know Her!

Whether or not Baruch Spinoza (1632–1677) was an atheist wunderkind who saw reason as the end of superstition or a heretic with a semi-decent Latin teacher, he changed the course of intellectual history with his *Ethics*. Say what you will about what happens next, but the mere fact that a seventeenth-century Jew can light upon the concept of reality as perfection without ever having attended a yoga class is reason enough to include him in this illustrious tome. Other big ideas: Man is free to think and feel as reason dictates, and it's not reality that blows; rather, it's our perception of reality. Snuggle up to that on a cold, dark night.

I'm a Bube Man: Martin Buber and Sexing the Divine

A Viennese Jew of means who was raised in an Orthodox home, Martin Buber (1878–1965) contended that in order for man to have an intimate relationship with God, he has to have an equally intimate relationship with his fellow man and that these two relationships are anything but mutually exclusive—i.e., man and God are in an open marriage where man can and should see other people. Clearly, everyone liked this idea. Buber's most famous work, *I and Thou*, outlines two ways of experiencing the world: the "I and It" approach, in which everything other than the self is experienced as a separate object, and the "I and Thou" approach, in which the "I" dissolves all boundaries between itself and "Thou" (God) without ever having to go to Burning Man. In other words, Jew complete me.

Hannah's Not My Sister

Hannah Arendt (1906–1975) was a German American philosopher and political theorist whose writings mainly focused on the nature of freedom, the meaning of power, and the, like, total buzzkill of totalitarianism. Important works include *The Origins of Totalitarianism*—a study of the Nazi and Stalinist regimes that garnered tremendous criticism from the left—*The Human Condition*, and *Eichmann in Jerusalem: A Report on the Banality of Evil*. Regarding this last work, let's just say some Jews no likey. Why? Because they perceive in it a certain lack of sympathy toward the Jewish victims of the Holocaust. Fun fact: Martin Heidegger (who, FYI, was a Nazi) was Arendt's on-again-off-again lover.

DID JEW KNOW?

Leon Czolgosz, the unemployed factory worker and meshug who shot President William McKinley, claimed he had been inspired to do so after hearing Emma Goldman give a speech.

> **DID JEW KNOW?** Johannes Gutenberg, the possibly Jewish inventor of movable type who changed forever the accessibility of books, not to be confused with Steve Guttenberg, the absolutely Jewish actor best known for his tour de force portrayal of Carey Mahoney in the *Police Academy* movies. Clues that good ol' Johannes was Jewish: His home was located in Judenberg, which translates as "Jewish Hill." Also, he was born in Mainz, which was a major hub of European Jewry during the fifteenth century. Plus, he had a beard.

My Son's a Genius! Judaism's Brainiac Triumvirate

Time was, the planet didn't know from commies, shrinks, or $E = mc^2$. While this might have made for exploited workers, repressed neuroses, and easier college curricula, there was half as much to sound off about at hipster conventions when everyone gets tired of talking about Ayn Rand. Enter the father, the son, and the holy roast: three Jews whose ideas would define the way the world thinks about working, *schtupping* its mother, and nuking its enemies. Let's face it, these activities have more or less existed ever since Eve sank her chompers into the forbidden fruit, but these three guys took breakdowns to a whole new level. Let's take a gander.

The Other Marx Brother: Karl and the Invention of Sharing

If there's one Jewish boy who knew from what's yours is ours, it was infamous philosopher and revolutionary Karl Marx (1818–1883). Marx coined a whole new class, the proletariat or the workers, who, after the Industrial Revolution, owned less than nothing, controlling neither the means nor the end result of their labors. Thing was, rather than just identifying the problem and calling it a day, Marx posed a solution: Communism.

Regardless of whether you think this system is viable, it has influenced leaders and thinkers from Mao to Ghandi to Bertolt Brecht. The idea is this: Rich people are exploitative meanies who made their dough by breaking the back of the worker, and the time had come for the worker to dismantle the system to emancipate himself. Slogan: "Workers, Unite! Take back the might!" Based on Marx's ideas, one-third of the planet turned communist, a tack the other two-thirds were less than thrilled about. Say what you will about private property, but communism seems all too often to lead to totalitarian regimes as well as the occasional bed-hopping hippy commune, both dirty systems that give a whole new meaning to the phrase *party town*.

Depending on whom you talk to, Marx and his buddy Engels' great work, *The Communist Manifesto* (published in 1848), is a short but sweet publication that is either the world's most touted or kvetched-about political manuscript. It outlines an approach to the class struggle and the major problemos of capitalism soon to be replaced by socialism (communism lite) and then finally by communism itself. This publication didn't win Marx any popularity contests with the capitalist factor, but as Karl and his commie buddies would agree, Jew can't have everything.

Hot to Trot: Leon Trotsky on Ice

Born Lev Davidovich Bronstein in 1879, Leon Trotsky rose to prominence in a party that wrested power from the richies and turned the world on its *tuchus*. Inspired by Marxism, Trotsky started playing hooky from school to organize a workers union, an extracurricular activity that, rather than getting him into a good college, got him exiled to Siberia, where he married and spawned before escaping to London in 1902.

In London, Trotsky met Vladimir Lenin, and the two began their rocky bromance. Getting wind of Bloody Sunday, Trotsky hightailed it back to Mother Russia, where he went Menshevik to Lenin's Bolshevik and landed right back in the Siberian slammer for supporting an armed rebellion against the still-powerful autocracy. Escaping yet again, Trotsky wended his way west for a ten-year spell before returning to Russia in 1917, where he joined the Bolsheviks and became a major player in the Russian Revolution, second only to Lenin.

> "Everything is relative in this world, where change alone endures."
>
> —LEON TROTSKY,
> THE REVOLUTION BETRAYED

Trotsky had been considered Lenin's heir-apparent, but alas, Stalin had a different plan in mind. Shortly after Lenin died in 1924, Trotsky was booted from the party and exiled, eventually settling in Mexico in 1936. There he occasionally canoodled with the likes of Frida Kahlo and penned critiques of Stalin. On August 20, 1940, Ramón Mercader, a Spanish communist, stabbed Trotsky in the head with an ice pick. Trotsky died the next day.

On Our Backs: Freud, Jews, and Psychoanalysis

Much like their brethren in other hoity-toity occupations, Jews were often excluded from full participation in the academic and scientific life of Western and Central Europe. In many cases, their involvement was titular and/or relegated to specified fields. In more extreme cases, including in Austria and Germany, Jews were not permitted to work in established specialties, such as surgery. As a result, they went into fields that were less attractive to their non-Jewish colleagues, such as psychiatry (the "Jewish science"), neurology, dermatology, pediatrics, pathology, and gynecology. On some level you could say that anti-Semitic restrictions on Jews and medicine gave rise to one of the most culturally transforming, life-changing Jews of the twentieth century: Paging Doctor Freud!

Sigmund Schlomo Freud, the father of psychoanalysis, began his doctor days as a neurologist with a penchant for cocaine and playing daddy dearest to a goodly number of hysterical Jewish females. His theories, even those that posterity has debunked, have exerted a vast influence on the various forms of "talking cures" that form the warp and weft of therapy as we know it. Whatever you may think of Victorian attitudes toward sex and women, or Freud's almost pathological obsession with *schmeckles, schvantzes,* and schmucks, one salient fact emerges: That cigar-chomping Jew might have been sexist, but he sure had the gift of gab!

Oedipus, Schmedipus: As Long as You Love Your (Jewish) Mother

While Freud's Oedipus complex has become a clichéd pop-culture explanation for a smorgasbord of neurotic behaviors, the analytical couch (his invention) has become a cultural icon. Ditto his theories of repression, sublimation, and projection. His concept of the oral, anal, and genitourinary stages of sexuality spoke to humanity's age-old preoccupations with noshing, pooping, and *schtupping* and how they make everyone act out either with their *schmeckle* or somebody else's. Freud also believed that his own sexual

> "There is too much fathering going on just now and there is no doubt about it fathers are depressing."
> —GERTRUDE STEIN

development hinged on a minor moment from his early childhood in which he peeped at his mama undressing. Then again, he was acting as his own shrink, so vat did he know?

DID JEW KNOW? Of the thirteen members of Freud's elite circle of headshrinkers, Carl Jung was the sole non-Jew. Also, most of the analytical patients were Jewish. Author Jonathan Engel posits that the reason for this demographic was that upper-middle class Jews were the only ones who had the scratch to fund a five-day-a-week couch habit. Also, since Jews are more comfortable discussing bodily functions, they also might have been more apt to blab about their sexual fantasies than their Victorian Gentile counterparts.

A Bunch of Jews Sitting Around Talking and Talking and Talking

Freud was raised in a highly assimilated Reform Jewish home, and he was an atheist who believed that religion was either an "infantile delusion" or attempt to control Oedipal urges. In fact, till the end, he repudiated the idea that analysis was in any way a Jewish science. Rather, psychotherapy started out as a discipline to treat the quintessentially "female" disease of hysteria—a symptom troubling and puzzling even to the Greeks. Freud didn't invent Oedipus and Electra. Or Jews. He just used one to treat the other, thus unintentionally birthing the nervous-breakdown industry otherwise known as psychotherapy and psychopharmacology.

It's All Geek to Me: Einstein and the Theory of Relativity

Even those who don't really know what it means know the equation $E = mc^2$. By the same token, even those who don't fully comprehend Einstein's impact on physics know about his impact on the Jewfro. Indeed, whether or not you can explain his theory of relativity, you probably know that Einstein came up with it and that he received a Nobel Prize for being the original science-fair geek, whose work, like Freud's, was pivotal in analyzing the stuff you can't see that drives the universe.

The *Reader's Digest* version is this: One day, German-born theoretical physicist Albert Einstein decided it was time to bump Newtonian mechanics up a notch, and so he developed Jew-tonian mechanics—a theory that transformed twentieth-century thinking about the things that go bump in the night and ushered in the

---

HE'S NO EINSTEIN! THE FOOLS OF CHELM

In Ashkenazi Jewish folklore, the city of Chelm is Eastern Europe's answer to New Jersey or Kamchatka: an actual place that became the butt of jokes about people who are less than brainiacs and dwell in a town quite unencumbered by culture. Chelm-ily enough, the real Chelm is in the vicinity of Lublin and is actually known for its Torah scholarship, while the fictional version, made famous by the likes of Isaac Bashevis Singer, is known for its Jewish morons, often ironically referred to as the Wise Men of Chelm. Chelm inspired other less than desirable fictional towns of Yid Lit such as Kabtansk (Poorville) and Sholem Aleichem's Glubsk (Idiotville).

A citizen of Chelm once asked his rabbi whether or not the sun was more important than the moon. "What a ridiculous question!" the rabbi replied. "Clearly the moon is more important! It shines at night, when we really need it. Who needs the sun to shine when it is broad daylight?"

---

nuclear era. Let's break it down: When Hitler came to power in Einstein's native Germany, Herr Doctor was visiting the United States, where he wisely decided to stay put. He also helped alert Prez Roosevelt that the United States should jump on the bandwagon in the arms race or risk being blown to smithereens by yet another bunch of Jew haters. This series of chitchats eventually led to what would become the Manhattan Project. Einstein would later write about the danger of atomic weapons and become a vegetarian.

The Womyn's Womb and the Birth of Feministory

As Jewish men were busy erecting throbbing systems that would penetrate the capitalist leviathan, defining hysteria as a side effect of a missing penis and design-ing weapons that promised the most explosive climax this side of Hiroshima, Jewish women began to realize that it was high time the vagina did some penetrat-ing of its own. Problem was, this plan was met with barriers greater than all the dental dams in va-China put together. What's more, Jewish women were getting it from both ends: the plain-old patriarchy and the Jewish patriarchy. And so some smart and serious ladies took Rashi's daughters to the next level, chiseling holes in the great reign of the phallus and testifying about their mistreatment by the stale, male, and pale.

Emma Goldman Never Met a Union She Didn't Like

Born in the Russian Empire, Emma Goldman (1869–1940) immigrated with her parents to Rochester, where life offered the spirit-crushing monotony of factory work and the depressing reality of an impotent husband. After she fled that soul-murdering scenario for New York City, she quickly fell in with a crew of anarchists and became a writer and impassioned orator on workers' rights, women's rights, and the anarchist body politic. During the entirety of her glorious soapbox career, Goldman was imprisoned several times for threatening to topple Papa Patriarchy by distributing info on birth control.

The Mighty Literati

A MATCH-UP QUIZ

A. Marcel Proust

B. Franz Kafka

C. Isaac Bashevis Singer

D. Saul Bellow

E. Primo Levi

F. Elie Wiesel

G. Grace Paley

H. Amos Oz

I. Philip Roth

J. Nadine Gordimer

K. Edna Ferber

L. Ayn Rand

M. Norman Mailer

N. Maurice Sendak

O. Judy Blume

_____ 1. Raised on Warsaw's Krochmalna Street, this Nobel Laureate and son of a Hasidic rebbe wrote novels and short stories that vividly captured the shtetls and cities of Eastern European life. One of these novels would go on to become a movie directed by and starring Barbra Streisand.

_____ 2. Born in Sighet, Romania, this Nobel Laureate, author, professor, and Holocaust survivor is the author of *Night*. Must-reads: *Twilight*—not to be confused with the sexy vampire novels—and *The Forgotten*.

_____ 3. This acclaimed illustrator and children's author de-monsterized monsters and produced the iconic *Where the Wild Things Are*, *In the Night Kitchen*, and *Chicken Soup with Rice*.

_____ 4. Canadian-born American writer who won the Pulitzer Prize, the Nobel Prize for Literature, and three National Book Awards for Fiction. Note: He is the only author to win this award three times! Must-reads: *Mr. Sammler's Planet*, *Herzog*, *The Adventures of Augie March*, and *Humboldt's Gift*.

_____ 5. Born in Newark, New Jersey, this novelist won the National Book Award for Fiction for his breakout novella *Goodbye, Columbus* and then went on to fetishize and sexualize neurosis, anemic shiksas, and liver. Alter ego: Nathan Zuckerman. Id: David Kepesh.

_____ 6. This Pulitzer Prize–winning American novelist and playwright was a member of the Algonquin Round Table. Must-reads: *Show Boat* (made into a musical) and *Giant* (made into a movie starring Rock Hudson, Elizabeth Taylor, and James Dean).

_____ 7. This best-selling author has tackled such hot-button topics as bullying, masturbation, and menstruation in her novels. In one of her all-time best-sellers, the protagonist's boyfriend's penis is named Ralph.

8. Italian Jewish writer and chemist best known for his autobiographical *Se Questo è un Uomo (Survival in Auschwitz)*. Fun fact: Magician David Blaine has this author's concentration camp number, 174517, tattooed on his left forearm.

9. Born in Prague, this author is regarded as one of the twentieth century's most visionary and influential writers of fiction. What's more, his name inspired an adjective that has come to mean complex, detached, and down-right weird. Must-reads: *The Trial, The Castle,* and *The Metamorphosis*.

10. This Bronx-born short-story writer and social activist was among the first American authors to explore the lives of Jewish New Yorkers, whom Margalit Fox calls "the women that Roth and Bellow and Malamud's men had loved and left behind."

11. No upper-middle-class ninth-grader's library is complete without this Russian-born American author/deep supporter of capitalism's two major works: *The Fountainhead* and *Atlas Shrugged*.

12. This Israeli writer's memoir/family history *A Tale of Love and Darkness* is considered one of the ten most important books since the creation of the State of Israel.

13. This South African political activist and Nobel recipient's work grapples with racial issues, especially apartheid in her native land. Must-reads: *July's People, Burger's Daughter,* and *The Conservationist*.

14. This novelist/journalist, New Jersey native, and early innovator of the creative nonfiction genre wrote the following powerful tomes: *The Naked and the Dead, Tough Guys Don't Dance, Executioner's Song, The Deer Park,* and *Harlot's Ghost*. Fun fact: He was married a total of six times.

15. An outspoken activist in favor of Jewish army officer Alfred Dreyfus during the Dreyfus Affair, this French author's cousin was the philosopher Henri Bergson. Magnum opus: *À la Recherche du Temps Perdu*.

ANSWERS

14. M	12. H	10. G	8. E	6. K	2. F
15. A	13. J	11. L	9. B	7. O	5. I	3. N	1. C	4. D

Caught in a Trap: Betty Friedan

Yet another great left-wing Jewish intellectual, Betty Friedan (1921–2006) did for North American housewives what Freud did for penises: She made them stand up and come to the head of the class. Her 1963 best-seller *The Feminine Mystique* spoke to the trapped, isolated "is that all there is" feeling shared by many suburban American housewives and sparked "second-wave" feminism. Friedan also founded and was first president of the National Organization for Women.

Kickin' It to Jew Old Skool: Gloria Steinem

Gloria Steinem (1934–) is one of the foremothers of the women's liberation movement, a staunch defender of reproductive rights for women, and the cofounder of *Ms.* magazine. Her 1969 article "After Black Power, Women's Liberation," written for a then-fledgling *New York* magazine, gave Steinem insta-celebrity as a member of the vagina vanguard. Her beef: It wasn't so much that women wanted work, which they did, it was also how they were being treated as second-class citizens in the workplace. Fun fact: Steinem, who once said "a woman needs a man like a fish needs a bicycle," was actor Christian Bale's stepmother. He doesn't like her either.

> "Once upon a time— say, ten or even five years ago—a Liberated Woman was somebody who had sex before marriage and a job afterward."
>
> –GLORIA STEINEM

Tootie Faludi

Susan Faludi's 1991 book *Backlash: The Undeclared War Against American Women* argues that the 1980s saw an outbreak of negative stereotypes against women in the workplace. Her 1999 follow-up *Stiffed: The Betrayal of the American Man* asserts that as much as it sucks to be a woman, it sucks to be a guy, too, mostly because individuals have no power and everyone's working for the man, even people with genitals on the outside of their bodies. So at least sisterfriend is balanced.

THE GOLEM: JEWISH FRANKENSTEIN, PROTO SUPERMAN OR PROTO HULK? JEW DECIDE!

In Jewish folklore, a golem is an anthropomorphic being made from clay that is then animated by the word *God* or the word of God. One version of the legend recounts how Rabbi Loew of Prague created a golem to defend the Prague ghetto from ceaseless pogroms. After gathering clay from the banks of a river, he fashioned a giant being and animated it by carving the Hebrew word *emet*, meaning "truth," on the golem's forehead.

DID JEW KNOW? Mild-mannered Jews came up with Superman, Batman, Spider-Man, Captain America, Green Lantern, The Fantastic Four, the Hulk, and the Justice League.

Dworkin It!

Andrea Dworkin was a hardcore rad femme whose whole anti-schtick schtick found voice in her crusade against pornography as a form of rape, particularly in her books *Pornography: Men Possessing Women* and *Intercourse*.

A Wolf in Sheep's Clothing

Naomi Wolf's 1991 best-seller *The Beauty Myth* argued that, like everything else, beauty is a social construct that Papa Patriarchy rides hard and fast so that he can continue to be Big Papa Patriarchy. In other words, the reason Jew go to Zumba and get mani/pedis and wrinkle fillers is to pump up the man-machine so that it can get bigger and stronger while you wither away from an eating disorder.

The People of the (Comic) Book: How Jews Invented the Superhero

Jews created practically every comic-book superhero but Wonder Woman (alas). Indeed, Michael Chabon chronicles the vast Jewish contribution to this very world of Jewish American mythology in his Pulitzer Prize–winning novel *The Amazing Adventures of Kavalier & Clay*, the protagonists of which are loosely based on the cocreators of Superman. The themes, storylines, and unconscious longings of these comic-book storylines are also innately Jewish and frequently lifted from the pages of Jewish history and the Tanakh.

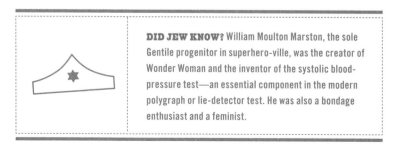

DID JEW KNOW? William Moulton Marston, the sole Gentile progenitor in superhero-ville, was the creator of Wonder Woman and the inventor of the systolic blood-pressure test—an essential component in the modern polygraph or lie-detector test. He was also a bondage enthusiast and a feminist.

Super Jews

Superhero(es)	Creators	Era
Superman	Jerry Siegel and Joe Shuster	Late 1930s
Captain America	Joe Simon and Jack Kirby	1940s
Spider-Man	Stan Lee (born Stanley Martin Lieber), first drawn by Jack Kirby	1960s
Hulk	Stan Lee, first drawn by Jack Kirby	1960s
X-Men	Stan Lee	1960s

Jewish Elements

Like Moses, Superman was cast out as an orphan and then taken in and raised in a foreign environment in which he was always the noble, long-suffering outsider. The destruction of Krytpon is an allegory for Israel, and his exile is the Jewish exile. Finally, Superman's story mirrors the Jewish immigrant experience—he has left the old world behind to come to the new world where he assumes a thoroughly American identity to which he never fully adjusts because he can never really reveal himself. His powers represent a Jewish nerd's wish fulfillment to go from a glasses-wearing, mild-mannered reporter to a man in tights with a six-pack who kicks Nazi ass.

The original cover showed the eponymous hero punching Hitler in the face. Captain America's origin was not some far-away planet but Manhattan's Lower East Side, locus of the nation's most recent emigrants and home of Captain A's alter ego, Steve Rogers, a sickly orphan. Captain A's nemesis murders his elderly Jewish adoptive parents, is taken under the wing of Hitler himself, and becomes the Red Skull. While Captain America had Jewish roots, he was still a blond-haired, blue-eyed uber-mensch, representing both authors' desire for assimilation in a nation that favored Biff McJogsalot over any Jew.

Spider-Man/Peter Parker follows the Jewish paradigm of a smart, bespectacled nebbish by day who is transformed into an all-powerful superhero by night. Stan Lee himself has drawn comparisons between Spidey and the handsome biblical King David, whose life is saved by a spider's web, a creature whose purpose the great king had famously doubted.

Robert Bruce Banner is a nuclear physicist who becomes a green muscle-head when his angry inner child is let loose. The Hulk is, essentially, the golem with a graduate-level education. Or rather, he is the embodiment of the Talmudic concept of *yetzer hara*, mankind's inclination toward selfishness, and *yetzer hatov*, the inclination toward all that is good. The Hulk is an outward expression of unconscious rage to the max, a greener version of the biblical Samson with an award-winning anger-management problem.

The X-Men are all mutants (read: Jews), shunned and feared by society for being different, forever wandering the earth. This is a running theme in all of Stan Lee's work. More striking, however, is the story of Magneto, an Auschwitz survivor who stayed alive by working as a member of the *Sonderkommando* for the Nazis, helping them kill countless other Jews. Rather than turning him into a crime fighter like Spider-Man, his unresolved guilt has left him a complex villain, committed to exacting vengeance instead of justice.

Let Me Tell You Somethink: Jewish Advice Columnists

While advice-giving might seem a specialty of your neighborhood yenta, it's actually a booming Jewish business that predates Emily Post. From Dear Abby to Ann Landers to Miss Manners, Jewish advice columns have been at the forefront of a movement that attracts a vast readership while it cranks out a social history of daily life rich enough to be called Jewish but lower in calories.

> **Dear Abby: My** boyfriend is going to be **20 years old next month.**
> I'd like to give him something nice for his birthday.
> What do you think he'd like? — Carol
>
> **Dear Carol: Never** mind what he'd like, give him a tie.

In 1906, the Yiddish paper *The Forward* started a column called "A Bintel Brief," Yiddish for "A Bundle of Letters." This column served as a cultural guide for newly arrived immigrants trying to navigate the values and customs of the New World. The topics ranged from intermarriage to landlord disputes, questions that the immigrants might once have taken to their rabbi back in the shtetl, but now found addressed to a more secular consigliere.

And then, in 1918 and on the Fourth of July no less, twin sisters whose names would forever be synonymous with advice were born in remote (and Gentile) Sioux City, Iowa. Their names were Esther "Eppie" Pauline Friedman and Pauline "Popo" Esther Friedman. Though Eppie and Popo would be well into their thirties before they entered the professional side of the advice-giving business, they took to the task like a Jew to creamed herring, garnering combined readerships in the multiple millions.

In 1955, Eppie won a contest to replace the original author of "Ask Ann Landers," a column in the *Chicago Sun-Times.* By 1993, she was the world's most widely syndicated columnist. In 1956, Popo took off on her own with her volcanically popular column "Dear Abby," a move that led to some bad blood between the sisters. "Dear Abby" is now written by Pauline's daughter Jeanne, who continues to dish out advice on matters of etiquette and the heart. Meanwhile, Eppie's daughter Margo writes the advice column "Dear Prudence." I know. I'm kvelling.

Shopping and *Schtupping*: Jacqueline Susann and the Invention of the Beach Read

If there's one thing a Jewish girl knows, it's that shopping and *schtupping* are the shpice of life. And no one was more familiar with this truism than Jacqueline Susann, the authoress who created the genre of trashy best-seller and knew from buzz. Here's her story: After Jacqueline moved to New York City, she had affairs with the likes of Eddie Cantor and Joe E. Lewis but wised up and married press agent Irving Mansfield, né Mandelbaum.

After Mansfield managed to get her name in news columns, Susann realized the power of exposure and used it to turn her second novel, *Valley of the Dolls*, into a runaway best-seller. *V of the D*, as it is lovingly called by its biggest fans, is a vivid soap opera with larger-than-life characters loosely based on Judy Garland and Ethel Merman. While Susann's writing style was, shall we say, less than literary, she had an unparalleled understanding of how to draw readers in and keep 'em there: melodrama and tacky rich people doing tacky things in tacky places. Novelist Gore Vidal once unkindly (but with perhaps a hint of jealousy) said of Susann's writing style, "She doesn't write, she types!"

Where Susann really made a name for herself, however, was her relentless book touring. Apparently, she and Mansfield shamelessly drove from shop to shop, giving readings and signing books so that stores wouldn't be able to return any unsold copies to the publisher. She also sent thank-you notes to almost every fan who sent her a letter or came to hear her read. Soon, *Valley of the Dolls* was a both a phenomenon *and* a genre: the guilty-pleasure trashy best-seller featuring beautiful women, hot hunks, and sex scenes so steamy they would curl the hair on Yul Brynner's head. She followed up *V of the D* with *The Love Machine* and *Once Is Not Enough.*

High-wattage Jewesses who have continued Susann's legacy of tasty yet tasteless tomfoolery include Judith Krantz, who basically invented the TV miniseries and cobranding with her book-to-small-screen combo specials such as *Scruples* and *Princess Daisy,* and Danielle Steel, whose novels are too numerous to cite—every one of them is a best-seller—and which follow the formula of rich families facing dark forces such as blackmail, suicide, or fraud.

The Write Stuff

Whether or not the People of the Book invented the actual alphabet (the Phoenicians did that) or the first actual bound book (the Romans did that), they did invent the trashy best-seller, Nathan Zuckerman, and Superman. They also wrote the scrolls that made the Western world stand up, face the Eastern wall, and get their pray on. What's more, no matter who wrote what when, not even Judaism's greatest detractors can deny that the Jews have been deeply involved with the written word since Moses first brought his mighty pen to papyrus. In fact, the Jew and his book's enduring and symbiotic relationship fits the classic paradigm for codependency: The Jew is fixated on the book for sustenance, and the book needs the Jew to remain psychologically dependent. That said, they're both still a match for the ages: They have the same values and belief systems. They finish each other's sentences. Indeed, who else but the People of the Book would buy a book about the People of the Book's books?

CHAPTER 9

BAD FOR THE JEWS:
Schnooks, Crooks, and the Son of Sam

Thou shall not kill. Thou shall not commit adultery. Thou shall not steal. Thou shall not bear false witness against your neighbor. Thou shall not covet your neighbor's house. Thou shall not covet your neighbor's wife, his manservant, his maid servant, his ox, his donkey, or anything that belongs to your neighbor.

EXODUS 20:13–14

In case you thought the Gentiles had the market cornered on illegal activity outside white-collar crime, think again. Let's face it: Much as the Chosen Tribe is a relatively temperate one—fewer barroom brawlers, murderers, gamblers, and pimps per yarmulke—there do exist amongst its holy ranks more than a handful of Jewish no-goodniks who would give the likes of Tony Soprano a run for his shekels.

Bernie Madoff aside, there's a certain secret pride among the home team regarding the nefarious Yids who put the crook in crooked, the hell in hellacious, and even the ew in Jewish. The Hebrew Bible devotes its fair share of sacred parchment to Hebrew and Shebrew transgressors, and not just those whom YHWH had the foresight to wash away in the flood. (If only it had been Michael Bolton!) Whether running booze, passing atomic info to the Soviets, or getting caught red-handed with a hand in the play-for-pay cookie jar, there are some righteously unrighteous Jews who make good look boring and give being bad a good name.

Jews and . . . Booze?

Purim and Pesach aside, the Israelites are for the most part a sober people, more likely to snack than imbibe. (Exam question: Compare and contrast sitting shivah and a wake.) That said, when Prohibition (1920–1933) rendered the United States drier than a Mormon prom, the production and distribution of alcoholic beverages immediately went immigrant and underground, falling right into the capable mitts of none other than the mob, who, as luck would have it, were then heavily Jewish. In fact, according to historian Howard Sachar, in 1921, 100 percent of the bootleggers in New York City were Jewish. These savvy Jewish street-toughs used the skills of catch-as-catch-can to parlay their black-market booze into gelt and make a mint on the dark side.

Funnily enough, the law allowed Jewish households a wondrous 10 galllons (38 litres) of kosher wine per annum on the grounds that anything else was an

DID JEW KNOW? The going hypotheses for why there are generally fewer criminals amongst the kosher set include insular and tightly knit communities, high educational standards, and (allegedly) more moderate consumption of alcohol. Add to this the fact that the Jews have their own intra-*eruv* legal system that has been painstakingly set forth in such tomes as the Torah, the Mishnah, the Talmud, and the Shulchan Aruch. So, while the Hebrew Bible might often read like a penny dreadful, it's pretty darn clear on how a Heeb should eat, live, and worship, and clearer still on how a Heeb should *not*! Those rules are then enforced by the Jewish legal system: both the rabbinate and the various related groups of judges (see chapter 5).

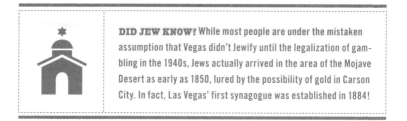
infringement on religious freedom. Thanks, God! That said, unlike the Catholic Church, which was afforded a similar dispensation, the rabbinate got a little more, let's say, loosey-goosey with what exactly constituted ritual vino. In fact, more than a few rabbis were arrested for doling out ersatz sacramental hooch—i.e., brandy, champagne, and vermouth—on the sly.

Meantime, in case the rebbe wasn't wetting enough whistles, various hard-working underworld types stepped in, most notably:

- **The Purple Gang:** a predominantly Jewish bunch of bootleggers, hijackers, and murderers who ran their operations out of Detroit in the 1920s. Michigan had banned booze even earlier, in 1916, necessitating immediate black-market smuggling of booze from Canada, thus making the Wolverine State the perfect hub.

- **Sam Bronfman:** the head honcho of a giant smuggling empire between Canada and the United States who bought Seagram's distillery and made a bundle selling the hair of the dog. In fact, Bronfman schlepped his product across Lake Erie so many times that it became known as "Jewish Lake." When Prohibition ended in 1933, Bronfman paid a fine, bought out New Jersey's biggest bootleggers, Joseph Reinfeld and Abner Zwillman of Newark, and went square and legit.

JEWISH ENFORCERS OF PROHIBITION

While the news of the Prohibition era was rife with stories of Jewish involvement in the sale and distribution of alcohol, causing lots of teeth-gnashing among teetotaling Jews, two federal party poopers named Izzy Einstein (1880–1938) and Moe Smith (1887–1961), both Jews, took it on themselves to shut down illegal speakeasies and arrest bootleggers like it was going out of style. This dynamic duo made a total of 4,932 arrests and confiscated about five million gallons (nineteen million litres) of booze between 1920 and 1925.

La Kosha Nostra: The Jewish Mafia
(and I Don't Mean the Weinstein Bros.)

Jewish gangsters played a quintessential role in shaping organized crime in the United States during the 1920s and 1930s. Yet again, a gang of scrappy, visionary Jews seized the opportunity to build a fledgling, unregulated empire with the signature aplomb of God's chosen. Only this time, rather than biblical patriarchs looking for a homeland or first-generation Jews looking to start their own country club, the gang was a bunch of second-

> "My mother was actually part of the Jewish mafia. But now she's in the witness overprotection program."
> —ROBERT CAIT

generation Jews clawing their way out of the ghettos of New York's Lower East Side as well as Brownsville, Brooklyn, Maxwell Street in Chicago, and Boyle Heights, Los Angeles.

BENJAMIN "BUGSY" SIEGEL (1906–1947): the prototypical gangster's gangster whose movie-star looks and natty style of dress made the perfect foil for his charismatic yet ruthless sociopathy. Bugsy's considerable charm also made him a surefire hit amongst the swishy Hollywood set, some of whose unions he had been running since the 1930s. Though he wasn't Nevada's first mobster—Capone had actually been absentee-running a casino in Reno since the 1920s—Siegel conceived and opened the lavish Flamingo Club in Las Vegas, a Pollyanna-ish if risky endeavor for which many now consider him the father of the corporate-owned theme park that is Vegas today.

Though his handsome *punim* served to belie his ruthless side, Siegel also did a fair amount of his own dirty work; he was both a hit man and a member of the notorious Murder, Inc., a coffee-klatch crime syndicate that took out the who's who of underworld dealers and squealers (see page 208). Some of Bugsy's big-name assassinations included Abraham "Bo" Weinberg (mob boss Dutch Schultz's former aide-de-camp) and Sicilian mega-boss Joe Masseria. Siegel was gunned down in Virginia Hill's Beverly Hills home in 1947.

For these mostly poor and uneducated Jews, America was a conundrum that simultaneously offered limitless promise while excluding them from the various fancy-schmancy "white shoe" legit professions. And so, rather than building a world for themselves where they might live the American dream on the up-and-up, this group of thugs, toughs, and sociopaths decided it was high time to exploit lucrative illegal markets, such as bootlegging, gambling, prostitution, and selling narcotics. Like their brethren in Hollywood, these Jewish gangsters created a world where a Yid might hobnob with the cream of the celebrity crop, even if they had to irrigate the desert or kill to do it.

MEYER LANSKY (1902–1983): Though Siegel basically had all kinds of dirty business with the top dogs of organized crime, including Lepke Buchalter and Lucky Luciano, the Frick to his Frack was famed gangster and mob brain Meyer Lansky. Known as "the Mob's Accountant," Lansky managed Mafia funds and ran their highly effective extortion department. His considerable mathletic gifts also helped him juggle various successful numbers rackets as well as control a gambling empire that stretched from Saratoga to Havana and from New York to Las Vegas.

Speaking of Vegas, Lansky was instrumental in convincing the mob to bankroll the Pink Flamingo Hotel, the high-rolling if money-hemorrhaging venture that possibly cost pal Siegel his eyeball and his life. In fact, rumor has it that Lansky at first tried to dissuade the mob from taking out a hit on his BFF but then ultimately agreed with the decision. *Nu*, what's a gangster to do? Lansky died of lung cancer in 1983.

GANSTER Trading Cards!

LEPKE BUCHALTER (1897–1944): One of eleven children, Lepke Buchalter was among the most notorious mobsters to grace the teeming tenements of New York's Lower East Side. In and out of the joint for various larceny charges in his twenties, Lepke commanded a veritable army of gangsters, extortionists, and hit men. He also developed a system of "protection" in which he strong-armed workers to protect the interests of manufacturers and created rival unions to maintain control of the work force and make a buck or six doing it.

Meantime, he also ran legitimate businesses in much the same way he controlled the unions. Those who tried to resist found themselves at the wrong end of an acid bath. When the manufacturer at last cried uncle, Lepke would install his men in the factory to protect his investment. By the early '30s, he was in charge of many industries in New York, including garment workers, motion-picture operators, the shoe trade, bakery drivers, and fur truckers, making him the "feudal lord of New York's underworld."

In 1941, Lepke was finally indicted for the murder of Joseph Rosen, a garment trucker. Fun fact: He was the sole organized-crime celeb of his era to be executed for murder. He died in the electric chair at Sing Sing Correctional Facility in 1944.

ARNOLD ROTHSTEIN (1882–1928): A refined boychik from an affluent family—his brother was a rabbi!— Arnold Rothstein was referred to as "the Brain." He was known as one of the patriarchs of organized crime, not to mention the inventor of the floating craps game. His million-dollar empire began with gambling parlors and racetracks, included a bootlegging stint, and ended with Rothstein as "financial overlord" of the narcotics trade.

The feather in Rothstein's criminal *kippah*, however, was his scheme to fix the World Series of 1919, also known as "the Black Sox Scandal." In 1921, eight players were banned for life from organized baseball. Since Rothstein had never actually met any of the players, he was acquitted and "exonerated" of wrongdoing. He died of a gunshot wound in 1928, possibly in a Schultz-ordered hit. When police asked Rothstein on his deathbed who shot him, he famously retorted, "You stick to your trade. I'll stick to mine."

DUTCH SCHULTZ (1902–1935): Born Arthur Flegenheimer, Schultz began his criminal career in the Bronx. He served seventeen months in prison for a B&E—his only jail time. After he was released, his crew began calling him "Dutch Schultz." He ran booze for Arnold Rothstein, later establishing his own bootlegging business to New York speakeasies.

He went to war with notorious Irish gangsters Legs Diamond and Mad Dog Coll, both of whom his henchmen gunned down. After Prohibition ended, Schultz moved into the Harlem numbers racket, extorting money and fixing odds at racetracks.

In 1933, U.S. attorney Thomas Dewey set his sights on Schultz, indicting him for tax evasion. Schultz was tried twice; once in New York City, where his lawyers convinced the judges that Schultz couldn't get a fair trial, and again in the small upstate town of Malone, where Schultz buttered up the locals and was ultimately acquitted of all charges.

Schultz then approached the Syndicate to have Dewey assassinated. The request was denied, but fearing Schultz would take matters into his own hands, the Syndicate ordered Schulz's execution, placing the onus on Murder, Inc.'s capo Lepke Buchalter to carry it out. At 10:15 PM on October 3, 1935, Charlie "the Bug" Workman and Mendy Weiss gunned down Schultz and his associates at the Palace Chop House in Newark, New Jersey.

Murder, He Wrote

In 1934, Louis "Lepke" Buchalter was instrumental in creating and organizing the Syndicate, a united coalition of Italian and Jewish crime bosses from New York. The brilliant (and fundamentally Jewish) idea behind the Syndicate was that each boss would have his own territory but would regularly convene with a board of directors to dictate policy and solve disputes. (Think alternate-universe Twelve Tribes of Israel packin' heat and sans Hashem.) Some of the Syndicate's earliest board of directors included Gambino capo Albert "the Mad Hatter" Anastasia (dubbed "Lord High Executioner"), Frank Costello, Lucky Luciano, Johnny Torrio, Dutch Schultz, Abner Zwillman, and Bugsy Siegel.

The Syndicate protected its interests by establishing a "crack corps of killers" to serve as their on-call enforcement and execution squad. Dubbed Murder, Inc. by the press, this section of the Syndicate's charter was based out of Midnight Roses, a humble twenty-four-hour candy store in Brownsville, Brooklyn, that served as the war room for the bulk of the era's approximately 1,000 contract slayings. Some of the Jewish members of Murder, Inc. included Harry "Pittsburg Phil" Strauss, Allie "Tick-Tock" Tannenbaum, and Seymour "Blue Jaw" Magoon. Eventually turncoat Abe "Kid Twist" Reles revealed the Murder, Inc. roster to the Feds, who then executed many of its members. Reles was later flung from a hotel window.

A NEW KINDA CANAAN

In the 1940s, a gang of Jewish racketeers followed Siegel to the Nevada desert. (Canaan). There they sacrificed, toiled, and spent vast amounts of the mob's cabbage to turn a stretch of sand into the Promised Land redux. Bugsy was Vegas's answer to Uncle Abe; he even had his own shiksa version of Sarah: actress Virginia Hill.

Your Mitzvah or Your Life!

While there is no doubt that the members of the Kosher Nostra were bad guys, their deeds weren't always dastardly. A few were highly supportive of world Jewry. Others, it should be noted, alchemized their blood money into *tzedakah*, or charity. Many gangsters funded synagogues and Jewish day schools. For instance, the day school at Temple Ner Tamid in Las Vegas was named for bootlegger, casino owner, and gangster Moe Dalitz.

According to historian Robert Rockaway, when New York state judge Nathan Perlman wanted to put the unofficial kibosh on some German American Bund rallies, he contacted Meyer Lansky and asked him to "disrupt." Subsequently Lansky and some guys from his Jew posse broke up Brown Shirt gatherings all over town, cracking skulls and defenestrating their fair share of vociferous Hitler-ites. To quote Lansky, "I was a Jew and felt for those Jews in Europe who were suffering. They were my brothers."

In 1945, Haganah emissary Reuven Dafne approached none other than Bugsy Siegel seeking funds to help free what was then Palestine from the Brits. Bugsy was moved by the idea of Jews fighting. Next thing you know, suitcases containing five- and ten-dollar bills began arriving at Dafne's doorstep, some $50,000 all told, all from that nice boychik Benjamin Siegel!

Public Frenemy: Jews and Political Assassination

While nothing excites a mobster more than breaking laws and skulls to roll his dough into a healthy piece of American pie, some Yids break the sixth commandment for political reasons and then skip dessert. For this special brand of assassin, the cause takes precedence over the punishment, despite Judaism's three cardinal no-no's: murder (especially premeditated), adultery, and idolatry.

Yigal Amir

A schlepper on a mission, Yigal Amir became a cause célèbre for assassinating Israeli prime minister Yitzhak Rabin. A born-and-raised Ortho, Amir attended religious schools and then a *hesder* yeshiva—a yeshiva that combines Talmud study with military training—before serving in the Israeli Defense Forces. While attending Tel Aviv University, Amir became especially vociferous in his vehement disregard for the 1993 Oslo Accords, a treaty that Rabin had signed with Palestinian leader and terrorist extraordinaire Yasser Arafat. During this time, Amir revealed to a friend his plan to kill the prime minister.

On November 4, 1995, both Rabin and President Shimon Peres were in attendance at a rally in support of a peaceful accord with the Palestinians. As Rabin made his way to his limo, Amir shot him twice with a semiautomatic pistol. Rabin died of blood loss at a nearby hospital. Amir was swiftly apprehended and sentenced to life imprisonment.

Jack Ruby

A Dallas nightclub owner with possible ties to the mob, Jack Ruby (born Jacob Leon Rubenstein) shot Lee Harvey Oswald, the alleged assassin of John F. Kennedy, on November 24, 1963. Oswald was being moved from Dallas police headquarters to county jail, and a crowd of press had assembled to film his departure. Suddenly, Ruby emerged from the crowd and shot Oswald in the abdomen, fatally wounding him on live television. As police nabbed Ruby and wrestled him to the ground, he shouted the now infamous, "You all know me. I'm Jack Ruby."

In March of 1964, Ruby was convicted and sentenced to death by the electric chair. He appealed the conviction and death sentence and died of a pulmonary embolism from lung cancer before his new trial date was set.

Kosher Killers

We also have bad Jews who are worse for the Jews, especially those they encounter on a cold, dark night after talking to the neighbor's dog or reading too much Nietzsche. Beyond their chilling and gruesome narratives, the best that can be said about these seriously psycho-Heebs is, thank God there aren't more of them! Who knew Jews could be so unorthodox? Answer: Hitchcock and Spike Lee!

The *Shanda* of the Century: Leopold and Loeb

Nathan Leopold and Richard "Dickie" Loeb were teens from an exclusive Jewish neighborhood in Chicago when they committed what would be the crime of the century: the premeditated murder of their neighbor (and Loeb's cousin), fourteen-year-old Bobby Franks. Through no uncertain miracle, and a famous goyishe lawyer's gift of gab, they were subsequently sentenced to life imprisonment rather than the death penalty.

A summary: Dickie Loeb, a charming looker with a penchant for detective novels, had graduated from the University of Michigan and was planning to start law school at the University of Chicago in the fall. Nathan Leopold, his neighbor and erstwhile love, was already a law student. While Loeb was smitten-kitten with the notion of the perfect crime, Leopold was obsessed with his Dickie as well as with Frederick Nietzsche's concept of the "Superman," the idea of a superior man whose supreme values and brilliance could save the human race. Put both boys together and you have a pair of Jewish prodigies bent on hatching the perfect crime as committed by the perfect man.

On May 21, 1924, after planning the murder for seven or so months, Leopold and Loeb lured Bobby Franks into their car, where they stabbed him to death with a chisel. Next, they poured hydrochloric acid on his body, stuffed it in a culvert, and sent a $10,000 ransom note to Franks' parents for the return of the body. Alas for the less-than-dynamic duo, the body was discovered before the Franks could pay the ransom. Additionally, Nathan "Four Eyes" Leopold had left his eyeglasses at the scene, glasses that had a particular hinge mechanism that was easily traced to a Chicago optometrist.

Being Jews, Leopold and Loeb's progenitors hired Clarence Darrow, the best criminal attorney that money could buy and a staunch opponent of the death penalty. Darrow (and the boys' families) knew that both boys were going to be convicted for the capital charges of murder and kidnapping; his goal was to keep them alive. While the expectation was that Leopold and Loeb would plead not guilty by reason of insanity, Darrow advised them to plead guilty so that they might avoid a trial by jury, which was likely to result in the death penalty. Darrow's closing argument served as the brilliant tipping point in his already brilliant uberplan; he admitted the guilt of his clients but blamed nature and Nietzsche—and the uberjudge bought it. The boys were sentenced to life in prison.

On January 28, 1936, a fellow inmate at Stateville Correctional Center attacked Loeb with a straight razor. Loeb later died from the wounds. Leopold was released on parole in 1958. He died of a heart attack in 1971.

The Hair of the Dog: David Berkowitz and the Summer of Shmuel

David Richard Berkowitz (born David Richard Falco) is a Jewish American serial killer also known as the Son of Sam. Arrested in the summer of 1977 following a yearlong shooting spree in which he killed six people (five of whom were young women) and wounded seven, Berkowitz became famous for the apocalyptic and deranged letters he sent to the media and police. These letters chronicled his intention to keep up the bad work and taunted police for not being able to stop him. The most infamous letter was sent to then–*Daily News* columnist Jimmy Breslin.

By the time Berkowitz was arrested—based on a tip and a parking ticket, no less—a huge team of 200 New York City detectives had been amassed in the manhunt for the killer bent on terrorizing Gotham. Berkowitz confessed to all the killings and then claimed that he had been commanded to do so by a demon that had apparently possessed his neighbor's black Labrador retriever. He pleaded guilty at his 1978 trial and is now serving the remainder of his 300-plus-year sentence at Sullivan Correctional Facility in upstate New York.

In 1987, Berkowitz became a born-again Christian. (Their loss.) Since this miraculous conversion, his moniker has switched from Son of Sam to Son of Hope. He continues to be denied parole.

Commies, Pinkos, and Spies, Oh My!

While the Red Scare in the United States would eventually become what some call "Cold War Hysteria" and what others call a clear-eyed view of Stalin's reign of terror, one fact remains: Jews have been among the most ardent supporters of socialism, if not its very inventors.

Julius and Ethel Rosenberg and the Cold, Cold War

Julius Rosenberg (1918–1953) and his little missus Ethel Greenglass Rosenberg (1915–1953) were the first and only U.S. civilians executed for espionage. They met at a meeting for the Young Communist League in 1936, married three years later, and had two sons. In 1942, they became full members of the American Communist Party but dropped out a year later so Julius could devote himself fully to his espionage activities for the KGB predecessor known as the NKVD.

DID JEW KNOW? BAD JEWS = GREAT MOVIES!			
BAD JEW(S)	**MOVIE**	**DIRECTOR**	**STARRING**
Leopold and Loeb	*Rope*	Alfred Hitchcock	Jimmy Stewart, Farley Granger
	Compulsion	Richard Fleischer	Orson Welles, Dean Stockwell, Diane Varsi
Jack Ruby	*Ruby*	John Mackenzie	Danny Aiello, Sherilyn Fenn

Said activities included providing thousands of top-secret documents from the National Advisory Committee for Aeronautics that contained information on various atomic weapons, specifically info from the Manhattan Project at Los Alamos, where Rosenberg's brother-in-law, David Greenglass, was employed as a machinist. Turns out, a number of Manhattan Project members, including Greenglass, were also diehard commies who were handing over secret info to the Soviets so that the red, white, and blue wouldn't have a monopoly on atomic weapons. On June 17, 1950, Julius Rosenberg was arrested for espionage after his brother-in-law named him and a handful of others as having stolen sensitive documents and fed them to the Soviet succubus.

The Rosenberg trial began in March of '51 and immediately polarized the country, mostly regarding Ethel's level of involvement. According to her brother, she had typed notes for her husband containing sensitive nuclear information, notes that then wended their way, via mostly Jewish couriers, into Soviet hands. While all the other spies started flapping their yaps and naming names, the Rosenbergs pled the Fifth about their involvement in the Communist Party. The biggest yap flapper was David Greenglass, who confessed to having handed over secret info about atomic weapons to the USSR, implicated his sister, and claimed that she herself had recruited Greenglass for her husband.

On March 29, 1951, Judge Irving Kaufman (Jew) convicted the Rosenbergs and summarily sentenced them to death, a decision that orphaned their two young sons. While some believe that such a stringent conviction served to ignite mass hysteria and paranoia about the Cold War, including the passionate efforts of Senator Joseph McCarthy, others believed the sentence was completely warranted, especially Judge Kaufman, who was quoted as saying that the Rosenbergs were responsible for as many as 50,000 deaths caused by the Korean War.

The Rosenbergs were executed on Friday, June 19, 1953. After their deaths, it was discovered that the documents Ethel Rosenberg had typed were of questionable value to the Soviet cause. Additionally, Ethel's brother had sold his sister up the river to reduce his own sentence and protect his family. The topic of the Rosenbergs remains controversial to this day.

Fanya Kaplan: Hit Me With Your Best Shot

Born in Ukraine, Fanya Kaplan was a political revolutionary who was arrested in 1906 after the accidental explosion of a bomb she carried killed a maid in her hotel. Sentenced to a life of forced labor at sixteen, she did time at a few Siberian gulags until she was released during the February Revolution of 1917. During this time, conflicts arose among the various parties, including Lenin's Bolsheviks. Since Kaplan was an anarchist to the nth degree, she decided that Lenin's Bolshevism was too namby-pamby and that the time was nigh to assassinate him.

On August 30, 1918, Lenin was set to deliver a speech at a factory in Moscow. As he departed the main building, Kaplan shot Lenin several times, hitting him in his left shoulder and jaw. She was taken into custody, where she was interrogated by Soviet security. This was her statement: "My name is Fanya Kaplan. Today I shot at Lenin. I did it on my own. I will not say from whom I obtained my revolver. I will give no details. I had resolved to kill Lenin long ago. I consider him a traitor to the revolution."

When it became clear that Kaplan wasn't about to implicate her accomplices, she was shot to death. Some historians do not believe Kaplan was the actual shooter, mostly because she had lost most of her eyesight when she was in the gulag, and that she took the hit for the good of the revolution. Regardless of who pulled the actual trigger, Lenin's assassination attempt kicked off the Red Terror.

Greed Is Good: White-Collar Crime

Forget usury. It's so 1400s. Not to mention the beginning of the negative association of Jews with money and quite possibly the origin of the stereotype of the greedy Jew. Instead, fast-forward about 500-plus years to ye olde boom-era 1980s, when the time was ripe for a shady Jew to make a bushel of beans beating a wholly holey system from the inside out. In fact, much in the same way that bootlegging was the perfect career for your average tenement dweller willing to take a risk, insider trading provided the white-collar world a chance to bet bigger, win bigger, and lose more money than Jew could shake a *lulav* at.

Big Brother Is Watching Jew: Ivan Boesky and Michael Milken

Ivan Boesky is the Wall Street stock trader and arbitrageur who played a key role, if not *the* role, in an insider-trading scandal that rocked Wall Street in the mid-1980s. Like any man who wins big, Boesky also fell big, taking down a number of high rollers and, for better or for worse, changing the Exchange forever.

When our story opens, Boesky had already reaped big-time profits (two hundred million dollars, give or take a mill) from arbitrage trading of various company stocks that were soon to be acquired, which is to say that Boesky purchased the stock before the deal went public and the stock price skyrocketed. Now, this move is actually legal, providing that the information is public. For

DID JEW KNOW? The character of Gordon Gekko in the 1987 flick *Wall Street* is somewhat based on Boesky, especially Gekko's iconic "Greed, for lack of a better word, is good" monologue, which derives from a speech Boesky delivered at a commencement ceremony at the University of California, Berkeley, Haas School of Business in 1985, in which he actually said, "I think greed is healthy. You can be greedy and still feel good about yourself." Well, it *was* the '80s . . .

Boesky, "public" had a slightly looser definition that also encompassed exclusive tips from corporate insiders, but let's not quibble. It was the '80s, and laws prohibiting insider trading were still pretty lax, or at least they would be until Boesky made one brazen purchase too many and the Feds slowed his roll.

Meanwhile, over at Drexel Burnham Lambert, a Wall Street investment firm that went belly up in 1990, a bad-for-the-Jews Jew named Michael Milken was underwriting debt for leveraged buyouts with mega-high yields. In case you don't speak Yiddish, that means he was turning one man's junk into another man's gold and raking in the cash doing it. Through Milken and Drexel, Boesky started raising debt capital in the hundreds of millions, which he then used to make arbitrage trades. In other words, Milken helped Boesky get even richer!

Meanwhile, Uncle Sam was dying to slam some rules and regulations on the whole white-collar scene, mostly because it had gotten completely out of hand and Uncle Sam can only turn a blind eye to so much before he puts on the smackdown. The Feds knew that if they could just get Milken and Drexel, then the junk-bond market would go under and the mean, green leveraged buyout era would bite the proverbial dust. In 1986, the Feds clocked Dennis Levine, a managing director at Drexel, distributing inside information. Next they caught Boesky buying inside information from Dennis Levine. Oops. To save his own *tuchus*, Boesky cut a deal with the Feds to start wearing a wire and toppled the whole insider trading bizz, including Milken, who may or may not have been unfairly implicated in the whole mess.

Boesky paid $100 million in fines, was sentenced to three years in prison, and was released after twenty-two months. Milken was fined $200 million plus another $400 mill in an SEC settlement and $500 mill in a civil lawsuit with Drexel, plus sentenced to ten years in prison. He was released after less than two years. The Milken Family Foundation is one of America's leading charitable organizations, supporting education and medical research.

The Worst for the Jews: Bernie Madoff and the Phantom Menace

Bernard Lawrence "Bernie" Madoff, a former stockbroker and investment-banking *gonif*, perpetrated the largest Ponzi scheme in U.S. history, defrauding thousands of investors and charitable institutions billions upon billions of dollars over a period of more than twenty years. While Madoff claimed this scheme began in the 1990s, federal investigators assert that the fraud began as early as the 1970s (!) and that Madoff's whole operation may never have been legit. Since some of the client "gains" were fabricated, the amount of missing money was initially totaled at $65 billion, though the estimation of actual losses is about $17.3 billion, at least $600 million of which came from the coffers of Jewish charitable funds.

Arrested in December 2008 following a "confession" to his sons, who then reported their father to the authorities, Madoff was charged with securities fraud. He pleaded guilty to a whopping eleven felonies and admitted his business was naught more than a humongous Ponzi scheme. On June 29, 2009, Madoff was ordered to pay billions of dollars in fines and forfeitures and sentenced to 150 years in prison. Compounding the tragedy, one of his sons committed suicide in 2010, on the second anniversary of his father's arrest.

In addition to the pension funds, universities, and charities that had invested with Madoff (including Holocaust survivor and author Elie Wiesel's Foundation for Humanity and Steven Spielberg's Wunderkinder Foundation), private individuals had handed over their life savings, some even scant weeks before Madoff confessed. What's more, many hardworking celebs also invested and summarily lost money with Madoff, including former New York governor Eliot Spitzer, talk-show host Larry King, *Daily News* owner Mort Zuckerman, thespian husband-and-wife team Kevin Bacon and Kyra Sedgwick, DreamWorks CEO Jeffrey Katzenberg, actor John Malkovich, and Hollywood legend Zsa Zsa Gabor.

Bros Before Hos: A *Bissele* History of the Jewish Skin Trade From the Hebrew Bible to Heidi Fleiss

As we all know, the Hebrew Bible is pretty darn explicit on the topic of sex, especially in terms of what thou shalt do and not do with whom and how much thou shouldst pay for it. While the former has understandably caused great consternation amongst those whose sexual preferences are labeled an "abomination," the latter, *zenut*, or prostitution, is clearly outlawed and yet figures prominently in several essential and somewhat odd biblical narratives.

Predictably, a double standard applies, the shameful onus of which falls mostly on the female perpetrators of the world's oldest profession: "Do not profane thy daughter to make her a harlot, lest the land become lewd, and the land become filled with depravity." (Leviticus 19:29) Yet, those Jewesses who earn their shekels on their backs are not the only ones to fall under the broad and pejorative category of *harlot.* In fact, lewd behavior in general is ultimately discouraged, as Hashem wants everyone to keep their legs closed and their robes on (unless, of course, they are married and multiplying): "There shall not be a promiscuous woman among the daughters of Israel, and there shall not be a promiscuous man among the sons of Israel." (Deuteronomy 23:18)

The Son Will Come Out Tamar-a: The Good Book's Best (and Bravest) Prostitutes!

Though you might think the Hebrew Bible can't get any clearer on the topic of prostitutes, it does include stories of working girls whose actions are nothing short of heroic, if also risky and risqué.

The Story of Tamar, Widow and Erstwhile Prostitute

Jacob's son Judah has three sons. A comely lass from around the way named Tamar marries Judah's eldest son, Er. Eventually, Er ceases to be a mensch and God decides it's time for Er to meet his maker. Due to the laws of levirate union—in which the brother of the deceased husband is obligated to marry the widow—Er's brother Onan marries Tamar. Oddly enough, even though Tamar is a hot mama, Onan doesn't want to make her an actual mama, so he spills his mighty Jew sperm on the ground, simultaneously invent-

> "For a harlot is a deep ditch, and the strange woman is a narrow well. She, too, lurks to snatch and multiplies the faithless among men."
>
> PROVERBS 23:2–28

ing both the pull-out method of contraception and masturbation. This displeases God and He kills Onan, too. Judah is now reluctant to have his youngest son Shelah get with Tamar and tells her he'll call her when Shelah is of marrying age.

And so, like many gals, Tamar waits by the phone. And waits. And waits. When Shelah doesn't show, she knows something is up but decides to keep at it. Meanwhile, Judah's wife dies and he decides to take a trip to the nearby suburb of Timnah. Hearing this news and wanting to get some holy seed, Tamar dresses up like a prostitute, including the prerequisite ancient hooker-by-the-side-of-the-road veil, and waits for him near the city walls.

When Judah arrives on the scene and sees the veiled woman, not recognizing Tamar, he decides a little action is in order. Tamar agrees to sleep with him in exchange for a goat, for which transaction Judah leaves her his seal, staff, and cord as an IO-Jew.

Three months later, Tamar is knocked up and accused of being a prostitute. A stickler for the law, Judah orders her to be burned to death, but Tamar sends him his seal, staff, and cord by way of telling him he's the baby-daddy. Judah releases Tamar, and she gives birth to his twin sons, Perez (an ancestor of King David) and Zerah.

DID JEW KNOW?

Before they escaped, the Hebrew spies promised to spare Rahab and her kin. They advised her to mark her house by hanging a red cord out the window. Some scholars believe this may be the origin of the "red-light district."

The Story of Rahab, Innkeeper/Madame and Convert Extraordinaire

Joshua, the leader of the Jews, decides it's time to sack Jericho and sends a couple of Hebrew spies to assess the situation. They arrive at Rahab's grocery store of ill repute and clandestinely bivouac there. Somehow, the king gets wind that the spies are at Rahab's and sends some soldiers to see what is up. Only Rahab, being a nice prostitute who is also on the lookout for a Jewish boyfriend, has hidden the spies on her rooftop under bundles of recently harvested flax. The soldiers return empty-handed, the spies head back to Joshua, and soon the Jews sack Jericho, pillaging the populace as expected. As a reward for her sacrifice, Rahab and her family are spared and Rahab converts to Judaism.

She Works Hard for the Money: Jewish Prostitution in the Post-Biblical Period

Talmudic rabbis were none too keen on prostitution. To encourage modesty and prevent *mamzerim,* or people born from forbidden relationships (including brother and sister), the sages decreed that any sexual contact between an unmarried man and woman constituted prostitution *(zenut).* "Consorting with many women and not knowing with whom, or if she has had intercourse with many men and does not know with whom—he could marry his own daughter, or marry her to his son." (*Mamzer*; Sifra, Kedoshim 7, 1–5)

In general, condemnation of organized prostitution persisted throughout Jewish history. Illicit relationships between Jews were considered bad enough, but those between Jews and Gentiles were actively dangerous, as Jews lived in fear of actions that might catalyze their disfavor with the Gentile majority. This was especially true during the medieval period. Many rabbis tightened regulations against prostitutes and those who frequented them. By the close of the Middle Ages, the law stated that if a married Jew took a trip to the cathouse, he was obliged to give his wife a divorce.

Much like its not-so-distant cousin bootlegging, prostitution of Jewish women increased greatly during the late nineteenth and early twentieth centuries, possibly as a direct result of increased poverty and a much-reduced list of semi-decent employment options. In big cities such as Warsaw, Odessa, Cracow, and Vilna, there were dense populations of Jewish brothels overseen by Jewish pimps. What's more, Jews had a hand in white slavery. Some historians assert that Jews even ran brothels in Shanghai, Argentina, Brazil, and India.

In Russia, where the Jews were stuffed into the Pale of Settlement, Jewish women officially registered as prostitutes were legally permitted to remain outside the settlement to tend to business. In other words, *zenut* allowed women freedom to earn money and to live beyond the confines and squalor of the settlement. Some of the registered Jewish prostitutes also received permits to live in St. Petersburg or Moscow so that they could acquire higher education.

That said, the increase in prostitution among Jews during the great waves of migration that began in 1880 was mostly the result of hardship, poverty, and loss of shtetl community leadership. Disbanded and desolate, some Jews took a chance and made the schlep to that great cathouse of opportunity otherwise known as the United States. In fact, historian Howard Sachar reports that by 1911, 75 percent of the prostitutes in New York as well as other major cites were Jewish and 50 percent of the brothels were owned by Jews.

What Ho, the Jewish Princess: The Legend of Heidi Fleiss

While the Hebrew Bible and the Talmud have plenty to say about prostitution, they're kinda quiet on the subject of lady-pimpin' (otherwise known as being a madam). Unless, of course, either the meat you happen to be hawking (or the customer) is 100 percent grade-J kosher, in which case it's a total no-go. This begs the question: Who's zoomin' who and for how much?

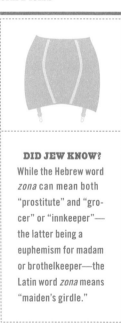

The woman with the answer to these age-old questions is none other than the grand dame of madams, Heidi Fleiss, the "Million-Dollar Madam." In the early '90s, Fleiss ran a high-end ring of call girls, counting numerous Hollywood A-listers among her clients, and living high on the kosher hog until she got busted for pandering. In case you were wondering what "high on the hog" means, Fleiss claims that she made $10,000 in profit on a slow night.

Following a twenty-month stint in the slammer for tax evasion, she was briefly engaged to Denis Hof, American pimp and owner of Nevada brothel Moonlite Bunny Ranch. Fleiss now lives in Pahrump, Nevada, where she owns a laundromat called Dirty Laundry.

DID JEW KNOW?
While the Hebrew word *zona* can mean both "prostitute" and "grocer" or "innkeeper"— the latter being a euphemism for madam or brothelkeeper—the Latin word *zona* means "maiden's girdle."

Houses of the Unholy:
Jewish Politic-hos and the Land of Second Chances

While some nice Jewish boys (and goils) use their political powers to prove to the world once and for all that Jews belong in the political arena, others can't seem to keep their naughty bits out of the public arena. Behold a few Jewish American politicians who couldn't keep a liddle on their yiddles:

Jerry Springer (1944–): Host of a low-shelf, eponymous TV tabloid talk show, Springer was once the mayor of Cincinnati, Ohio. *What?* Back in 1974, Springer resigned from the Cincinnati City Council after he admitted he'd hired a prostitute (but hadn't inhaled). Basically, during a raid on a Kentucky massage parlor, the fuzz discovered a check Springer had written for services rendered, a check that then bounced. Talk about the check is in the male! Somehow, Springer's honesty helped him win back his seat in 1975, and the very same Cin City Council chose him to serve as mayor in 1977. He even considered running for United States Senate in 2003, but then everyone remembered *The Jerry Springer Show* and convinced him to be on *Dancing With the Stars* instead.

> "If a woman called out to you as you walked down Allen Street [a busy street in New York's Lower East Side], you knew she wasn't calling you to a minyan."
>
> —JUDGE JONAH J. GOLDSTEIN

Eliot Spitzer (1959–): a lawyer and yid who served as New York governor from January 2007 until his resignation in March 2008 as a result of his "involvement" with a certain Emperors Club VIP, a high-end escort agency. Allegedly, Spitzer dropped thousands of dollars to dally with a shiksa prostitute named "Kristen," a.k.a. Ashley Dupre. Spitzer also became a talk-show host.

Anthony David Weiner (1964–): a former U.S. congressman and bush-league sexter who resigned from an almost twelve-year stint in Congress on June 16, 2011, after a naughty pic scandal now called Weinergate. Weiner allegedly sent some very personal penis pics to a twenty-one-year-old college student that somehow ended up in the hands of conservative blogger Andrew Breitbart— the pics, not the penis—who then published them. Weiner claimed the photos weren't of his actual *membrum virilis*. When Breitbart next posted a shirtless pic of Weiner that he had obtained from twenty-six-year-old Meagan Broussard, Weiner held a press conference in New York during which he apologized and admitted, "I have not been honest with myself, my family, my constituents, my friends and supporters, and the media." He then confessed to several naughty if only virtual relationships with various women conducted over Facebook, Twitter, e-mail, and the phone. Two years later, Weiner ran for mayor of New York City.

Monica, Monica, Monica

Monica Lewinsky may not be the most famous Jewess in the world, but she is without a doubt the most infamous White House intern, not to mention the owner of the world's most talked-about blue Gap dress and the most incriminating stain in the history of admissible evidence.

Lewinsky began her abridged career in politics as an unpaid White House intern in 1995. While interning, she allegedly engaged in a total of nine sexual encounters with then-president Bill Clinton, making her if not the first Jewish girl to perform fellatio in the Oval Office then at least the first one to free Willy.

On January 26, 1998, Clinton uttered the following amazing sentence: "I did not have sexual relations with that woman, Miss Lewinsky." Just to hear an American president say the word "sex" in the same breath as a Jewish woman's last name in a nationally televised White House news conference blew the minds of Jews the world over. Not since Marilyn Monroe had a humble Jewish girl with big thighs had it so good!

> Clinton: "What kind of a name is Lewinsky, anyway?"
>
> Monica: "Jewish."
>
> –FROM *MONICA'S STORY* BY ANDREW MORTON

After some interesting arguments about the semantics of the verb "to be" and who zoomed whom when, the president admitted to having a "relationship" with Lewinsky that was "not appropriate." Clinton was acquitted of all charges and remained in office. Monica became a bag designer and a reality star and then moved to the United Kingdom. Currently, she may be penning a $12-million tell-all about her dirty doings with the American president. And that's a helluva lot of dresses at the Gap!

Beyond the Jail

Whether they used crime as a schpringboard out of the ghetto or just as a way to put some extra bagels on the table, Jews have indeed lettered among the world's most notorious rebels, revolutionaries, and cold-blooded killers. While some formed coalitions and created their governance as their ancestors had in the land of Canaan, others took matters into their own hands and cranked up the heat on the Cold War. From the red-light district to the Red Scare, these Jews stuck to their guns and became the stuff of legend. You might not condone their actions or their tactics, but one thing's for certain: It pays to be a J! Mazel tov! Let's eat!

CHAPTER 10

LET MY PEOPLE NOSH: Jews and Food— A Love Story

They beheld God, and they ate and drank.

EXODUS 24:11

Forget Abraham and Sarah. Or, for that matter, God and the people of Israel. There is no relationship more enduring (or artery-clogging) than that between the Chosen Tribe and their chosen snacks. In fact, from the moment Eve sank her chompers into that infamous apple, food has played a quintessential role in the very identity of a people whose social life and religious rituals revolve around stuffing their faces with complex carbo yum-yums at every possible opportunity. Compare/contrast: the Spartan communion cracker versus the lavish Kiddush spread at temple following your cousin's bar mitzvah. An Irish wake versus a shivah call for any of your beloved great-aunts and -uncles. No comparison!

Here's why: While Hashem seemingly told the goyim to make a run for the bar and stay there, He commanded the Jews to head for the buffet, there to pile their plates according to His (and later Atkins') rules and regulations. In fact, when He commanded the Jews to get loaded for religious reasons, such as on Purim and Pesach, He also wisely commanded them to eat a giant meal. And so the Jews did eat . . . and eat . . . and eat their way from Canaan to Canada! Behold the love affair to end all love affairs: the Jews and food.

The Bible Made Me Eat It:
Feasts, Famines, and Fêtes in God's Cookbook

The laws of kashrut and manna aside, food and its procurement, eating and storing are yet another vital element of the Torah's narrative arc. While the first actual meal is the feast Abraham served the angels (Genesis 18:1–8), a more significant *mise en place* may well be the primogeniture battle between Jacob and Esau—a fight won with a red lentil stew. (Genesis 25:29–34) How do you like them apples? Meanwhile, Solomon's got a larder big enough to warrant extra trips to Costco (Kings I), and Samuel throws King David a sumptuous repast that includes bread, lentils, cheeses, butter, and honey. Additionally, God also sets forth the menu for the first Pesach meal in Egypt. (Exodus 12:1–11)

If you want to spice it up a bit, there's always the Song of Songs, a love poem to God that reads like *Fifty Shades of Grey*. The Song of Songs uses erotic language to invoke both the aphrodisiac and restorative properties of food. "Sustain me in exile with raisin cakes, spread fragrant apples around me to comfort my dispersion, for I am sick with love." (Song of Songs 2:5) "I came to my garden, my sister, my bride, I gather my myrrh with my spice, I eat my honeycomb with my honey, I drink my wine with my milk." (Song of Songs 5:1)

PETA's Not Just for Hummus:
God Wants Jew to Be Vegetarian!

Back in the ol' Garden of Eden, Adam and Eve happily snacked away on various leaves and fruits. From this limited yet blissful spa menu, some biblical scholars have concluded that God did not originally intend for man to eat meat. In Sanhedrin 59b, the Talmud uses verses from Genesis to prove that originally God gave Adam only plants to eat but after the flood He relented and permitted people to eat meat.

Rav Avraham Hacohen Kook, the first Ashkenazi rabbi of British Mandate Palestine, explains that while the ideal is to be vegetarian, most people aren't ready to give up meat; thus, it's better for people to eat meat in a controlled, that is, kosher way. Also, the manner in which the prophets describe the restored kingdom of God also implies that after the apocalypse, animals will cease to eat one another and all species will live in peaceful, tofurkey-eating harmony.

Let Them Eat Carbs Unto the Lord: The Middle Ages and the Middle-Aged Spread

Since the various expulsions of the Jews during the Middle Ages led to what can only be described as a far-reaching Diaspora, their cuisine expanded to include available local ingredients and dishes, as well as bringing traditional Jewish dishes, such as *charoset*, to far-flung lands. In fact, a great number of the dishes cooked by either the Ashkenazim or the Sephardim were often Jew-ified adaptations of those of their Gentile neighbors: e.g., the chicken paprikash of the Hungarians and the kasha and blintzes of the Russians and Poles. While the Jews of Rhodes subsisted like a bunch of models on veggies only, the Jews of Egypt enjoyed a more expanded menu of meat, cheese, and fish. Meanwhile, Yiddish literature from the period mentions such signature dishes as borscht and a "Shabbat pudding," otherwise known as kugel.

> "The food of the Jewish people is also the history of the Jewish people."
> —MARLENA SPIELER, *THE JEWISH TRADITIONS COOKBOOK*

Ashkenazi food traditions stem from an era when Jews settled in the Rhine Valley and then spread eastward. Their cuisine was a cold-weather one featuring fermented sauerkraut and pickles and, when it was available, smoked fish and meat. Meanwhile, the foodways of the Sephardim also reflected their climate and locale; the Jewish cooks of northern Spain were more Mediterranean-influenced, while those on the southern end were influenced by the Turks and incorporated their spice palette: Cumin, cinnamon, and nutmeg were prevalent, as were almonds, citrus fruits, and eggplant.

That said, most of what people think of today as Jewish cuisine derives from the foodways of the Eastern European Jews who immigrated to North America in the late nineteenth and early twentieth centuries, bringing with them the flavors of home—hearty meats seasoned with onions, brine, grease, and love. From this nostalgic gastronomy emerged the Jewish delicatessen, including the canon of dishes that are now recognized as old-school Jewish fare. Since Jews who immigrated to the United States predominantly ended up in New York City, and specifically the Lower East Side, the classic deli traditions took root and evolved in that quiet and idyllic little burg, there to super-size and carbo-load.

KEEPING KOSHER CAN SAVE YOUR PEOPLE!

While the book of Judith did not make the cut in the Hebrew Bible—too late, too philosophically problematic—it did make it into the holy grab bag that is the Apocrypha. The book presents the story of Judith, a brave and beautiful Jewish queen who, hearing her hometown was about to be sacked, took matters into her own lunchbox. As the story goes, the town elders had decided to wait for God to do something about the pesky Assyrians bivouacked by the town's sole water supply while the Jews went thirsty. Annoyed at the passivity of her peeps, Judith put on her sexiest outfit and went to eat dinner with the Assyrian king Holofernes in his tent. As part of her ingenious plan, she toted both her nubile young maidservant and a sack of wine and salty cheese—an offering the guards allowed because they knew that Jews could eat only their own specially prepared—read: kosher—foods. After the king got drunk and passed out, Judith cut off his head and stuck it in her sack and confidently moonwalked on out of there, saving the town's water supply and the Jews with naught but her luscious melons and a sack of kosher cheese!

It's a Sin in 'Frisco, When They Fry Their Latkes Up in Crisco: The Jewish Delicatessen and Why It's as American as Apple Pie

An establishment that features salami as decoration and serves such cliché Jewish delicacies as matzo ball soup and sky-high towers of various pickled meats on rye is actually a Jewish American derivative of a type of specialty store that originated in Germany. Indeed, lack of refrigeration necessitated the various forms of pickling and curing meat that were the progenitors of such crowd favorites as pastrami and corned beef, both somewhat easier to come by in the Land of Opportunity, where meat was more readily available than it had been in the shtetls and ghettos of Eastern Europe.

> "I love Jewish food, but when you eat, 72 hours later, you're hungry again."
>
> –RICHARD F. SHEPARD, REPORTER FOR THE NEW YORK TIMES

When German and Eastern European Jews began arriving in New York during the first wave of migration in the late nineteenth century, they first

KOSHER VERSUS "KOSHER STYLE"

Just as you can't be kinda pregnant or really unique, you also can't be sort of kosher. That is, unless you're "kosher style." Kosher style refers to food that isn't strictly kosher according to Halakhic standards but could be if it had been slaughtered and prepared thusly. Generally speaking, kosher-style food does not contain meat from *treif* animals such as pigs or shellfish, but it is prepared without kosher supervision. Also, the meat is generally not slaughtered according to the laws of kashrut, regardless of whether the recipe or style of preparation is traditionally "Jewish." Some famous kosher-style delicatessens include both Canter's and Langer's Delicatessan in Los Angeles, Schwartz's Deli in Montreal, Schmaltz Deli in Chicago, and Katz's Delicatessen and Russ & Daughters in New York City.

GRIBENES: DELICACY OR DEATH SENTENCE?

A favorite snack among Ashkenazi Jews, *gribenes*, literally "scraps," are poultry skin cracklings that are a byproduct of the process used to make schmaltz. As the fat is lovingly rendered, the bits of skin are then fried along with small pieces of onion. Considered Jewish bacon by those in the know, *gribenes* are typically associated with Hanukah, when they are served along with potato kugel or latkes.

encountered German delis selling traditional pickled and smoked beef/pork and pondered how best to Jew-ify this specialty idea and schlep with it. Since real estate was expensive and hard to come by—the Lower East Side was then the most densely populated area on Earth—the People of the Book put their *kops* together and prayed unto the Lord, until at last it hit them like a ton of mustard: pushcarts! How better to serve an unassimilated population packed into tenements and basically trapped there by a lack of decent public or private transportation!?

By 1910 or thereabouts, Jews had become New York City's largest immigrant group, and the Jewish version of the German delicatessen began popping up all over town in the form of small specialty shops and pushcarts. By the time the deli business wended its sodium-infused way indoors, traditional Eastern European Jewish foods had already become synonymous with *delicatessen*, a term the Jews had pretty much singlehandedly ushered into popular parlance. By the 1930s, as Jews were moving from the Lower East Side to the south Bronx and Brooklyn, the city had as many as 1,500 kosher delicatessens. Today there are only about two dozen. Sad face.

Though New York contained far more delis than any other North American city, similar Jewish eateries could be found in other cities with sizable Jewish populations, such as Morris & Schiff's in Boston, Cohen's in Los Angeles, Batt's in Chicago, and Schwartz's in Montreal.

DID JEW KNOW?

Carciofi alla giudea (Jewish-style artichokes) were a specialty of the Roman ghetto as well as one of the most popular preparations of Roman Jewish cuisine.

Knish Alley, Here I Come

More than heart attacks waiting to happen, the Jewish delis, cafeterias, and appetizing stores were also places to gather with other landsmen, left-wing intellectuals with thick accents of origin whom writer Isaac Bashevis Singer called the "cafeteria-niks," referring specifically to the crowd at the Garden Cafeteria, one of Singer's favorite haunts. There they would sit for hours, sipping hot tea from a glass, kibitzing, reading the Yiddish *Forverts*, or discussing current events.

Katz's Delicatessen, a legendary kosher-style New York deli, was founded in 1888. When the three sons of the owners were serving in the United States armed forces during World War II, the family tradition of sending food to their sons became the Katz's trademarked logline: "Send a salami to your boy in the army!"

Ratner's, the now defunct dairy restaurant founded in 1905, had two locations, on Delancey Street and on Second Avenue, the latter a favorite hangout spot for Meyer Lansky.

Sammy's Roumanian Steakhouse is the only restaurant in Manhattan that still keeps a pitcher of rendered chicken fat, or schmaltz, on every table. The late comedian Alan King once joked, "Whenever I go to Sammy's Roumanian restaurant, I make two reservations: one at Sammy's and one at Lenox Hill Hospital."

Yonah Schimmel Knish Bakery, founded in 1910, began its life as a humble pushcart schlepped by none other than Rabbi Yonah Schimmel himself. When the eponymous Romanian rebbe arrived on the Lower East Side, he quickly realized that there were more rabbis than you could shake a *yad* at and decided that the only way to support himself was to start selling knishes—mashed potatoes wrapped in dough—from a pushcart. The family-run business is now in its sixth generation and going strong.

Russ & Daughters, a renowned appetizing store, was founded by Joel Russ in 1914 and is now in its fourth generation. Russ & Daughters is also believed to be one of the first businesses to have "and daughters" as part of its title. In the author's humble opinion, Russ & Daughters sells some of the best smoked fish and whitefish salad on the planet.

Second Avenue Deli was founded in 1954 by Abe Lebewohl, a Polish-born Jew of great moxie and generosity of spirit who survived Stalin and the Nazis and opened one of the all-time great New York delis. On March 4th, 1996, Lebewohl was tragically murdered en route to the bank to make a deposit. After the deli closed in 2006, Lebewohl's nephews decided to carry on the family tradition and reopened the deli in Manhattan's Murray Hill, where it continues to thrive.

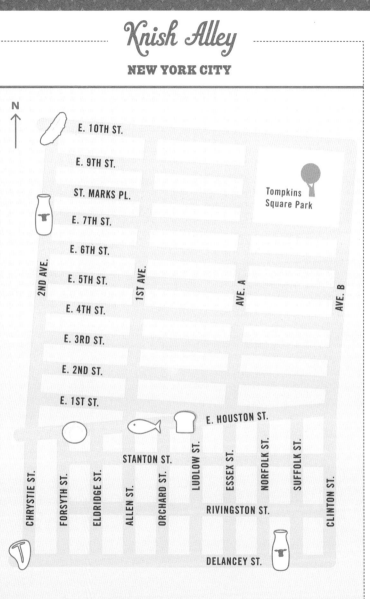

What Am I, Foie Gras? A Brief Exegesis of Chopped Liver

Along with gefilte fish, chopped liver is one of those love-it-or-hate-it Jewish indelicacies that often bring people to plead temporary vegetarianism on Shabbat and/or Passover. Made with chicken livers, schmaltz, and sometimes hard-boiled eggs, chopped liver is served at any kosher-style deli that calls itself authentic. The history of this seemingly pre-masticated substance may be traced back to medieval Germany, where Jews bred geese—in fact, the earliest manifestation of chopped liver was made with goose liver. Eventually, Eastern European Jews also used chicken and beef livers, and it was these recipes that made it across the ocean, through Ellis Island, and into the burgeoning New York deli scene of the late 1800s. A second theory of origin for chopped liver relates to the poverty of the Jews, which meant that all parts of the chicken would be consumed, including the bits that, unless you're Alexander Portnoy, would otherwise seem unappetizing.

> "Do not make a stingy sandwich;
> pile the cold cuts high!
> Customers should see salami
> comin' through the rye."
>
> —ALLAN SHERMAN, COMEDY WRITER

Speaking in Tongue:
Pastrami, Corned Beef, and the Muscle That Moos

Over the years, many a Jewish deli favorite has faded to near extinction, the victim perhaps of a more multi-culti palate and the Western world's extreme preoccupation with healthful eating. Regardless of waistline watching and quintuple-bypass avoidance, many of these old-school faves have emerged as classics worthy of a cholesterol-and-saturated-fats bender, especially some of the cured and pickled meats of the hot pink variety. While the startling hue and soft consistency of these Jewish American meats might confuse or gross out the novice deli-goer, not all meats are pickled equal.

Corned beef is the result of a pickling process using "corns," or large grains of salt. The beef is then boiled or steamed for umpteen hours. A cheaper alternative to the Irish corned pork (bacon), corned beef was a staple of the Irish American diet. Due to the abundance of beef in the New World, what had once been corned pork became corned beef. The same is true for "Jewish" corned beef: Jewish immigrants adopted it as a go-to, affordable meat during the late nineteenth century.

DID JEW KNOW?

A delicatessen sells meats, whereas an appetizing store sells fish and dairy products, i.e., whitefish and cream cheese, or rather, the food one might heap or schmear upon a bagel.

Some food historians theorize that the proximity of Jewish and Irish immigrants in New York City is one possible reason that corned beef became a culinary anchor of the descendants of both groups and that Irish immigrants purchased brisket as corned beef from kosher butchers. (And let's not forget that the Irish may or may not be one of the Ten Lost Tribes of Israel!) That said, the brines vary: The Jewish tends to be more sweet and garlicky, whereas the Irish is more aromatic and uncircumcised.

Pastrami was created as another way to extend the shelf life of meat before modern refrigeration. One main difference between pastrami and its kissing cousin corned beef is that the latter, generally the navel end of a brisket, is first brined, then dried and seasoned, then smoked, and finally steamed. While there is also a Turkish variation called *pastrama*, the Romanian version was introduced to North America during the first influx of Romanian Jewish immigration in the late nineteenth century. In fact, early references in English use the original Romanian spelling rather than the later, more familiar *pastrami*, which was considered to sound more like the Italian *salami* and thus have broader appeal.

DID JEW KNOW?

The word *delicatessen* derives from the Latinate *delicatus*, meaning "delightful" or "pleasing," and the German *essen*, meaning "to eat." The word has since come to refer to specialty or prepared foods.

KOSHER FRAUD!

During the first half of the twentieth century, laws regarding who could sell kosher meat were "on the books." Problem was, these books weren't centralized, and so some butchers sold treif meat and passed it off as kosher—the discrepancy between kosher and nonkosher prices was too high for some to resist going in for crooked profit. Eventually, the New York kosher world went Montague and Capulet: The ultra-Orthos adopted the mark of Glatt Kosher as their alimentary be-all-and-end-all. NOTE: *Glatt* literally means that the meat comes from an animal that has been inspected for smooth lungs, but informally it implies that the food in question is held up to a "higher standard of kashrut." This more-kosher-than-thou distinction emerged with the waves of Hasidic immigrants to New York following World War II.

Spelling aside, the origin of the pastrami sandwich remains in dispute. Sussman Volk, the owner of a delicatessen (formerly butcher shop) on New York's Delancey Street, is often credited with making the world's first pastrami sandwich in 1887. While the founders of Katz's Deli assert that Volk's claim is, in fact, a load of pastrami, Volk claimed that the recipe came his way from a Romanian pal. Allegedly, Volk then prepared the pastrami and served it as a sandwich in his butcher shop. The sandwiches caught on like gangbusters, and Volk then had to convert his beloved shop into a restaurant to sell the sandwiches.

Pickled beef tongue, sometimes referred to by the overly generous moniker "the other red meat," is a Jewish delicacy not for the faint of tastebud. Here's how it happened: Though European Jews were barred from owning land until the late eighteenth century or later, a fair share of cattle merchants were Jewish. Since many Jews couldn't afford the better cuts of meat, they invented dishes that used the lesser cuts of meat such as the aforementioned chopped liver, gooseneck, and tongue, which they then pickled and boiled.

Tongue is experiencing a popularity resurgence as of late, due perhaps to increased interest in "nose-to-tail" butchery. It has sparked a nostalgia strong enough to send foodies to their local butcher to purchase a muscle that formerly spent much of its life masticating cud and uttering a plaintive cry that rhymes with

DID JEW KNOW? *P'tcha*, otherwise known as calf's foot jelly—yes, calf's foot jelly—is an Ashkenazi delicacy served on chopped eggs on Shabbat or as an appetizer at a wedding. And while foot jelly at a wedding might sound distinctly like starting off on the wrong foot, *p'tcha* is as economical as it is rich and savory. Mazel tov! You're married! Have some foot jelly!

Jew. Traditionally pickled for several days with a brine of salt, pepper, garlic, and spices, tongue is braised for at least eight hours to tenderize the muscle. Some Jewish preparations for tongue include cold and sliced on sandwiches, "sweet" for Rosh Hashanah and Passover, and finally Polonaise, or sliced and broiled in a sweet-and-sour raisin sauce, a specialty of the Second Avenue Deli.

What Makes a Pickle Kosher (Besides a Bris)

Jews did not invent the pickle. Sad, but true. Also, a kosher pickle isn't kosher in the strictest sense of the word. It is simply a pickled cucumber made with a generous amount of garlic; in other words, in the traditional style of Jewish New York City pickle picklers. Deli mavens will tell you that the tastiest cuts of pastrami are also the fattiest; they also know that eventually the fat dulls the flavor of the meat. Just as sorbet cleanses the palate between courses, the pickle cleanses the palate between bites, so that the flavor of the pastrami can be fully experienced. Thus the deli pickle became ubiquitous. Fun fact: The word *pickle* derives from the German word *pokel*, meaning "salt and brine."

Man-O-Manischewitz! Wine for Jews

In 1888, Lithuanian-born Rabbi Dov Behr Manischewitz founded the Manischewitz Company in Cincinnati, Ohio. He and his sons forever revolutionized the production of matzo by changing the shape of its more labor-intensive round predecessor and by using machines to roll and bake the matzo, thereby making his company the world's largest producer of Passover matzo. By the 1920s, Manischewitz produced an estimated 1.25 million of these holy crackers per day.

Capitalizing on its successful foray into matzo territory, Manischewitz then branched out into other kosher staples such as gefilte fish, matzo ball soup, and borscht. In 1947, it licensed a line of sweet kosher wines produced by the Monarch Wine Co., a move that would forever link the brand with the cloyingly sweet wine chugged at many a Passover Seder. The company's advertising slogan "Man-O-Manischewitz!" became such a far-flung tagline that Apollo 17 astronaut Eugene Cernan possibly exclaimed it during his famous 1973 moonwalk.

DID JEW KNOW?
Challah's distinctive braid possibly derived from a local bread in Germany.

To Ess, Divine!

THE BIG CHART OF JEWY FOOD

Blintz	Jewish crepe, variant of the Russian blini, rolled enchilada-style and filled with jam, fruit, or sweet cheese.
Cholent	Beef stew prepared on Friday night and cooked slowly overnight to be eaten on Shabbat, when it is forbidden to cook. *Fun fact:* The word *cholent* derives from the French *chaud* ("warm") and *lent* ("slow"). So fancy schmancy! Who knew?
Gefilte fish	Jewish sushi/ Jew-shi. Cold, poached fish burger (generally carp, whitefish, or pike) made with eggs, onions, and matzo meal.
Knish	A round or square-shaped brick of baked or fried dough filled with mashed potato, ground meat, onions, cheese, or kasha. Less traditional fillings include tofu, sweet potato, spinach, or black beans.
Kasha *varnishkes*	Bow-tie-shaped noodles (*varnishkes*) mixed with cooked buck wheat groats (kasha). The Russian-influenced Jewish equivalent of pasta salad.
Kishke (a.k.a., stuffed derma)	Beef intestine stuffed with chicken or beef fat, onion, matzo meal, and seasonings.
Kreplach	Small boiled dumplings filled with either meat or mashed potatoes and served in chicken soup. Considered the Jewish wonton.

DID JEW KNOW? The Vlasic Company claims the record for the biggest pickle: 19 inches (47.5 centimetres) in length! (Don't tell the *shiksas*!)

AVERAGE PICKLE: 6 in/15 cm

BIGGEST PICKLE: 19 in/47.5 cm

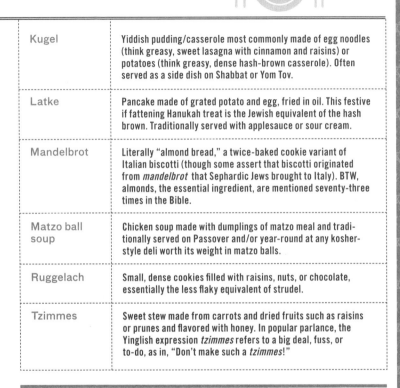

Kugel	Yiddish pudding/casserole most commonly made of egg noodles (think greasy, sweet lasagna with cinnamon and raisins) or potatoes (think greasy, dense hash-brown casserole). Often served as a side dish on Shabbat or Yom Tov.
Latke	Pancake made of grated potato and egg, fried in oil. This festive if fattening Hanukah treat is the Jewish equivalent of the hash brown. Traditionally served with applesauce or sour cream.
Mandelbrot	Literally "almond bread," a twice-baked cookie variant of Italian biscotti (though some assert that biscotti originated from *mandelbrot* that Sephardic Jews brought to Italy). BTW, almonds, the essential ingredient, are mentioned seventy-three times in the Bible.
Matzo ball soup	Chicken soup made with dumplings of matzo meal and traditionally served on Passover and/or year-round at any kosher-style deli worth its weight in matzo balls.
Ruggelach	Small, dense cookies filled with raisins, nuts, or chocolate, essentially the less flaky equivalent of strudel.
Tzimmes	Sweet stew made from carrots and dried fruits such as raisins or prunes and flavored with honey. In popular parlance, the Yinglish expression *tzimmes* refers to a big deal, fuss, or to-do, as in, "Don't make such a *tzimmes*!"

AVERAGE MATZO BALL:
3 in/7.5 cm

BIGGEST MATZO BALL:
17 in/43 cm

DID JEW KNOW? This biggest matzo ball ever was made in Canter's Deli in Los Angeles. It weighed in at over 25 pounds (11.3 kilograms) and measured 17 inches (43 centimetres) long. Now, that's a mighty big ball! The "world's largest matzo" was made by the Manischewitz Corporation. The matzo measured 82 square feet (7.6 square metres) and marked the grand opening of the new Manischewitz matzo factory in Newark, New Jersey.

Ancient Chinese Secret: Jews and Chinese Food

These days, everyone and their uncle knows the Jews-love-Chinese-food cliché—there's even a Chinese restaurant in Los Angeles called the Genghis Cohen—but this mixed marriage was actually forged long, long ago on New York's Lower East Side, where the two foreign foodways managed to meet and mate. As the Yiddish Book Center asserts, this match made in heaven was due partly to some strange similarities between Chinese and Jewish cuisine, in that both featured hot tea served without milk, chicken broth, boatloads of garlic and onions, and vegetables cooked until you no longer need to chew them. Additionally, Chinese food is dairy-free and can therefore be considered kosher style, especially if you ignore the pork and shellfish.

A Jewish guy and a Chinese guy are having a chat.
The Jewish guy tells the Chinese guy how much he respects the
wisdom of the Chinese people. "Yes," replies the Chinese guy.
"Our culture is over 4,000 years old. But you Jews are also
a very wise people." The Jewish guy nods and says,
"Nu, our culture is over 5,000 years old." Incredulous,
the Chinese guy looks at the Jew and retorts, "That's impossible!
Where did your people eat for a thousand years?"

–CLASSIC JEWISH JOKE

Though Jews had been hitting New York's Chinese restaurants since the late 1800s, the city was bereft of a kosher option until 1959, when Solomon Bernstein opened Bernstein-on-Essex, or "Schmulka Bernstein's," as it was commonly known. This now-defunct kosher restaurant proffered both typical Jewish deli fare and Cantonese-style dishes such as moo goo gai pan and the immutable "lo mein Bernstein."

Bialystok & Bloom: The Bagel's Boy Wonder

Outside New York City, the bialy lives in near obscurity, while the bagel gets all the props (and all the cream cheese). Surprising, because this yeasty, round, flat, chewy roll is as delish as its more famous and fattening sidekick. Some history: In the early 1900s, bialys came to the United States via Bialystok, Poland, and hit the streets of the Lower East Side rolling. New Yorkers in the know sometimes refer to the Lower East Side as "Bialy Central," an apt moniker considering that even if you went to Bialystok itself, you wouldn't find a single bialy, or a married one either. Seems these tasty rolls didn't manage to survive the Holocaust.

So, what makes a bialy a bialy? Well, *kindela*, unlike a bagel, a bialy does not have a hole in the middle. It has an indentation that is filled with either onion or garlic. Also, while a bagel is boiled and baked, a bialy is just baked. So if you end up in the Big Apple, hit up Kossar's Bialys on Grand Street and belly up to the bialy bar for a bit of Bialystoker heaven.

The Schmear Campaign:
The Truth about Everyone's Favorite Roll With a Hole

Bagels arrived in North America along with the influx of Ashkenazi immigrants to the United States and Canada in the late nineteenth century. To this day, there is a fair amount of contention over which major city can lay claim to the better bagel: New York or Montreal. While New York bagels are bigger and denser, Montreal bagels are boiled in honey water and baked in wood-burning ovens and are therefore sweeter than their New York brethren. Meanwhile, the Holy Land also touts its own version of the bagel, the Jerusalem bagel: a softer, oblong-shaped, sesame-studded variation that is either eaten solo or dipped in *za'atar* (a Middle Eastern spice combo of oregano, thyme, sesame seeds, and salt).

> "Why did the onion fall in love with the bagel? Because she was his everything and had gorgeous lox!"
> —COMEDIAN STEVE CARPI

French toast aside, the origins of this Jewish breadstuff—on some level more quintessential to Jewish life than challah—remain somewhat murky. For the sake of argument, let's agree that these dense, boiled-n-baked, ring-shaped bread rolls were born in Poland in the early seventeenth century. Food scholars point to a document from 1610 in Cracow that alludes to "beygls," round rolls that were given as gifts to women in childbirth and to newborns for teething. Another origin story has to do with the 1683 Battle of Vienna. As legend has it, King Jan Sobieski was the first king not to confirm a decree limiting the production of certain breads to the Cracow bakers' guild, thereby allowing Jews to bake bread within the city walls. What's more, when Sobieski saved Austria from the Turks, a baker commemorated the event with a pastry in the shape of the king's stirrup, and dubbed it a *beugel*, Austrian German for "stirrup."

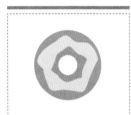

DID JEW KNOW?

The disparaging quip that a bagel is nothing but an "unsweetened doughnut with rigor mortis" originated in a *New York Times* article from May 1960.

But why the hole? Yet another bagel dispute! When bagels migrated from Poland to Russia and then to New York, vendors threaded the holey bread on dowels or strings to hawk on street corners. Another less likely but more exciting legend comes from the small Jewish villages in Russia. Seems that the tsar, in the best of times a pain in the *tuchus*, levied a bread tax on Jews stipulating that the tsar receive one-tenth of all bread baked from the middle of each loaf. Thus, the bagel. When the tsar's minions came to collect the tithe, the villagers presented the rolls-with-a-hole and the soldiers left empty-handed.

Cut to the United States in the 1950s: A Jewish boy named Murray Lender bought a freezer and realized that he and his father, a wholesale bagel man from Poland, could ship frozen bagels to retailers and that the thawed bagels would maintain both their flavor and consistency. With the advent of the miraculous frozen-food aisle, this Ashkenazi delicacy could suddenly be shipped to such exotic locales as Ohio and Utah and other parts of the country that didn't know from bagels. Thus the humble country bread from Poland made it into the backcountry, and bagelmania was born!

The Sunday Schpread

AN APPETIZING SMORGASBORD OF JEWISH DELICACIES

As Chinese food is to Christmas and *matzo* to Mosesmas, bagels, cream cheese, and lox (and its variants) are to Sunday brunch. In case the fish counter at your local Jewish delicatessen still seems a sea of pink on ice, here's a handy-dandy guide to the fish that have festooned the holy (and holey) bagels of your ancestors.

Lox 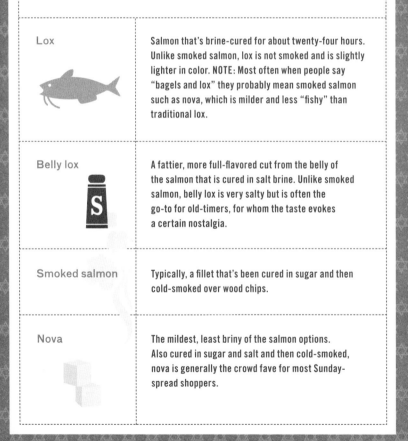	Salmon that's brine-cured for about twenty-four hours. Unlike smoked salmon, lox is not smoked and is slightly lighter in color. NOTE: Most often when people say "bagels and lox" they probably mean smoked salmon such as nova, which is milder and less "fishy" than traditional lox.
Belly lox	A fattier, more full-flavored cut from the belly of the salmon that is cured in salt brine. Unlike smoked salmon, belly lox is very salty but is often the go-to for old-timers, for whom the taste evokes a certain nostalgia.
Smoked salmon	Typically, a fillet that's been cured in sugar and then cold-smoked over wood chips.
Nova	The mildest, least briny of the salmon options. Also cured in sugar and salt and then cold-smoked, nova is generally the crowd fave for most Sunday-spread shoppers.

I'm Still Here: Herring

Among the classic Ashkenazi foods, nothing evokes paroxysms of revulsion or joy with quite the same alacrity as herring—the fish Jew love to hate and hate to love. Indeed, there is no fish as closely linked to the Old Country as pickled herring, especially when served in the traditional style with marinated onions. A little history: Herring became popular with Eastern European Jews for the same reason it was popular with the Scandinavians—it was cheap and abundant, if quick to go rancid. According to food historian Gil Marks, Jews were prominent figures in the herring trade, importing the pickled fish to Russia, Poland, and Germany, where they sold this poor-man's delicacy from pushcarts. Eventually, herring wended its stinky way to North America via the Lower East Side. Though these days herring has lost some of its mojo, it still appears on Yom Kippur breakfast tables. True, no one but your grandmother will eat it, but it's there . . . in that bowl, by the tuna salad.

And Now a Brief Jew's Who of Herring:

- *Matjes* herring: *Matjes*, literally "maiden" in German, is a more mild preparation that is made from young female herrings, resulting in a more ladylike fish with a smoother, subtler taste.
- Shmaltz herring: A fatty, more mature, and pungent herring that has been cured in brine and brown sugar and/or marinated in rendered chicken fat.
- Creamed herring: Marinated herring and onions that is smothered in sour-cream sauce.
- Chopped herring: Also known as *forshmak*, chopped herring is pulverized pickled herring spread often served on brown bread or matzo.

The Enigmatic Egg Cream:
No Eggs, No Cream, All Heeb, U-bet!

Back in the day, when delicatessens and soda fountains were as ubiquitous as fast-food joints today, the egg cream was the popular beverage equivalent of the significantly more caloric (and pricey) Frappuccino. Made with milk, seltzer (or "Jewish champagne"), and chocolate syrup—Fox's U-Bet if you want to do it right—this delicious, frothy beverage's genesis and name remain in dispute. Some theories:

- A Jewish immigrant by the name of Louis Auster invented the egg cream in the 1890s at a Brooklyn candy store. Food historian Gil Marks says Auster called it an egg cream because of the "egg-white-like foam that rose to the top."
- Yiddish-theater star Boris Thomashevsky, who also brought the first Yiddish play to New York, had apparently experienced a similar drink in Paris called *chocolat et crème* and decided it was high time to have it made in New York. The "et crème" allegedly later morphed into "egg cream."

- In the 1920s, a candy store on Second Avenue and Eighth Street in Manhattan began making the drink with seltzer, syrup, and real cream, held together by eggs as an emulsifier. During the Depression, the eggs and cream were necessarily eliminated.

"When I was a young man, no bigger than this,
a chocolate egg cream was not to be missed.
Some U-Bet's chocolate syrup, seltzer water mixed with milk,
you stir it up into a heady fro, it tasted just like silk."

–LOU REED

A Nation of Nibblers

For many Jews in the Western hemisphere, Jewish cuisine is its own religion—or rather, the culinary equivalent of that history lesson you never paid attention to in Hebrew school. For others, Jewish cuisine is an oxymoron on the level of kosher jumbo shrimp. It seems like a good idea until you eat too much and have to lie on your back all night like a beached whale. Regardless of your opinion on the quality of the cooking, one thing's for certain: The force that has shaped Jewish food with all its disparate elements and desperate diasporas is Judaism itself. Challah-braiding, *cholent*-warming, pastrami-fressing, bialy-toasting, pickle-popping, egg-cream-consuming, matzo-ball-soup-slurping Judaism. Its dietary laws, family-centric celebrations, and even the religious symbolism of certain dishes set a bounteous table that is as varied as it is unified, not to mention fun and loud. So load up your bagel, pull up a table, and take a *bissele* bite of history. Go ahead, Jew know you want to.

MAKE YOUR OWN EGG CREAM AT HOME!

INGREDIENTS:

- 2 tablespoons (30 ml) Fox's U-Bet Chocolate Syrup
- 5 ounces (170 ml) ice-cold whole milk
- 3 ounces (90 ml) seltzer from a seltzer siphon, the kind that uses CO_2 cartridges

Pour the chocolate syrup into the empty glass, then add the milk. Squirt the seltzer as you bounce the spoon up and down, thereby mixing in the chocolate syrup without actually stirring, as this will reduce your authentic egg cream to a flaccid chocolate soda. NOTE: Some egg cream aficionados begin with milk first, then seltzer, then pour the chocolate directly into the foam and stir. Others make chocolate milk and then add the seltzer.

CHAPTER 11

THE OYS OF YIDDISH:
Yiddish Words and Phrases Even an Irish Cop Would Know (and Some He or She Might Not)!

Du zolst nor fahrtsn in dred.
(You should only fart
in the ground.)

—YIDDISH CURSE

The *mameloshn* ("mother tongue") of Ashkenazi Jews, Yiddish is a vernacular linguistic hybrid of German and Hebrew that also borrows from other Eastern and Central European languages to develop its own rich and evocative pastiche. While some Yiddish words have entered the English lexicon, it is the nuance rather than the literal meaning of the words that shoulders both the weight of Jewish history and the resilient if gallows humor of its people. In other words, if you need to be sarcastic, melodramatic, hyperbolic, disparaging, insulting, demonstrative, or dirty in three words or less, Yiddish is the ideal language! What's more, if you throw a good eye roll in there, you'll appear a native speaker faster than you can say, "She's a real *baleboosteh*."

> Man comes into the world with an *oy!*— and leaves with a *gevalt!*
> –YIDDISH PROVERB

What happened to Yiddish?

Not so long ago—less than a century—an estimated eleven to thirteen million of the world's eighteen million or so Jews spoke Yiddish; that is, until the Holocaust systematically wiped out around 85 percent of the world's Yiddish speakers. Although some would survive the war, assimilation in new homelands such as the Soviet Union, the United States, Canada, and Israel also contributed inestimably to the language's continued decline. So, *nu*, liven up your lackluster communiqués and curses with some Yiddish words and expressions sure to shock your *bubbe*, delight your *zayde*, and/or hopefully guarantee a *schtup*fest to end all *schtup*fests with your Jew boo.

DID JEW KNOW? Ladino, a hybrid of Spanish and Hebrew, is the "Yiddish" or international mother tongue of the Sephardim, i.e., the Jews of Spain, Portugal, the Middle East, South America, and North Africa. Some choice Ladino phrases to bandy about at Purim parties and impress your Sephardic friends include:

- *Si Mose morio, adonay quedo.*
  Moses may be dead, but God endures.

- *Quien al cielo escupe, en la cara la cae.*
  Whoever spits at the heavens hits himself in the face.

- *Quien no sabe de mar, no sabe de mal.*
  He who knows nothing of the sea, knows nothing of suffering.

- *Si ten dan, toma: si te ajahvan, fue.*
  If they give you, take; if they hit you, run.

- *Si los anios calleron, los dedos quedaron.*
  If the rings fell off, at least the fingers stayed.

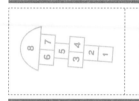
Just for Beginners: Oy!

To quote the great Leo Rosten, "*Oy* is not a word; it is a vocabulary." Whether expressing joy, surprise, disgust, horror, or a panoply of options in between, *oy* is practically its own soliloquy. Indeed, never have two letters managed to say so much to so many with so little. Let's take a look at the expletive that invokes a heck of a lot more than its pallid cousin *oh*.

Oy!

Literal: Oh! (in the sense of "oh no!")
Conveys: Dismay, frustration, exasperation, vexation, disappointment.
Usage: *Oy*, this printer is always jamming. *Oy*, Aunt Sadie is coming for the whole weekend?

Oy vey! Oy vey iz mir!

Literal: Oh, pain/woe! Oh, woe is me!
Conveys: Anguish, exasperation, lamentation, agony, or excitement.
Usage: *Oy vey*, Sadie's husband just left her. *Oy vey iz mir*, the dishwasher is broken and the guy can't come to fix it until Monday!

Oy gevalt! Or simply, Gevalt!

Literal: Oh, force/violence!
(Less literally, Oh, my God! Hell, no! Good grief! Holy s**t! Enough already!)
Conveys: Fear, shock, tribulation, deep distress, alarm, amazement, astonishment.
Usage: *Oy gevalt*, I think I broke my ankle! *Oy gevalt*—stop texting and driving! Do you want to kill us all? *Gevalt!* The baby just spit up on the new sofa! Don't have such a *gevalt*; I only slept with him once!

MORE YIDDISH WORDS FOR *PENIS* THAN YOU CAN SHAKE A SCHTICK AT

Schmuck (also used figuratively to mean "jerk" or "dickhead"), *putz* (*putznasher* is therefore one who sucks the *putz*), *schmeckle, schlong, schvantz.*

Yiddish Words
JEW SHOULD KNOW

Baleboosteh: A top-notch homemaker, a bossy woman.

Bashert: One's beloved/affianced/soulmate.

Bissele: A little.

Bubbe: Grandmother.

Bupkes: Literally, goat or rabbit droppings; used with derision to mean something worth nothing, something pointless or ridiculous.

Chozzer: Pig/glutton.

Chozzerai (also khazeray): Trash, junk, food that is low-end or awful, stupid TV shows.

Chutzpah: Nerve, guts, balls, effrontery.

Fartutst: State of being discombobulated, confused, mixed up and kinda freaked out about it.

Feh: Interjection bearing the connotation of *ew* or *bleh*.

Fleyshik: Meaty, made with meat; see also *milkhik*.

Frum: Deeply religious; connotes intense piety or stringent adherence to Jewish law.

Ganef/gonif: Thief, crook, shady character.

Gelt: Actual money, or chocolate coins used for purposes of degenerate gambling on Hanukkah.

Goy, goyim (pl) (also Hebrew): Literally, nation (other than Israel); a non-Jew, a Gentile. Often used to imply someone of a lesser intelligence than a Jew and/or someone who might turn you in to the Nazis for a kilo of sugar. Think Rolfe in *The Sound of Music*.

Heimish: From the German word "home." Used to mean friendly, nice, homey, unpretentious.

Mazel: Luck.

Kibitz: To offer advice, converse idly, gossip.

DID JEW KNOW? The word *Yiddish* derives from the German word for "Jewish." One theory on the origin of Yiddish as a language is that it stems from the tenth-century migration of Jews from France and Italy to the German Rhine Valley. In the late Middle Ages, when Jews settled in Eastern Europe, Slavic elements were also incorporated.

MORE YIDDISH WORDS JEW SHOULD KNOW

Kippah: The round skullcap worn by observant Jewish men to show their constant devotion to God; see also *yarmulke*.

Kosher: From the Hebrew *kasher* meaning fit, proper, or permissible, usually used in reference to dietary laws as writ in the Tanakh. Can also be used to mean legitimate or appropriate.

Kvell: To express happiness and pride.

Kvetch: From the German word for "squeeze." Used to mean complain, gripe, bitch (verb). As a noun, a *kvetch* is a person who complains a lot.

Macher: Big shot, someone who has connections, someone who fixes and arranges everything, can also connote one who is very wealthy.

Mamzer (also Hebrew): Bastard, illegitimate, untrustworthy. *Mamzer* can also be used admiringly to mean a clever person.

Mazel tov (mazal tov in Hebrew): Literally, good luck, as in "what good luck!" Used to mean congratulations.

Mensch: A good guy, an upright being.

Meshugge: Crazy. A crazy man is *meshuggener*. A crazy broad is *meshuggene*.

Milkhik: Made with milk; see also *fleyshik*.

Mishegas: Literally, insanity. More often used to mean nonsense, absurdity, or silliness.

Naches: Feeling pride/gratification in another person's achievements, often a parent's pride in the achievement of his/her progeny (as opposed to schadenfreude). As my father once said, "My children think that *naches* is something you order in a Mexican restaurant." NOTE: You don't have *naches*, you shep *naches*.

Nebbish: An insignificant/unlucky person, a person to be pitied. Can be used as an interjection to mean "Poor thing!" To quote Leo Rosten, "When a nebbish leaves the room, you feel as if someone came in."

Nosh: Snack (noun or verb).

Nu: Interjection used to mean "So?" or "Well?" Also used to mean "Well, now," "What's new?" or "How do you like them apples?"

Nudnik: A pain/pest.

Pisher: From the German word for "piss." Used to mean a young, inexperienced person or a squirt.

Potch: To spank.

Plotz: To burst, explode, be outraged.

Schlemiel: A habitually clumsy or inept person.

Schlep: To drag, haul, delay. A *schlepper* is someone untidy, rundown, or a drag.

Schlimazel: A person who is chronically unlucky, a bungler or born loser (*schlim*, bad or wrong + *mazel*, luck). As the saying goes, "The schlemiel is one who always spills his soup. The schlimazel is the one in whose lap it always lands."

Schlock: Something cheap, junky, or inferior.

Schmaltz: Melted chicken fat. Often used to mean excessive sentimentality.

Schmatta: A rag. Also used to mean "junk."

Schmegegge: A non-talent, a drip, an idiot. Also used to mean hot air or BS.

Schmutz: Dirt.

Schnorrer: From the German word for "beg." Used to mean moocher, cheapskate, bum, loser.

Schnoz: Nose, generally size large.

Schtup: To have intercourse, more in the sense of "to screw" rather than "to make love."

Schvartze: Black—while this word has come to have a derogatory, racist connotation in most American cities, in Yiddish it originally meant black.

Schvitz: To sweat.

Sheygetz: A derogatory term for a non-Jewish male.

Shiksa: A derogatory term for a non-Jewish female, especially one who is captivating the heart and *schvantz* of an otherwise eligible Jewish male.

Shtetl: A small, usually poor, insular and Jewish town or village in pre-Holocaust Eastern Europe.

Shul: Synagogue.

Treif: Not kosher.

Tsuris: Troubles, worries.

Tuchus: Backside, bottom, rear end.

Verklempt: Choked up (as in with emotion).

Yarmulke: Round skullcap worn by observant Jewish men to show their constant devotion to God; see also *kippah*.

Yenta: A gossipy/talkative woman, a busybody, rumormonger.

Yontef (from the Hebrew yom tov): A Jewish holiday during which work is forbidden.

Zaftig: Stacked, full-figured.

Zayde: Grandfather.

WORDS JEW DIDN'T KNOW WERE YIDDISH

Dreck: Literally "crap." Used to mean worthless merchandise. $0.00

Klutz: Literally "wooden beam." Used to mean a clumsy person.

Maven: An expert.

Mishmash: A hodgepodge or jumble; from the Yiddish word *mishn*, meaning "to mix."

Schmooze: To converse informally, make connections; or to chat in a friendly yet persuasive manner so as to advance one's career.

Tush, tushy: Backside, rear end, butt. Derived from *tuchus*.

A SAMPLING OF COLORFUL AND KOOKY CURSES

While the Irish might bless you with such kindly and hopeful benedictions as "May the wind always be at your back," the Yiddish speaker's choice of idiom leans more toward the blessing's inverse and comprises a host of hilarious exhortations, such as:

- *Khasene hobn zol er mit di malekh hamoves tokhter.* He should marry the daughter of the Angel of Death.

- *Gut zol oyf im onshikn fin di tsen makes di beste.* God should visit upon him the best of the Ten Plagues.

- *Hindert hayzer zol er hobn, in yeder hoyz a hindert tsimern, in yeder tsimer tsvonsik betn un kadukhes zol im varfn fin eyn bet in der tsveyter.* A hundred houses shall he have, in every house a hundred rooms and in every room twenty beds, and a delirious fever should drive him from bed to bed.

- *Zoln dayne beyner zikh brekhn azoy oft vi di Aseres Hadibres.* May your bones be broken as often as the Ten Commandments.

- *Du zolst nor fahrtsn in dred.* You should only fart in the ground.

Say It, Don't Pray It

Indeed, Yiddish is like a kugel; it's rich, heavy, and stays in your system for a good, long time. More than merely evocative or colorful, it's a language in which you can say a lot with a *bissele* or, in the case of my *bubbe*, a *bissele* with a lot. In fact, add a question mark to any Yiddish phrase or the adverb *no* and unleash an array of subtle and not so subtle negative connotations, as in, "My son-in-law, he's no genius."

Finally, lest Jew think the *mameloshn* is on the verge of going the way of the Automat and the cassette tape, think again: More than a few scholars and universities have added Yiddish to their linguistic curricula to keep that jam alive and kicking, as are the ultra-Orthodox populations of Israel and New York who continue to speak Yiddish at home and around the way. So, start spreading the news (and the Jews), get fruitful and multiply, and bring that beat back. Otherwise, to invoke a favorite Yiddish curse, "May you be a person of leisure and take a daily nap, so that the lice in your shirt marry the bedbugs in your mattress and their offspring take up residence in your underwear."

AND, TO BE BIPARTISAN, SOME YIDDISH WORDS FOR VAGINA
Schmundie, knish, pirge/peergeh, pirog (literally "meat-pie"), *mutersheyd* (literally "mother-sheath").

INDEX

Born in New Orleans and raised
in Brooklyn, **Emily Stone** is
a writer and a yoga teacher
living in New York City.